Postcolonial Theory and Literature

Postcolonial Theory and Literature

Edited by

P. Mallikarjuna Rao
Rajeshwar Mittapalli
K. Damodar Rao

ATLANTIC

PUBLISHERS & DISTRIBUTORS (P) LTD

Published by

ATLANTIC

PUBLISHERS & DISTRIBUTORS (P) LTD

7/22, Ansari Road, Darya Ganj, New Delhi-110002
Phones : +91-11-40775252, 40775214, 23273880, 23275880
Fax : +91-11-23285873
Web : www.atlanticbooks.com
E-mail : orders@atlanticbooks.com

Branch Office: Chennai
Phones : +91-44-48531784, 28291383
E-mail : chennai@atlanticbooks.com

Printed & bound in India by Atlantic Print Services

Introduction

In colonial and postcolonial societies, the nationalist aspiration of liberation and active resistance to colonialism is closely linked, in one way or another, to the socio-political movement of decolonization. As it gained momentum, it demanded a re-location of power and a concomitant symbolic overhaul. Postcolonial literatures are an articulation of this process of replacing structures/myths of power reshaping dominant meanings. In this effort, they have produced a whole counter-narrative. As Edward Said rightly observes, literature has contributed massively "as the shaper, creator, agent of illumination within the realm of the colonized" and played a crucial role in the "re-establishment of national cultural heritage in the re-instatement of native idiom in the re-imagining and re-figuring of local histories, geographies, communities."[1] As a part of the process of decolonization, postcolonial literatures dismantled historical and textual monoliths and demonstrated the possibilities of (alter)native texts and perspectives. The single-voiced authority of colonialism and colonial writing was challenged by postcolonial writings that are marked by multiplicity, plurality and plentitude.

In the first phase of postcolonial literatures, articulation of national/regional/racial consciousness occupied centrality. The narrative texts of liberation that formed part of resistance process in the colonized societies, emerged as a contingent need to realize the "truths of the nation."[2] In fact, the development of national literatures became fundamental to the whole enterprise of postcolonial studies. It is the beginning of what Soyinka calls the process of 'self-apprehension.'[3] However, he was the one creative writer who did see the dangers of untutored nationalism and made it the main theme of his play, *A Dance of the Forests,* written in 1960 on the eve of celebrations of Nigerian Independence. Frantz Fanon, even while stressing the enabling condition of the narratives of the nation, cautioned against essentialist formulations that might lead to nationalist/religious orthodoxies. The subsequent appearance of various generals, mullahs, advocates of untutored religious and racial configurations only proved what Fanon and Soyinka had projected in their texts. The celebration of national independence forms the theme of such diverse novels as *Kanthapura* and Ngugi's *A Grain of Wheat*; the theme of influence of a foreign culture on the life of contemporary postcolonial societies is evidenced in Achebe's *No Longer at Ease* and George Lamming's *In the Castle of my Skin*.

In the second stage, postcolonial writers engaged themselves with the poetics of subversion; they closely scrutinized the imagery of dominance/subordination by questioning the bases of European, British worldview. Writers like Wilson Harris, George Lamming, Patrick White, Salman Rushdie, Chinua Achebe, Ngugi wa Thiong'o, Margaret Atwood, Margaret Laurence and Jean Rhys interrogated the philosophical assumptions of the metropolitan centre. They opened up possibilities of a new language and new way of seeing the world. Received history is rewritten and reconstructed in a space that annihilates time and defeats imperial purpose. G.V. Desani's *All About H. Hatterr*, Salman Rushdie's *Midnight's Children* and the novels of Wilson Harris deliberately set out to disrupt received notions of history and the ordering of time. As an alternative to the monolithic construct of colonial perspective, these writers were busily engaged in promoting hybridity which acted as the source of literary and cultural redefinition. They interspersed their texts with a lot of extraneous things; the practice of past, present and future intersecting in their narratives became all too common. This enterprise defied the boundaries of disciplines and genres. In 'writing back' to the centre, they resisted the notion of the grand narrative so close to the colonial enterprise. Besides, the appropriation of English language for purposes of specific cultural contexts assumed centrality. However, in postcolonial countries such as India, Nigeria and Kenya, where alternatives to English exist, a re/turn to writing in regional languages is often advocated for the decolonization programme. A notable example, in this respect, is that of Ngugi wa Thiong'o who has taken to writing in his native Gikuyu.

In the Indian context, the fine mosaic of regional literatures opens up possibilities of narratives of liberation and resistance. In fact, many texts written in indigenous languages of India have emerged as potent and powerful elements in postcolonial self-assertion. As a case in point, one can cite the example of Mahasveta Devi who writes in her native language Bengali. Her fiction, essays, journalistic writings and her activism among the adivasis in India could be described as one body of articulation, one mode of resistance to imperial stratagem, one gesture of self-assertion.

In recent times, postcolonial studies have occupied the centre-stage of academic discourse and, in effect, these have proliferated so much that the authors of the pioneering work, *The Empire Writes Back* (1989), in their recent volume, *Key Concepts in Post-colonial Studies* (1998) observe that the term post-colonialism is now used to refer to "a remarkably heterogeneous set of subject positions, professional fields and critical enterprises."[4] In the broad areas these critics have configured, emphasis may have been transferred to national literatures, but the critical practice and models have essentially remained European and American. The theoretical assumptions and critical perspectives made in many instances clearly point to replication/mimicry of the European and American establishment. By its failure to alter the terms of discourse, postcolonial criticism participates implicitly in the discourse operated by imperial power. When Salman Rushdie upholds the elevated status of Indian Writing in English at the cost of regional literatures, the same mechanism is at work. The dangers of such critical practice, both implicit and explicit, in postcolonial studies are enumerated by K. Purushotham in his article, "First World within the Third World: The Universalist Fallacy in Criticism" included in the present volume.

In addition to the inner contradiction of the absence of viable critical models to match the creative spectrum of postcolonial literatures, machinations and counter-appropriation policies of the Metropolitan Academy and Theory pose another danger, this time external. Sometimes it is misleading and at times it is reductive but either way it makes attempts at re-colonizing postcolonial literatures. In an article entitled "Political *Re*turns: *Ab*uses of the Academy" D. Venkat Rao disputes some of the claims and assumptions made by Robert Young. In his set questions indicating the nature and problems of contemporary postcolonial studies, Robert Young asserts that the rise of postcolonial studies coincided with the end of Marxism as the defining political, cultural and economic objective of much of the third world. Venkat Rao, in his response, sets the record straight by mentioning that the rise of postcolonial studies does not coincide with even the virtual disappearance of Marx; that social movements emerging from the third world, India in particular, do not necessarily divide the realms of the economic, political and cultural; that questions of decolonization could be traced back to the sixties and even earlier periods. He also disputes the claim of Young that the radicality of postcolonial scholars has only served their assimilation into the liberal values of individualism. The article provides a pointer to the various means of the imperial centre to falsify, mythicise and control postcolonial studies. By implication, it stresses the need to develop local/national models of criticism and theory. One could cite Emmanuel Obiechina's *Culture, Tradition and Society in the West African Novel*, Soyinka's *Myth, Literature, and the African Society*, Ngugi's *Moving the Centre*, G.N. Devy's *In Another Tongue* and Susie Tharu and K. Lalitha's *Women Writing in India: 600 B.C. to the Present* as some of the pioneering attempts in this direction.

In postcolonial societies, translations of regional literatures fill the enervating void left by creative writing in English and act as the aesthetics of liberation. These translations represent the forces and concepts of the once-colonized countries to challenge the canonical and the hegemonic. In fact, the interplay between the categories of the oppressor/oppressed, colonizer/colonized, canonical/subversive has been dealt by the writers in regional languages in much better way than those writing in English. This is particularly true of the Indian context. Such Indian writers as Mahasveta Devi, Ismat Chughtai, U.R. Ananta Murthy, R.V. Sastry, O.V. Vijayan have immensely contributed to the growth this poetics of resistance. If the translated text is the site of interpretation carrying on it the stamp of multiple agenda, the enterprise of translation itself emerges as an act of defiance, "of political defiance."[5] Hence, translation is a potent weapon in the hands of anti-hegemonic and decolonising forces. The intricacies involved in the translation programme, in the context of India, are addressed to by P. Shiv Kumar in his article, "Towards a Translation Protocol in Post-colonial India" included in the present volume.

As part of the process of defiance, the practice in the realm of the postcolonial studies has been to question the validity and sanctity of the notion of standard English. Many writers attempted, through demonstration, to subvert the notions of language and meaning, particularly the notion that meaning resides in standard usage. G.V. Desani's *All About H. Hatterr* and Gabriel Okara's *The Voice* could be regarded as the earliest examples of this process of appropriation. In the Indian scene, some of the ways in which standard English has been nativized by the "Fourth World" of Indigenous people offer an instance of "abrogation and appropriation."[6] T. Vinoda's article on Arundhati Roy's *The God of Small Things* while making a stylistic analysis of the novel offers interesting insights into the many ways in which the standard/authentic notion of language has been subverted.

In addition to the mappings of theoretical re/figurations, the present volume includes articles that closely examine individual texts from specific standpoints: D. Ramakrishna explores and interrogates the Swamy motif that constitutes a binary opposition between materialism and spirituality as depicted in postcolonial Indian English fiction and Bhabani Bhattacharya's *A Dream in Hawaii,* in particular. Syed Mujeebuddin charts the problematic of double marginalisation and the sense of entrapment the Indian women are confronted with taking Anita Desai's *Clear Light of Day* for closer scrutiny. The 'Third Theatre' of Bengali playwright, Badal Sircar, and his avowed aim of awakening the urban audience to an awareness of exploitation in rural India and rural audience to a sense of its power receive attention in E. Renuka and Shampa Bhattacharjee's article.

The Canadian novelist, Margaret Laurence, in a fascinating fictional account, presents the interplay of male/female, urban/rural, and European/settler categories. While the question of nationalism in Laurence's *The Diviners* is addressed to by P. Mallikarjuna Rao and M. Prabhakar in their article, her Manawaka fiction is sought to be analysed in terms of regional ethos by K. Damodar Rao and M. Surendra Kumar in their article entitled, "The Context of Regionalism in Margaret Laurence's Manawaka Fiction."

Shelley Walia's article with its wider sweep unfolds "an understanding of the construction of the colonial power and reaction to it through a liberating narrative and discourse." He illustrates his argument by citing Raja Rao's *Kanthapura.*

R. Saraswati explores the recurring pattern in Bessie Head's novels in which the characters resolve their inner trauma by striking a harmonious relation with the outer reality and thus combine "private with the social." The "internal struggles" Elizabeth faces in the novel are metaphoric of the struggles ensuing out of cultural colonization.

In his article, Ashok Mohapatra discusses three different models of self-acknowledgement in the novels of three black writers from three different continents namely, USA, Kenya and Nigeria. Despite their disparate backgrounds these novelists exemplify how the postcoloniality plays out in "varying forms with varying implications" in different contexts.

In "R. Parthasarathy and postcolonial discourse," P. Mallikarjuna Rao traces the growth of the Indian poet in English in the postcolonial situation and illustrates how the alien cultural influences which operate through the medium of language shape the poetic sensibility of a writer. He argues that unless a writer is conscious of the cultural forces and suitably bend the language to his needs he tends to become alienated and derivative.

In her article, "*Jane Eyre* and Jean Rhys: 'Gendering the subaltern'" Rama Kundu while pointing out the differences between western feminist theory and feminist discourses within the third world context, argues that the latter had to "grapple with a complex challenge that subtly combined imperialism with androcentrism and patriarchal domination." She analyses this contrast by taking Jean Rhys's *Wide Sargossa Sea* for closer examination. She views the novel as an interrogation of exclusivist assumptions about the racial other as depicted in Charlotte Bronte's *Jane Eyre*.

Concentrating on postcolonial aesthetics Prasenjit Maiti in his article on Othello's Otherness examines the marginality of Othello. While asserting that Othello has always remained as a stranger, the outsider, whose "modalities of interaction cannot be addressed by white narrative," he presents Othello as one who has to negotiate the role performances of Desdemona and Iago.

NOTES

1. Edward Said, "Figures, Configurations, Transfigurations," *From Commonwealth to the Post-colonial*, ed. Anna Rutherford (Aarhus: Dangaroo Press, 1992) 3.
2. Frantz Fanon, *The Wretched of the Earth*, trans. Constance Farrington (New York: Grove Press, 1990) 23.

3. Wole Soyinka, *Myth, Literature and the African World* (Cambridge: Cambridge UP, 1976) xi.
4. Bill Ashcroft, Gareth Griffiths and Helen Tiffin, *Key Concepts in Post-colonial Studies* (London and New York: Routledge, 1998).
5. G.N. Devy, "Translation Theory, An Indian Perspective," *In Another Tongue* (Madras: Macmillan, 1995) 136.
6. Bill Ashcroft *et al.*, *The Empire Writes Back: Theory and Practice in Post-colonial Literatures* (London and New York: Routledge, 1989) 40.

CONTENTS

1

Political *Re*turns: *Ab*uses of the Academy

D. VENKAT RAO

In my part of the country (India) this is the harvest season. This January saw suicides of 100 farmers who wanted to reap the "white gold"—cotton.[1] These farmers have all moved from reaping paddy, onions, groundnuts to cotton—the globe demanded this move. But the move forced them to move out of life. They all succumbed to their blighted crop by gulping the same pesticide that they sprayed, in vain, across their pest-ridden crop. How to turn my tribes eyes toward this disaster? The obscenity of Indian middle class has no limits. What kind of strength, obduracy and optimism does one require to turn its eyes? What literacies do we have to incorporate to stomach these indigestible events of our times?

Yet, but truly, what can be done with the delay—the time-lag? Our profession kept us securely away from those "social hieroglyphics" which need re-decipherings. There are always formalizations and capturings of this institution that manages "our" work (of mourning). But even when there is no such professional imposition (as at my work place in India)—how does one deal with the time-lag? My writing a paper/report may see the light of day weeks after (if I am lucky) it is written. But that period is the most crucial and disturbing gap and delay. The text will wait but both the textile maker and the cotton-farmer have no time to wait or they will be condemned to wait in perpetuity. What does it mean to think and write in the face of sudden death? In the face of denials of the death-event? Also what does it mean to write other than as a reporter, journalist, social scientist etc? Can writing for speaking at conferences be used to think about these issues?

What about the risks? When Gaddar (a poet composer-performer and singer of my region) writes songs about these peasants and handloom weavers—his life is under gun. The time-lag is also a source for someone like me to write about these songs of death. What are my own risks—especially when I am talking in a company which may not yet have much to share?

On February 18 this year the *Wall Street Journal*—a journal in small print but with big deals—published a human interest story on the front page. The pesticide deaths appear important enough to have found place on the front page of this journal of pure calculations with returns. It tells a "good story." It tells about the new lure of the cotton crop, the new banking regulations on farm lendings, the blood-sucking moneylenders, the unscrupulous pesticide dealers, the killer pest, and above all the glaring disparities in the access to "benefits" of new economic reforms: the "economic expansion is by passing some of India's most impoverished rural areas [...]."

Would it be pertinent to ask why are Wall Street audiences interested in Warangal—"a region so backward that it spawned India's most violent guerrilla movement?" It's a shocking tragedy—the reporter glosses. The hubris of this tragic subject—the reforming India—is entirely and essentially internal to the subject: feudality and politicians: "many people, like these cotton farmers, are trapped in a feudal time warp." Politicians have used them only for votes. The help from outside, the *deus ex machina* of global capital flows could benefit these people but the tragic flaw comes in the way. A very American (or Wall Street) story indeed.

How can we, academics outside and in the academy, and others begin to unravel this narrative of tragedy? How can we solicit the outside so that the conceptions of the tragic can be transformed?

As a standardized penacea for all fatal flaws in the world, the World Bank offered its magic wand to the state of Andhra Pradesh recently. In a confidentially circulated document of the Bank, released in the middle of 1997, one can see a symmetrically divided plot. To overcome the fiscal crisis the state can choose between the "Status-quo scenario" and the "Adjustment scenario." As one goes through the plot one recognizes that it is no longer literary texts alone that can change mind-sets (as the colonial epoch plotted once) but even these documents of the "real" (despite the rebarbative language-use) world have the capacity to change minds in no time (or in the given time). The simplicity of the plot and its conclusions are disarming. In the SQ scenario the fiscal crisis would aggravate and the current proposed 4.3% Gross State Domestic Product (GSDP) would decline to 3.5% in another five years. Whereas the ADJ scenario, as the wand waves, the GSDP will shoot up to 6.5%. Even idiots, both Marx's and metropolitan, would love this ending. The latter applaud.

But the outside needs space to move (*i.e.*, move-in), the wand has to swivel. As anyone who is familiar with this magic knows, the space that needs cleared for this movement is people-intensive areas: agriculture, subsidies, public-sector employment etc. (the "non-interest expenditure" in the Bank lingo). Even the *Wall Street* story-teller points out that "subsidy cuts have made seeds, fertilizer and electricity more costly...," as if the agency of these measures is some despicable barbaric feudal lord. Indian agricultural sector, after the so-called Green revolution experiment and more recently the Bank's new measures in agriculture, requires a thick description and a new form of writing than the one that time, space and expertise would allow me here (*Cf.* Public Interest Research Group Reports in general and Vandana Shiva's work more specifically). The space that the Bank mandates for its movement in "sectoral" issues such as power, irrigation, health care is total. As anyone familiar with Indian scene of "reforms" knows major international bidders have moved into these areas.

The Wall Street's shocking tragedy will be effective only when the machinations or mandates of the outside are kept out. This keeping out will keep intact the long-cherished great divide between the aiding West and the reset of them.

But where is the academy in all this? What can the academy do today? Here I wish to examine a new venture from the academy announced recently. Robert Young, an Oxford academic, circulated an announcement about a new journal last year. The announcement carried with it a set of seven questions indicating the nature, problems and limitations of contemporary postcolonial studies. Responses to the questions were solicited. Before attending to the questions in detail let me briefly comment on the Preamble to the questions included in the announcements.

The journal—*Interventions*—is projected as a founding and naming act. The journal seeks to "forge the identity of contemporary postcolonial work so as to foreground its interventionist possibilities." Despite such founding aim, the inaugural issue commits itself to unraveling the hidden ideologies of the postcolonial (discourse). These ideologies, notwithstanding the dominant characteristic of self-conscious inquiry in postcolonial studies—are tracked as its eclecticism, its "truth of experiential knowledge" its privileging of location, its fundamental dependence on "historical realities" etc. Here the division between ideology and critique remains conventionally governed. Is postcolonial discourse a critique or an ideology, Young asks? If it is the latter (that is, ideology) "what are the ideologies of the postcolonial writing, whether literary, cultural or critical/theoretical?" he queries.

In accordance with the agenda, the questioning and the inaugural gesture both project the journal itself as an interventionary critique (that which exposes false consciousness, the "hidden ideologies" etc). Further, the entire announcement places firmly the agent of this critique outside the business of postcolonial studies. Indeed so, for the postcolonial studies is represented here entirely as an activity of the migrants, ex-colonials, or people of colour: it is a transaction "within and across postcolonial nation-spaces." These formulations, despite undoubtedly good intentions, do not suggest the necessity or possibility of a thinking together. On the contrary, they seem to emerge from the science of critique. The substance and method of these formulations reinforce this dubious division. Such formulations can give rise to deeper suspicions about these befriending gestures.

Yet, as I am in solidarity with the effort I commit myself to thinking along with these questions as far as possible and see whether a thinking together can help us in reformulating the issues of our (common) concern.

> **Q 1** Who and where is the postcolonial? Does contemporary postcolonial and related writing overemphasise the cultural impact of migrancy and dislocation? Certainly migrancy has constituted a major feature of global order since World War II, but to privilege the migrant condition as representative of the postcolonial down-plays the historical experience of the far greater numbers who have not migrated, who have migrated to non-metropolitan places, as well as of the vast numbers who migrated in the past. The emphasis on cultural hybridity in the reading of contemporary diasporas, implies a contrasting homogeneity in the past that the long histories of slavery, indentured labour and political exile refute. How are these interests to be reconciled?

It seems to me that postcolonial studies if there is such a thing-ought not to consolidate and privilege a certain historical temporality. At the same time, one must see the ways in which those other experiences (of slavery and indentured labour) can be articulated beyond the empirical, disciplinary productions. In other words, can those experiences as substantive sources be used to rewrite disciplinary perceptions—and through these articulations address contemporary institutionalized structures of making sense of the world? That is, the fundamental condition of postcolonial studies—that of displacement—must be radically practised here. The originality, the specific as the cathected source of origin must be displaced. Even for all practical and substantive purposes, and necessarily, if we engage with those unique and historically specific experiences and language and gestural uses these uses are, in the ultimate analysis, not in the service of fetishizing and congealing the moment into a disciplinary icon for some "domestic benefit."

Q 2 The question of representation: why has "recognition" of minorities become a key political issue, often apparently put above access to employment and other (un)equal opportunities? Does it still implicitly assume a Hegelian master-slave recognition structure? Who is being given the agency of doing the recognising? Are they still located at the metropolitan centre? In a related way, the topics of identity, subjectivity and "voice" have become of primary significance for contemporary cultural theorists: but to whom is the voice addressed, which listeners are being spoken to, who is supposed to hear and how are they supposed to respond?

This question, in implying a hierarchy of "minority recognition" (master-slave relation) over "access to employment and other (un)equal opportunities" seems to suggest that these could be exclusive and opposed entities of a structure. In this hierarchisation the "key political issue" of recognition is still formed in Hegelian master/slave narrative. The question still seems to have arisen in the metropolitan academic context of affirmative action. But precisely this context is seen to be the basis for postcolonial minority recognition syndrome. Whereas the site on which both these narratives (reception/access) are being made visible is certainly academic university as the institution of the principle of reason. Although the questions concerning the agency and audience of the postcolonial articulations (of subjectivity, identity and voice) are pertinent they have a curious ring when postcolonial cultural theorists are asked to think about their voices, agencies, audiences and their desired responses, as if the onus is on the postcolonialists alone to address these questions. Consequently, the larger possibility of addressing the very structures of constitution—rational academic subject, the university, civil society (in short the legacies of the so-called enlightenment)—an addressing that could be glimpsed through the breaching of the postcolonial gets foreclosed.

The abuse of the legacy of the enlightenment (if one wishes to retain the term) can possibly be envisaged when the division and separation of minority recognition and access to opportunities is displaced. Such a displacement is made possible by the impinging of questions of life, living and land on the academy and other structures. And it seems to me that to trace the provenance of these questioning acts to some unified origin of European enlightenment is not just a gratuitous gesture but even false piety that could perpetuate a certain violence. Indeed, this is where the principle of what do you do with what you have must be put to practice radically. That is, the modes and material of specific articulations and locations must be attended.

Yet the practice must guarantee no certainty of a ground—however specific and local that might be. The question of provenance as much as the issue of destination, and the question of agency (and subjectivity) as much as the matter of reception must be divided and displaced. For example, elemental questions concerning land, water, air, body and living could be addressed once again from the specific contexts of endangered and dispossessed lives. At the same time, the resources at hand in those contexts in terms of languages, practices, gestures and relations must be received with care for the purposes of unforeseen living as thinking. Thus the received division between empirical and philosophical or economic or moral could be re-thought.

Whereas Robert Young's question (regarding agency/ destination of critique) still addresses the subject of the academy. (Crassly put, Young's question might run polemically thus: given the sophisticated and inaccessible idiom of so much of postcolonial discourse—psychoanalysis, deconstruction and locationalism who are these people addressing? Can these claims of empowerment have any meaning if their implied subject [the subaltern] has simply no access to these accounts? In short, isn't postcolonial theory simply another academic turf battle?)

Q 3 How far does the high profile of class, race, ethnicity and gender issues in postcolonialism sustain the view that postcolonial studies are really the product of contemporary multiculturalism in the US? Has theory really travelled or have the theorists rather travelled to theory in the metropolis? Does the related argument that postcolonial studies are a predominantly Western phenomenon confined to Western institutions mark a productive political intervention in an era of transnational communities?

The third question predictably emphasizes and makes explicit the locational politics of postcolonialist theory. Isn't postcolonial theory largely a western, metropolitan academic creation? Can such a discourse make effective political intervention in an era of transnational communities?

Here, once again, it seems to be a matter of the distance and difference between phrase and content, promise and fulfilment. Postcolonial theory is supposed to have claimed radical cutting edge interventions—its frame, its promise is being questioned here. Such questioning must necessarily be done. Indeed the promise must be brought to crisis by interrogating the nature of contents that are being transported or incorporated under the promising banner. Yet, curiously, why this questioning of promising form (the consolidating label) is being done in the context of postcolonial theory alone? Shouldn't such questioning be undertaken as a general practice—a practice that moves across and beyond all the regional consolidations (canons, disciplines, and institutions)? Shouldn't Young's question be unleashed in the general context of the concept of the university itself?

Whereas his regionalizing of postcolonial studies makes his question rather polemical. On the contrary, a certain kind of questioning, certainly emerging from the terrain of the postcolonial thinking, is advancing precisely this problematic of the general. This is not to say that regionalizing and field-making and area-consolidating efforts are absent in the so-called postcolonial ventures. But this regionalizing and totalizing of postcolonial studies is inattentive to the general force of that other thought. While insisting on the singularity of this other take (this moving *itaratra*), this force of the general need not be valorized under the regionalized phrase or phrases that have turned into dogmatic cliches. This critical thinking of the general, for instance, is not emerging from the so-called postcolonialist studies in India. In fact, postcolonialist studies for that matter, are not part of a majority of the universities at all. The critical thought of the general, the thought of living are emerging out of concerns for the elemental, the irreducible sources of life and land.

> **Q 4** Does "postcolonialism" mark the end of the "Third World?" A recent article in *The Investor's Chronicle* suggested that India might be a good place to invest in now that it is "shedding its postcolonial ideological shackles." So from capitalism's point of view, postcolonialism describes the third world's adoption of the Marxist anti-capitalist ideologies in the past. Most nations in Africa and Asia had a choice of economic and political system upon becoming independent—either a Western free-market demand economy, or a Sino-Soviet Marxist centralised one, or an indigenous mixed economy, such as in India. With the collapse of the Soviet block, and the conversion of China to a form of controlled capitalist economy, today there is effectively no longer any choice *de facto* there is now only a single world economic system. One implication of this is that with the demise of the second world, a third world no longer exists. Indeed the emergence of postcolonial theory could be viewed as marking the moment in which the third world moved from an affiliation with the second world to the first. The rise of postcolonial studies coincided with the end of Marxism as the defining political, cultural and economic objective of much of the third world. But if it still seeks an oppositional role, what form of critical participatory economics should postcolonial analysis look to?

One wonders why the poor postcolonialists are being upstaged and put in the dock. Why postcolonialist theory is being asked to carry the burden of the world's evils and calamities. Can't postcolonial theory's "historical situatedness," Young questions, be conflated with global capital flows and the "economic migrant?" But, to make a minor point first, the *Investor Chronicle*'s declarations regarding India shedding its "post-colonial shackles" indicate a different chronology and mapping from the one drawn by Young. For the *Chronicle* the ending of postcoloniality marks the inauguration of "globalization" (in the Indian case, specifically, 1991-92). But Young's recounting of this declaration takes on the rhetoric of the end of ideology, end of history narratives. But even chronologically postcolonial studies do not begin with globalization/financialization of the world. Questions of decolonization can be traced back easily to the sixties and even to earlier periods. "Marx" continues to be an animating or haunting force of these questions in the so-called decolonization. Here it could be even pointed out that "Marx," at least in certain parts of India in this period, did not come simply from above as such. The academy, with minimal exceptions, in decolonization was deeply anti-Marxian (in terms of curriculum and material). The persistence of Marxian notes can be distinctly identified in the social movements—largely composed of the marginalized and grass-roots communities. The haunting of Marx from below is still palpable in the Indian context.

It is, however, amusing that Robert Young's questioning should make postcolonial studies responsible for an alternative to the devastating rapacity of globalization. Why should a regionalized "critical" discourse carry the burden of responsibility of such magnitude? Especially, when such a discourse is affiliated with the so-called third world? However important the question might be one could ask, how many critical ventures and movements that seek their origins in a certain West have been forced to face such questioning? "Without a substantive economic basis for its critique," writes Young, "postcolonialism runs the danger of merely reflecting the globalization of capital flows that has been such a feature of Post-Soviet Union history...." Is such a danger peculiar fate of Postcolonial theory alone? What about all such other post theories? Further, can the questioning emerging from colonial displacements—from epistemic violations—be reduced to spatiotemporal limits as Young seems to be doing here?

Yet it must be seen whether Young's questions can be addressed beyond polemical disputations. Even if today's world can be described as, as Young seems to do, "a single economic system," can capitalism be said to be absolute and total in its success? Can it be said to be entirely self-generating and self-sufficient? Has it ever existed in complete independence? As Raymond Williams said long ago, the word dominant always suggests subordinated elements prevailing. This is not to suggest that the subordinated, residual elements will in some desirable future reassert themselves and emerge as full-blown systems. On the contrary it is to remind that the unity and the supposed self-sufficiency of this "single economic system" are perpetually and constitutively dependent on the other devastated systems and modes. The rapacity of the globalizing forces, in their super accumulations deploy all modes of abstraction today: once again the elemental entities such as land, water, forest and lives are at stake here.

The logic of this "new" accumulation is in disfiguring the ecoscript. The blighted cotton crop and the sweating textile factory (75 handloom weavers committed suicide in the first year of liberalisation in India) continue to tell the story of deprivation and displacement that Marx first tracked over a century and half ago. Retrenchment and displacement are mandated by the new mochlos of governance today.

Capitalism fixes the human for its conceptual unity and for celebration of its visibility. The ends of the human are claimed to reach their glorious zenith in this supposedly self-sustaining structure. An undoing of this alleged unity of the concept and the destiny of the human must be first undertaken. Instead of asking for ready-made models as alternatives in the "blaming-the-victim" tone, detailed and specific practices of the undoing must be brought into effect. The barbaric nature of its civilizational claims can be made visible when the remote controlled suffering on which capitalism depends is addressed.

Further, the question of alternative to capitalism cannot be conceived in economic terms alone. Given that the human value is codified in terms of productivity and enterprise ethos, the alternative must be conceived in larger and general terms. Robert Young's assertion that "The rise of postcolonial studies coincided with the end of Marxism as the defining political, cultural and economic objective of much of the third-world" is too premature an assumption. This claim can be disputed factually. First of all the rise of postcolonial studies does not coincide with even the virtual disappearance of Marx. On the contrary, and more importantly, social movements emerging from the third world, especially India, do not divide the realms of the economic, political and cultural as Young indicates in the question. The economic is never articulated in isolation from the cultural and the political. This is so especially and patently in movements animated by the figure of Marx. Once again we are returned, in these articulations, to the question of the elemental. The elemental cannot be separated from modes of living in these contexts. There is indeed a general lesson to be learnt in these concerns for the elemental. In these articulations where concepts are turned into metaphors Marx is not just a predictive scientist—but more effectively and powerfully a figure for the voices from below. Yet in these catachrestic undertakings loyalty to provenances must be confounded. Marx, like any other figure, will be transformed.

Q 5 In the West, it was also the theories of post-structuralism which from the 1960s onwards challenged certain Marxist presuppositions, a challenge which took on greater momentum with the historical coincidence of the collapse of Marxism in the Soviet Union and the end of the Soviet Empire in Eastern Europe. Unexpectedly given its initial reception as a form of a political idealism, many of the precepts of post-structuralism were utilised in Europe and the US by minorities, particularly people of colour, who recognised the radical political potential of certain of its ideas and transformed its priorities in the process. If post-structuralism lost its idealism, this transformation also involved the renunciation of its radical anti-Enlightenment critique of humanism and a re-endorsement of the liberal values of individualism, together with the abandonment of economic arguments in general. Has the tendency to individualise experience meant that fundamental economic disparities, both within nations and between them, are considered in general terms but without the issue of poverty access to health care, and the benefits of political stability being addressed in any substantive way?

Can the Critique of Marxism emerging from post-structuralist thought be equated with the reasons for the "collapse" of the Soviet-style Marxism? That is, are these two events similar in their responses to Marxism? Can the so-called "Marxist pre-suppositions" be reduced to the Soviet experiment? Does this mean the existing uses of the concept-figure of Marx exhaust all possibilities of its other uses? Can uses of existing entities be determined in advance?

Further in the same question as we can see Robert Young sketches postcolonial uses of poststructuralist thought. Against the current of idealist receptions of poststructuralist thought, he suggests, people of colour have used this thought for radical political purposes in the metropolis. But curiously, he goes on to say that these uses of post-structuralist thought have renounced the latter's "radical anti-Enlightenment critique of humanism" and endorsed liberal values of individualism and abandoned economic argument. This is a strange claim. If post-colonial studies brought back or endorsed metropolitan liberal ethos wherein lies their recognition and forging of radical political potential of post-structuralist thought? Does this mean that the radicality of post-colonial scholars served their assimilation into liberal" ethos? The polemical/cynical thrust of the argument here is now a fairly well-known skirmish of metropolitan academy.

Robert Young's attempt to turn post-colonial studies from academic battles toward what could be described as material and institutional conditions of deprivation ("economic disparities," "health care" etc.) is a very pertinent and commendable one. But to make post-colonial studies and people of colour the respondents to such deprivations by a first world academic makes the attempt very intriguing. What was Western Marxism's—in its heydays—contribution in putting into practice

Marx's eleventh thesis? If postcolonial studies fetishizes "individual experience" and abandons substantive issues in the world we live in—then surely it would end up being a regional science sheltered in the academy. But very much like the other satellite fields that flourish under the rubrics of period, movement, name etc. poco studies too would safeguard its niche in the university.

The question that is being posed to postcolonial studies must be unleashed against the very structure or concept of the university itself. What has been the role and chance of the university itself in its entire historical existence with regard to the fundamental conditions of deprivation and displacement? This kind of questioning would suggest the necessity of abusing the very idea of the university (as a place for the subject of public use of reason). In such questioning one would be made to see that disciplinary knowledges that compose and constitute the structure of the university have largely functioned on regionalized and professionalized forms of knowledge production. An abuse of the university (and enlightenment) would require a deliberate forgetting, an abdication of knowledge and an abandonment of epistemophilic subject. It would require, of necessity, learning to do and live with what one has beyond and outside the frames within which what one has have been encoded. The provenance and destination of what one has cannot be foreclosed in advance. (More pragmatic activities can be outlined here—such as reading/writing reports from "below," tracking media narratives, bringing together policy, decision makers and those at the receiving end with necessary mediations, calling the bluff of "democratic" ideals in the context of their response to voices from below etc.) Whether a label or field should be consolidated to put into practice this abuse should not be turned into a specialist issue for debate. The maxim—what do you do with what you have must be put to work.

Q 6 Postcolonial writing, together with minority writing in the West and feminist writing generally, has achieved a revolution in aesthetics and the aesthetic criteria of the literary just at the moment when "the literary" was most under attack as an outdated category of elitist institutions. In institutional terms, the impact of feminism and postcolonialism has radically changed, the criteria of what makes authentic art by challenging the cultural capital from which notions of the literary were derived. Writing is now valued as much for its depiction of representative minority experience as for its aesthetic qualities. Postcolonial writing has decisively articulated itself through history and historical rewriting, reforming and retrieving an historical sensibility through the creative processes of contemporary writing. This suggests that in its own way, despite an appropriation of forms of thinking associated with post-structuralist and postmodernist antifoundationalism, in practice postcolonial studies can be strongly foundationalist, grounded in an epistemology which gives primacy to an authentic historical reality (a position decisively mapped out in the founding text of modern postcolonial studies, Edward Said's *Orientalism* of 1978). If it is this combination that orients postcolonialism in political terms and constitutes its distinctive cultural and theoretical identity, how does post-colonialism manage to lay claim to this foundationalism while at the same time reversing the premises of an earlier foundationalism grounded on universals, aesthetics, totality, homogeneity, purity, race and attachment to the land?

Robert Young's questions are concerned with philosophical and material implications of postcolonial studies. In this questioning sometimes the phantasmatic postcolonial scholar appears as an interview candidate who is obligated to answer questions. One such job-market question is: given that postcolonial studies as a critical discourse draws on radical foundational critiques of post-structuralist and post-modernist thought how can it (poco) at the same time epistemologically insist upon an "authentic historical reality" as its source as it appears to do? That is, while drawing its lessons and strategies of foundational critiques from European thought how can poco reconcile it with its claims for a distinctive cultural and theoretical identity?

Responding to the protocols of the format—it could be argued that post-structuralist critique of foundations could be understood more as confounding foundations rather than being anti-foundationalist. If one understands *foundation* as a condition (or set of conditions) for the possibility of significance—post-structuralist thought (especially Derrida's) did not deny such conditionalities. Anti-foundationalism suggests denial of conditions or contexts. Whereas post-structuralism clearly states that it is not that there are no contexts as such—but it is that there is no single context that can exhaust all possibilities of a significance. No context, as a foundational condition of significance, can have complete control over what it *appears* to generate. Post-structuralism has redeployed the concepts of origin and end as open-ended.

Secondly, the foundational patrix that post-structuralism was confounding conceives its elements as pre-interpretive, always already given (philosophy is European, reason western, Europeanization of earth etc.). Soliciting the house that he inhabited Derrida described this foundational legion as metaphysical. It is such ontologized and essentialized founding concepts that received critical interrogation from postcolonial scholars/critics.

Surely, these critiques when they insist on the specificity of contexts cannot be reduced to some foundationalist epistemology. The insistence on the specificity of context cannot be conflated with a metaphysical (pre-interpretive) will for purity, homogeneity, universality, totality, race and land. The insistence on the context has largely manifested, in practice and thought, in unravelling interested blindness, domestic benefits, that consolidated interpretations as transparent, self-evident truths (*cf.* subaltern studies).

It is difficult to see from Young's questioning which postcolonial critic is investing in the transparency of the so-called authentic, individual experience. In this kind of questioning, unfortunately, postcolonial studies appear more as a metropolitan imaginary with a unity and self-sufficiency which is hard to find in the symbolic of its manifestation. Above all, the emphasis on the contextual must be received as an invitation to interpretation and changing the conditions of possibility rather than a foreclosure for further thought.

But why should there be an inherent and essential peculiarity in the postcolonial theory that would guarantee against its joining a behive? Can anyone guard poco studies from becoming regionalized disciplinary study in the academy? Robert Young himself points out the assimilation of radical potential of post-structuralist thought in the liberal academy. Should we have, can we design fool-proof regulatory mechanism against such assimilations?

As suggested earlier, however, the questioning of decolonization can provide possibilities for thinking in general. Colonization, it could be argued, covered the territories under its control with a massive pedagogical programme: subject making enterprise. It bred its own "counter" pedagogics which, advanced themselves in ways that were outlined by the master pedagogy. The abuse of this pedagogy and the confounding of those outlines could be practised when provenances and destinations (time, space, nature and heritage) are not valorized and canonized. When exploring the ways of moving beyond, while deploying, the received pedagogic protocols, the confounding act must be practised as a mode of living. The energy and force of this questioning and living, or living as questioning (of the received and of provenance) cannot be exhausted by the specific contexts that seem to nurture them. The roots of these modes of living can spread deep and wide in soils across terrain.

This is what I have described as the concerns of the elemental. The necessity of embracing these concerns has been made imperative by the devastating forces in decolonization. What is at stake is living. The elements that weave this living are: water, space, forest, land and air. The unique and the singular, in terms of living must be addressed across all kinds of received frames and structures. Academy is just one such, but important, structure. And the university cannot teach us the pedagogy of its abuse. The hieroglyphics of such abuse must be learnt from a displaced "below" on the very sites of our "habitation." This concern for the elemental, this abusive pedagogy, I wish to submit, would return the very notion of the political.

Q 7 The notion of race and attachment to land opens up the questions of nationalism and the nation-state in relation to postcolonial studies, and the debates around their progressiveness, their viability, and their operativity in decolonized countries in particular. Can a politics of cultural nationalism only be sustained in postcolonial studies in relation to continuing colonial or quasi-colonial situations (for example, in Ireland, Palestine, and Hawaii)?

The last question whether national assertions (in terms of attachment to land and racial communities) are viable only in the contexts of colonial/quasi-colonial situations must be addressed beyond the claims of such assertions. For even during national liberation struggles nationalist rhetoric remained impervious to the radical heterogeneity of communities and languages that were subsumed under a homogeneous unity of the nation. In decolonization nationality question returns to breach the lid of unity imposed from above. But what needs to be seen in the nationality question in decolonization is that it is no simple rhetoric in the name of some cultural heritage or unified idiom. These questions are profoundly consumed with the elemental questions of survival, access to land, crop, water and living. They cannot be terminated into sublimation of some putative unity of heritage. However, the specificity of these questions, the uses of what is available in forging the questions, the singularity of these idioms must be carefully responded. The uses of nationality question therefore, beyond nationalist rhetoric or "liberation" movements, articulate a larger and more general agenda.

The abuse of the academy, need I repeat, must be for a thinking together for other openings. Unfortunately, Robert Young's inaugural announcement even as it desires for active concerns appears to formulate its idiom from an older divide.

Even as I write this the provincial government of Andhra is busily concocting a report on this "sudden" "mysterious" deaths of the cotton farmers. The enlightened are always there to help the state. This time the state sought the help of a group of psychiatrists (the most vocal of these claimed to be a member of the Royal Society of Psychiatrists of London) to render an expedient account. The account became necessary as the National Human Rights Commission, responding to a petition by a farmer for its intervention, demanded an explanation from the state.

The over educated experts had text-books that gave answers. The cotton farmers' suicides were, the psychiatrists explained, a kind of "mass hysteria rather than each thing happening individually.... People learn by seeing others. A kind of fashion has caught up." Farmers' greed for promised money (*ex gratia*) from the government to the bereaved families, they added, spurred these deaths. Among remedial measures the experts recommended (to the state) electric shocks, or in their lingo, "electro-convulsive therapy" to the surviving "depressed" farmers as the best treatment. These experts belong to a tribe that has become stenographers to the Bretton Woods bureaucracy in the last seven years. "Come Ugadi", said a farmer to the Wall Street Reporter, "so many people will kill themselves. What else can we do?"

"What is to be done, at present?" an old question is repeated by a French philosopher recently. "Where certainties come apart," wrote Jean Luc Nancy, "there too gathers the strength that no certainty can match." Elements of such strength can be gathered from the uses of the available in unforeseen ways. Such elements can be gathered in the gesture and speech, song and poem of the very region which has been living through this mourning without ends in the epoch of decolonization. These elements are forging questions in a language that has no representation in the region's public media, staging performances which have no recognizable precedence in the heritage: these are the question songs, mourning poems of the Telengana region which is struggling against postindustrial feudality and of late the capital flows of Bretton Woods. These are writings and showings with concerns for the elemental: land, living, life and water. Predictably these voices are under the constant threat of extinction.

"Of all the animals" says the oldest text of Indic past, "capable of *being* sacrificial victims, man is the sole creature who is also capable of proforming, of *doing* the sacrificial act." Today the beings that are called upon to perform, to do this act are coming forth from the margins and ends of the society: children, women and men of the othered (or itered) communities. Their acts sing and show an unending mourning as a yearning for an unforeseen future. Can we partake their mourning outside in the academy?

NOTE

1. This paper was presented at a conference on "Activism and the Academy: Opening Dialogues" organized at the George Washington University (USA) in the last week of March 1997. At the time of preparing this presentation the number of suicides was reported to be 100 in the Western Press. As is well-known now more than 400 deaths were reported subsequently.

2

Postmodernism, Discourse and the Colonial Perspective

SHELLEY WALIA

My choice of this subject derives from the premise that any criticism of colonial or postcolonial literature depends for its force on the recognition of its self-definition. It derives also from my concern that the interplay between past and present requires a continuing dialogue between historians. It is important to explore the subject position of the colonial writers within texts produced in the colonies and in Britain. Both kinds of texts coming from the two sides are constructed out of situations of power, and constructed differently. The ensuing analysis consists of an understanding of the construction of the colonial power and the reactions to it through a liberating narrative and discourse.

This essay forms the basis for the dialectics of cultural formation. Such an intention is pertinent to a postcolonial ethos where the colonial experiment changed the native framework that somewhat showed resistance as well as acceptance of the imperial intellectual position. The appropriation of native literature to such hegemonic control brings about the crisis in indigenous art forms when they collide with western art forms and theory. This colonial imposition taken as continual referents could only shape a lopsided view of history replete with notions of closure, exclusion, and bias. A cultural analysis of the multi-faceted experience in colonial and postcolonial literatures is essential because different cultural perspectives must recognize both the independence of the discourse of the colonised and its potential as an alternative, even though marginal in its capacity to re-examine the colonized experience. A movement away from Said's idea of a totalizing and monolithic Orientalism imposing itself on the passive colonial subject is necessary, and an interesting break is seen in the works of Nigel Leask and Homi Bhabha where hybridism and orientalist dichotomy between European paradigms of moral superiority and Asiatic violence and eroticism suggest models of colonial self-articulation which have the capacity to deconstruct the colonial space.

The following view sets out to show that no theory of colonial/postcolonial history or of literary criticism can be non-partisan but carries with it an ideology that fixes one's relationship in a culture and is reinforced by principles of power—academic, political and social. When new historicism is applied to literary (especially narrative) texts it often creates a disjunction between what the text is saying about history and what the historian is saying about the text. And as the historical moment changes, so does the meaning of the text or the sign. Behind the creation of such texts lie narrative histories as well as imaginative literary works.

We can discern only surface regularities across a wide range of texts. Underlying them are divergent discourses which, as Foucault says, are not simply those which "translate struggles or systems of domination, but are the thing for which and by which there is struggle." The colonial and postcolonial discourse is an area for studying struggles for meaning and to see how future writings would shape. Processes and struggles, power and knowledge, go hand in hand to determine the forms and domains of knowledge. Texts are determined by a range of discourses and there is a need to examine differences within and between texts because of factors of time, place, and the type of colonial intervention. As is often argued, I do not think that contemporary obsession with theory has in any way led to the disparaging of the anti-colonial discourses of colonial liberation. It becomes important for both the western and third world scholarship to pay full attention to the ways in which the investigative and interpretative exercises of the 'other' provide insights into the designs of imperialism. In one way the third-world scholar becomes the agent of the postcolonial state as well as a counterpart of the first-world scholar who seeks to interpret the third world and its politics of resistance and repression. The first-world scholar must not patronize or romanticize the third world, but instead learn from its investigations which in no way need to be corrected by the so-called "superior theory and enlightened compassion" of the West.[1] Compassion, in fact, can come more through the broad understanding that 'reality' is not just there, but "depends on the codes and conventions within which it is represented."[2] The linguistic insight threatens and unsettles the accepted hierarchies of reality/appearance, self/other by revealing them as effects held in place by discourse.[3] What needs to be emphasised is that all objective knowledge necessarily has the underpinnings of power and establishes its status by regarding oppositional discourse as being provisional and unauthoritative. For instance, early 19th century 'liberal imperialism' employed enlightenment attacks on "the tyranny and priestcraft of the *ancien regime* to justify the conquest of non-European societies and culture."[4] The discourse of racial superiority, or the rationale behind the employment of illiberal colonial policies along with fostering racial and sexual stereotypes became vital to the racial design of "participation in the civilizing mission of 19th century European culture."[5]

In the context of destabilising and transforming fixed ideas of history, 'orientalism' has been revealed to be little more than a body of strength and power—a "culture hegemony at work."[6] The imperial epistemology exclusively works through the centrality of western consciousness; the incestuousness of orientalist testimony results in ambiguous colonial perspectives and disillusionments replete with desires and projections, dogmatism and racism.[7] Such is the consciousness with which the European confronts the idea of colonization. Behind such epistemology, there is no passivity, but a conscious political and hegemonic awareness which slowly finds expression in literary and a literary text. It is in this context that the problem of textuality with the underlying ideological and institutional constraints constantly working upon the writer has to be studied.

The study of imperialism and its power structures challenges the official discourse by highlighting the viewpoint of the native writer or historian. I only make a case for a humanistic study which needs to focus itself on politics and multi-culturalism. It is, in fact, not merely the methodological individualism that I have in mind but methodological holism also which seeks to integrate the economic, social, cultural, and political history into a total history, necessitating an acquaintance with social sciences for any literary historian. There must be alternate systems of concepts and assumptions in whose terms an interpretation of imperial epistemology can be arrived at. Such an interpretation may be a potential counterforce to cultural imperialism which operates as an auxiliary of economic imperialism.

Imperialism, as it appears to me, is not so much an advancement or extension of geo-political influence as the urgency to perpetuate the rule often by creating its own epistemology. Culture influenced through subversive politics, educational systems patterned to create the Western hegemony of the non-European, and control of the colonial psyche through imperial economic power are the prevailing norms which need to be upset by new theoretical and literary models if any meaningful literary traditions have to be formulated.

It is the writer who can disturb the prevailing political dispensation without fear, who can grasp the ordinary people's anxieties and hopes in a period of rapid change to construct a new narrative in order that received images of history be dismantled to arrive at multilayered meanings that run through the text, thus throwing light on the extent of the authenticity of the historical event. It is here that language exfoliating the complicity between the colonizer and the indigenous elite becomes important. In this context, Fanon's remark that "every people in whose soul an inferiority complex has been created by the death and burial of its local originality" throws light on the cultural rupture and its political consequences.[8] To arrive at a meaning, one can only read into the text by seeking the mythology, old literary forms, religious and metaphysical perceptions in the native literature. The profusion of untranslated Sanskrit, Hindu, or Swahili words we find in the fiction of Raja Rao, Narayan, and many African writers, categorise the literature to be first, local and particular, and then universal. Without the knowledge of Hindu mythology or Yoruba myths, or an oral narrative tradition, such works will not be understood within the framework of native thought. The culturally coded defamiliarisation in *Kanthapura*, for instance, where Rao describes the worship of the goddess Kenchamma does not involve automatic intelligibility. To the reader skeptical of the logic of offering a gold trinket to the goddess to keep smallpox away would be unverifiable narration, having little claim to reliability. Consider, for instance, the following:

> O Kenchamma! Protect us always like this through famine and disease, death and despair. O most high and bounteous! We shall offer you our first rice and our first fruit, and we shall offer you saris and bodice-cloth for every birth and marriage, we shall wake thinking of you [...] and through the harvest night [...] we shall sing and sing.[9]

Literature here is a vehicle of a cultural tradition deeply implicated with unquestioning divinity, accepting the 'truth' laid down by received tradition in its making, therefore more authentic even though presented in English.

The importance of the reconstruction of traditional culture constitutes an alternative practice from the discourse of the colonizer or the master narrative. Horkheimer and Adorno's *Dialectic of Enlightenment* argues that the logic of the enlightenment project was doomed to alter the quest for human freedom into a logic of domination and oppression. The desire to dominate nature had the underlying lust for domination of human beings.[10] The oppressive power of purely instrumental reason had therefore to be countered through the ideas of continuity and difference in history, through the rediscovery of pragmatism and the shifting of ideas about the philosophy of science. While Euro-American post-structuralist theories offer exciting possibilities to postcolonial theorists, it is nevertheless important to break up such strategies for a recreation of an indigenous culture. As we all know, the main aim of postmodernism is not to commit a master narrative. But within this stipulation lies a paradox. Whereas on the one hand within cultural studies, the postmodernist view allows the minority or third-world cultures to undertake a comprehensive, synthesizing approach, this itself tends to move towards a totalizing project. Nevertheless this paradox is essentially and cannot be ignored if the colonial discourse is to dismantle the imperial by having an authoritativeness of its own. I would like to treat colonial politics as essential integral to postmodernism; the colonial practice of fiction-writing has to be integrated within post-structuralist theorizing about representation, subject, gender, and the interaction discourse and power—in short, the full repertoire of poststructuralist theoretical *topoi*.

From the point of view of the hegemonic powers, the political of imperialism would regard the minority discourse as a flexible conceptual structure, open an "ever-changing structure by which to order both our cultural knowledge and our cultural procedures."[11] This approach is adverse to the colonial perspective which endeavours to establish indigenous and new ways of perception that help to break down the closed epistemological structures of Third World oppression. The challenge, in the words of Njabulo Ndebele, "is to free the entire social imagination of the oppressed from the laws of perception that have characterized these societies."[12] For writers, this implies a step beyond protest, to free the creative process itself from these very laws. But for the colonial powers this must provoke anxiety at the existence of other discourses which compete with their own for authority and attention.

My concern here is primarily with the problems created by language and history which employ polyphony and hybridization both as a means of appropriation and control over the 'other' and paradoxically for providing models for cultural recognition. This would necessitate an evaluation of texts not as much through the criteria of observation, analysis, verification and application as by a comprehension of the multi-layered meanings inherent in that literature. It is notable that throughout *Kanthapura*, the unofficial discourse of folk culture with its transgressions against decorum moves along with the official as in the lawyer's repeated attempts to speak in Hindi. He has a little pot with a slit in the lid into which he drops a coin every time he accidentally speaks in English. And if any of his friends should utter an English word in his house, he urges them to drop a coin as well. It is important that Rao plays up such ambivalences, even as he writes his novel in English.

The central dynamics of the colonial system and its nature and form can be seen at work in the colonial narrative. A study of literary forms emerging from the colonial world uncovers the world view and assumptions behind the strategy of presenting history. The type of narrative produced concerning the colonial state and its history will depend upon the importance the writer gives to certain events.

The problem of literary representation is seen in all colonial discourse where the oppositional consciousness of the 'silent' other posits nothing less than new objects of knowledge and new theoretical models that "upset or at very least radically alter the prevailing paradigmatic norms."[13] It is within this perspective that colonial discourse and literary theory contend with problems of dismantling the science of imperialism. Real events are spoken about or narrated differently from imaginary ones, and this is what produces different discourses. The means of representation of different discourses are fundamentally "heterogeneous and unequal" according to Lisa Lowe.[14] These discursive apparatuses differ over time, and do not necessarily correspond across national and cultural boundaries. Yet, despite their essential non-equivalence, discursive means of representation overlap and are mutually implicated in one another at different moments in time.

The truth of the historical texts can be corroborated by reference to inter-textual historical narratives. History is intrinsic to all narratives and cannot be done away with. But in the context of postmodernism the very foundations of historical knowledge have become shaky.[15] Complex and delicate relationships between the researcher and the historical reality are thrown into doubt. The subject "has become at once much more important because he is seen as the centre of ideology and partiality, in effect of whatever undermines the objectivity of research, and also in some sense much less important because modern theorists such as Foucault, Derrida, and Althusser attack his autonomy, 'decentring' the subject by focusing especially on ways in which society, discourse, or ideology produce the subjects they want and need."[16] Under the influence of postmodernism and new trends in cultural and literary studies, the interdependence of all modes of interpretation is now recognized. Hermeneutics, the influence of Roland Barthes' principle of structuralism which separates the author from the text resulting from the act of writing, and new historicism, all envisage a close link between literature, history, and textuality. Positivistic assumptions are slowly discredited as any account of the past is only one more story. An M.K. Naik or a Shahane thus become relevant to the critical studies on Forster which before their participation might have remained biased. Self-reflexivity and relativism have replaced self-confidence in the objectivity of historiography owing to the postmodernist belief that all representation deforms 'reality.' Competent in objectively analyzing only factual documents, historians have ignored the synchrony and diachrony, or narrative and discourse which new historicism has encouraged.

The emergent challenges to Said's presentation of orientalism as a constant and monolithic discourse through the multiplicity of discursive formations also needs to be mentioned here, especially in the context of the interventions of Third World creative writers and critics. Every form of critique from the 'other' alters and shifts the dominant discourse. As Lisa Lowe points out, "power is not static, nor does it inhere in an agency or a position or practice in itself; rather, it is found in the spatial and relational non-equivalence of the discursive terrain, in the active shifting and redistribution of the sites of inscription."[17] Diplomatic politics, maps, literary material all conjoin to produce different pictures of the 'Orient' at different moments in time. Objects of knowledge or conditions under which discursive formations take place are always dynamic and therefore multivocal, irregular, discontinuous, and nonlinear.[18]

It thus becomes imperative to dislodge the logocentricism of the Western discourse, and the universality claimed by Western culture, its science, its social organization, and finally its bland rationalism. We must not ignore the voices crying out in tortured dissent, drawing world-wide attention to the nature of self, will, freedom of human identity, personality, and dignity and the manner in which they are abused. The West constructs images of the East through the production and elaboration of structures of narrative that "culture prepares for, ratifies and promotes imperialism"[19] as is clear in Said's latest work. There is a discernible history of European representation and appropriation of the Orient which has a definite relationship with the history of European colonialism. But it must be kept in mind that this construction of the Orient is not monolithic, as varying British and French constructions of the Orient are engendered by changing social and literary circumstances. A single determining univocal discourse is a fallacy and needs to be challenged especially in the Saidian camp which often overlooks "the heterogeneity of different textual, intertextual, and discursive situations."[20] The deconstruction of white mythologies within the context of recent political and geographical upheavals throws up new configurations and transfigurations of Orientalism, each internally complex, contradictory, and unstable. Culture, therefore, is not a mere reflex of imperialism, but the culture that promoted imperialism paradoxically also produced resistance. And this resistance took place by resorting firstly, to language, structures, narratives, and concepts of the imperial culture as in the works of Lamming, Selvon, Soyinka, and C.L.R. James, and, secondly, through the assertion and development of indigenous forms, languages, and methodology to asset their own identity and history. Nativism and nationalism or, in other words, the two forms of resistance through the notions of a superior national identity and ethnic culture are competent tools during an anti-colonial struggle, but essentially becomes oppressive in postcolonial times if allowed to generate a feeling of inordinate national pride.

To represent the culturally displaced, the biases in Third World literature have to be opposed by the independent voice of the subaltern. And this is difficult to accomplish as long as the demands for representation in neo-colonial literatures are assimilated within Western knowledge and authority. Emerging out of quietism, the colonial culture must dismantle the stereotypes of a false orient—a false portrait providing moral, cultural, and artistic justification for orientalism and for its underpinning ideology, that of the "racial superiority of the Caucasian over the Asiatic."

Helen Tiffin, in her article, "Post-Colonialism, Post-Modernism, and the Rehabilitation of Post-Colonial history," has stressed the connection between the erosion of the implicit and explicit universalist claims of Western epistemology and the increasing impact of other cultures on European thinking. She is of the view that the relativisation of native epistemologies is sustained by labels such as 'post-modern,' 'postcolonial' or 'post-structural' that are applied hegemonically to cultures and texts outside Europe as a "survival strategy against the reinscription of non-European realities into a dominant European system."[21] Although she acknowledges such 'neo-univeralisms' to constitute liberating practices from the discourse of the colonizer or the master-narrative, she also interprets it as a shrewd means of controlling the 'other.' Appropriation of native literature to such hegemonic control—a control that revives and invigorates the dialectic of self and other—brings about the crisis of one's indigenous generic forms that become peripheral when implicated in unquestioning compliance with the Western centre. It is a valid contention that European models undergo ontological fracture when the 'other' begins to formulate its own perspective and a vision of an independent identity brought about by exposing the politics of labels and metaphors, in refusing to accept the hegemonic forms of impenetrability. Such features are embedded in the imperial venture where the historical consciousness, a master-narrative, always works towards cultural control and limits any postcolonial definition of the self.

Among other Indian fiction writers, Raja Rao, R.K. Narayan and Salman Rushdie, have endeavoured, to a large extent, to recuperate the precolonial dynamism and vibrancy of Indian traditions and ceremonies in that the reader's perspective is assimilated into Hindu mythology in *Kanthapura* or implicated in the manifold indigenous experiences as in Rushdie's *Midnight's Children.* Again, *The Satanic Verses* demonstrates a displacement of an "Indian translated into English-medium"[22] by depicting Saladin Chamcha in battle with his localism. Though he dislikes being called 'toadji,' he admits to feeling giddy in the city he grew up "because it feels like home and is not. It makes my heart tremble and my head spin."[23] Acceptance is not easy for Gibreel either when Rosa, an English woman, makes a conquest of him: "Are you such exotics in your cold England?" he asks her, and answers his own question, "Senora, I don't think so. Crammed into that coffin of an island, you must find wider horizons to express these secret selves."[24] One of the purposes of *The Satanic Verses,* in fact, is to evoke questions of selfhood. The lack of a sense of history is a consequence of having been bred in a cultural vacuum and not being allowed to have access to a major portion of one's history. Where the incomplete accounts of the displaced historicist or of a homogenizing world-historical scheme and assimilates non-synchronous developments, histories, cultures, and peoples to it have been recovered by sciences like anthropology, linguistics or political economics, in Indian fiction. Rushdie and Raja Rao among others have shown a similar enterprise. Their projects are interventionist in nature, radically altering the norms of official discourse by self-consciously situating themselves against cultural stereotypes and representations.

I take the example of Raja Rao's *Kanthapura,* where the economic plunder of the nation by the conquerors as well as the symbolism of the Father of the land, the Mahatma, gathering the offerings of the village festival turns documented history into myth. Rao's representation of this myth approximates to a long-buried language stored within the individual consciousness in numerous heterogeneous and ambivalent layers. The destruction of the village and the insinuating presence of the British become illusory in the face of spiritual time. *Kanthapura* presents us with a ritualistic vision of the native writer who displays more dispersed images rather than a univocal concept.[25] The British economic incursion is thwarted by Indian metaphysics, and thereby, the controlling master-narrative is decimated throughout the novel that forges together remnants of the past with the present and dissolves the present in memories of the past. Many of the indigenous fictional forms employed resist the European master narrative and remould history through a fiction that struggles to break out from the ideological encirclement brought in by the dominant educational apparatuses we are schooled in. Similarly, in the subtly complex cultural maelstrom of the narrator's psyche in *The Serpent and the Rope* we are shown a modern expatriate Indian struggling to define himself, incorporating the fragments of modern 'provincial' pluralities into his persona even as he resists cultural alienation by constructing an uncompromising self-image based on monolithic tradition.

Thus we see that in the cultural tension implicit in his works, Raja Rao has the idea of a uniform vision of 'Indianness' though he moves away from the regional nationalist narcissism and the cultural closedness of *Kanthapura* to the open-ended cultural dynamics that underlies the postcolonial *The Serpent and the Rope.*

In both the pre- and neo-colonial literature of India, the struggle has been towards a recovery and mediation of cultural practices which have been and continue to be subject to oblivion. The resident or emigrant Indian faces the dual pressure of cultural dislocation interrupted by a desire to reconstruct an uncorrupted past. Undoubtedly, both exercise equal pressures for representation in neo-colonial literature : the demands of representing an assimilated Western knowledge and moral authority are as pressing as the counter strategies of developing a critique from outside its cultural hegemony. Nevertheless, in his detailed historical perspective of the culturally displaced native, Rao consciously seeks correlations and correspondences with the past, activating a torrent of political, religious, metaphysical, and regional articulations which run against teleological centring in Western authority.

"Our marginality can be our chief asset"—to use Abdul JanMohamed's phrase—if we examine our cultural tools and methods and the very categories of our epistemology, aesthetics, and politics which have been surrendered by the native in his desire to acquire the superior intellectual level of his rulers.[26] Transgressions against official discourse by highlighting the 'voiceless' subaltern can hold the possibility of recovery, finding a voice, discovering an identity, or seeking out an authentic sense of oneself. It is significant that Indian nationalism as represented by the elites is a consequence of the expectation of power and wealth which comes out of collaboration with British culture and institutions. Although theirs could well be a nationalist emergence with the idealist need to lead the country to freedom, nowhere does elite historiography tell us about the role of the masses independent of the elite. The masses are seen as involving themselves in the political process out of a blind devotion to the charisma of the elitist leadership. This narrow view, pro-elitist in that the power structure created by the British was finally perpetuated by the national elites, virtually ignores the existence of a society which, in spite of its subjugation, made itself felt in national politics by often breaking away from its elitist superiors, as is evident from the work of third-world writers like Rao or Rushdie.

The trans-national literary phenomena beyond geo-political cultural and linguistic boundaries can then be of some value. Even though the themes are predominantly based on indigenous native culture, the Indian English writer implicitly deals with cultural dualities since it is not easy to revive traditional modes amidst bicultural complexities and ironies. The realities of public history or private experience are never reduced to the absolutist constraints that the artist may want to impose upon them. The openness of the narration to various interpretations is his affirmation as an 'other' of the right to recognition as a subject of history. A relative, yet historically determined perception of reality is a precursor for the creation of a heterogeneous culture, a heterogeneity that implies more than just a denial of the hegemonic culture of the West, but one that combines the native present, the past, and the future in creating a culture which generates meaning without preempting it, by providing multiple voices within the narrative, creating both a world view and a typology of culture.

An anti-totalizing and a decentred consciousness provides the underpinning of attitudes or activities that aim at being secular and at opposite ends to monoculturalism or authoritarian systems. Critiques of imperialism and imperialist ideologies concomitant with the homogenization of histories are contested so as to evolve an epistemological critique of Western modernism and Eastern identity to reconcile the binary oppositions of colonizer and colonized. The function of all cultural criticism and struggle is to overcome these oppositions on which the passive acceptance of cultures is founded since overcoming the dominant culture and articulating the theoretical assumptions of third-world cultures can only be stages in a process of resistance.

NOTES AND REFERENCES

1. Gayatri Chakravorty Spivak, *In Other Worlds*: *Essays in Cultural Politics* (London: Methuen, 1987) 136.
2. Anthony Easthope, "The Practice of Theory," *The Sunday Times* 18 Sep. 1994: 7.
3. Easthope.
4. Malini Bhattacharya, "Decolonising Third World Culture," *Economic and Political Weekly* 11 June 1994: 1453.
5. Nigel Leask, *British Romantic Writers and the East: Anxieties of Empire* (Cambridge: Cambridge UP, 1993) 22. There is a distancing from the experiences of the third-world scholar and a lack of primary research in European and American scholarship as I discussed earlier on.
6. Edward Said, *Orientalism* (Harmondsworth: Penguin, 1978) 7.

7. See Rana Kabbani, *Imperial Fictions: Europe's Myths of Orient* (London: Pandora, 1988). To justify the slavery enforced on the people of the East, the European narrative of the 'other' stressed the conspicuous cruelty, the lechery, the perversity, and the inherent violence of the natives. The 'cosmetic can of *mission civilsatrice*' served to forge the imperial representation of the world. History, reason, and science were employed to meet the ends of its rule, not brute jingoism. Orientalist studies with such motives gave power and knowledge to the conquerors to sustain the Empire. But excessive dependence on the existing Orientalist scholarship reduces the orient to a set of archaic concepts and literary clichés which prejudice the Western observer. The orient becomes "a pretext for self-dramatisation and differentness; it is the malleable theatrical space in which can be played out the egocentric fantasies of Romanticism" (11).
8. Frantz Fanon, *Black Skin, White Masks*, trans. Charles Lam Markmann (London: Pluto, 1993) 18.
9. Raja Rao, *Kanthapura (*Delhi: Orient, 1938) 5.
10. Theodor Adorno and Max Horkheimer, *Dialectic of Enlightenment* (London: Verso, 1979).
11. Linda Hutcheon, *A Poetics of Postmodernism: History, Theory and Fiction* (New York: Routledge, 1988) 14.
12. Njabulo S. Ndebele, "Beyond Protest: New Directions in South African Literature," *Criticism and Ideology: Second African Writers' Conference* (Stockholm, 1986), ed. Kirsten Holst Petersen (Uppsala: Scandinavian Institute of African Studies, 1988) 205-16.
13. Edward Said, "Orientalism Reconsidered," *Europe and Its Others*, vol. 1, ed. Francis Barker, et al (Colchester: U of Essex P, 1985) 24.
14. Lisa Lowe, *Critical Terrains: French and British Orientalisms* (Ithaca and London: Cornell UP, 1991) 4.
15. See Joyce Appleby, Lynn Hunt and Margaret Jacob, *Telling the Truth About History* (London: W.W. Norton, 1994).
16. Margaret Jacob, "Telling it Like it Was," *Times Higher Education Supplement* 2 Sep. 1994.
17. Lowe 9.
18. Michel Foucault, *The Archaeology of Knowledge*, trans. A.M. Sheridan Smith (New York: Pantheon, 1972) 38.
19. Nicholas Tredell, *The Critical Decade* (Manchester: Carcanet, 1993) 167.
20. Lowe x.
21. Helen Tiffin, "Post-Colonialism, Post-Modernism and the Rehabilitation of Post-Colonial History," *The Journal of Commonwealth Literature* 23.2 (1986) 169-81.

22. Salman Rushdie, *The Satanic Verses* (London: Viking, 1988) 58.
23. Rushdie 46.
24. Rushdie 156.
25. Raja Rao has been criticised, however, for propagating an essentialistic category of cultural nationalism in his effort to thwart imperialism, which he magnifies to universal proportions. See Rumina Sethi, *Myths of the Nation: National Identity and Literary Representation* (Oxford: Oxford UP, 1999).
26. Abdul R. JanMohamed, "The Economy of Manichean Allegory: The Function of Racial Difference in Colonialist Literature," *"Race," Writing, and Difference,* ed. Henry Louis Gates, Jr. (Chicago and London: U of Chicago P, 1986) 78-106.

3

Towards a Translation Protocol in the Postcolonial India

P. SHIV KUMAR

> "I realised soon that in Indian arena I had to 'wash' English clean of alien colour, flavour, association."
>
> —Ranga Rao

From the point of view of the reader the success of an English translation largely depends upon its ability to approximate the experience of reading the source text, without subjecting the language of the translated version to avoidable strain. But this is a tall order, for the best of translations invariably missed out on at least a little something of the experience of the source text. However, close approximation of the experience of the source text in the English version is the ideal to which all translators ought to be committed in an ideal situation. But as it often happens, the teleology and ideology of the translators, coupled with their background, has always tampered with this ideal. Just as the poets have evolved critical canon to rationalise their poetic practice, the translators too have tended to put forth theories of translation that supported their practice, often ignoring their obligations to the text they are supposed to mediate. In the forties and fifties, for instance, the translators, very much like the earlier Orientalists, have thought it fit to anglicize the language of the source text in its English version. This trend continued into 60s and 70s. This probably was an easy way out of the insurmountable difficulties and dilemmas that confronted the translators of the Indian language literatures; their convincing *alibi* for this has been intelligibility and readability of the English of the translated text, especially for the English native. The carry-over functions of the translator were supplanted by his interpretive, paraphrasing roles. Such preferences were seen in the 70s and 80s as attempts to colonize the source text. Sensitive critics perceived in this political dimensions of the postcolonial power struggle. Susie Tharu and Lalitha, for instance, say:

> Formulations that setup the problem of translation as one of judging how faithful a translation has been to the original, or how well it reads in the target language, divert attention from the fact that translation takes place where two, invariably unequal, worlds collide, and that there are always relationships of power involved when one world is represented for another in translation (Susie Tharu and Lalitha, 1993: xx).

Taking for granted the asymmetry between languages, especially between English on the one hand and Indian languages on the other, some critics have observed that the use of the English language in the postcolonial Indian context has tended to acquire a subversive aggressiveness. Bill Ashcroft, Gareth Griffiths, and Helen Tiffin have astutely pointed out that these subversive tendencies have taken the form of "abrogation" and "appropriation" in the use of the English language. For the "abrogation" meant rejection of the notion of correctness of usage and of even the semantic structures that go with the English of the country of the colonisers. On the other hand, "appropriation" meant free adaptation of the English language to express the cultural experience of the postcolonial Indian context. In either case the aggressive translators brought about sweeping changes in the use of the English, in the process rendering it unrecognisable or even unintelligible to the alien international audiences. The self-indulgent linguistic experiments of quite a few translators and even of some creative Indian writers in English (like Raja Rao, G.V. Desani, Mulk Raj Anand) haven't exactly built bridges between India and other countries.

It must be said, that they have failed to communicate the Indian cultural experience through these strategies of "abrogation" and "appropriation." The example of these creative writers has in a sense encouraged a host of translators to use these strategies to a fault.

This subversion could be seen as a kind of backlash in the postcolonial era. It could also be seen as a reaction to the uprootedness perceived to have been triggered by the English language in the colonial consciousness. The uprootedness worked both for good and for bad. The good it did could be seen in the creative uses it was put to by gifted writers in the postcolonial context. In day to day life too the distance between the individual and society is determined by the degree to which he is close to the English language. The bad it did, of course, could be felt in the countless ways in which the English language wrought disorientation in the life of the individual. Interviewing V.S. Naipaul recently, Sadanand Menon formulated this problem into a question thus:

> Writers living and writing in India have experienced this problem, getting "otherised," not being able to penetrate their specific social context, experiencing the angst of producing 'good' literature but, simultaneously being treated like outsiders.... Well it is the classic contradiction between who you are when you write in your own language and otherwise.

The postcolonial writers writing in English have often been accused of the "colonial cringe." Not only are these writers said to write for English-speaking foreign reader, presenting them with images of Indian life that fulfil their expectations, but also their assumptions and attitudes are found to be so completely Westernized that their focus on Indian life is skewed. In all these weaknesses the English language is implicated in no small measure, for the language converted them, in ways hard-to-pin-down, to attitudes and assumptions that are essentially un-Indian. The recent Seminar on "Nativism" or "Desivad," whose discussions were put out in the form of a book by Makarand Paranjape, pleads almost unanimously for decolonisation and seeks solution to the crisis of alienation from history and culture that is confronting the Westernized elite in India. Some Indian writers who could write in English as well as the regional language that is their mother tongue, made a creative decision in favour of the latter. O.V. Vijayan, for instance, who chose to write in his native Malayalam language has said: "But I have chosen to write in Malayalam and not in English, although it would have been more profitable to [...] Indo-Anglian writing is the East India Company in reverse. And is culturally untenable" (*Outlook*, October 27, 1997, p. 126). There are many impressive writers and critics who subscribe to the view that one cannot participate in one's own civilization by writing in the language of another culture. The Seminar on Nativism supports this view and makes a call for decolonisation. This call for going "native" is akin to Emerson's call for declaration of intellectual independence in America during the last century. However, the point to be noted here is that in India there is a growing recognition of the problem that the use of the English language poses for the writers whose approach to Indian reality is coloured by a mindset moulded by the cultural baggage that goes with the English language. Indian writers in English stand in stark contrast to the writers writing in native languages not merely on account of the language they use but owing to a subtle, hard-to-pin-down, complex set of assumptions and attitudes that have completely set apart their focus on Indian reality. To understand this phenomenon clearly one only has to put side by side a novel originally written in English by an Indian writer and a good English translation of a novel originally written in a native, language. The differences between the two texts are most likely to be seen in the assumptions and attitudes implicit in their focus on the aspects of life selected for portrayal. One could even venture to think it possible to see patterns of differences in the choice of areas of experience, of subject matter, of details of life, etc. that the writers writing in English and those writing in the native languages make for their creative expression. These patterns of difference should surely suggest radical differences in their world views and in their complex conditioning factors.

One could hazard the view that all these differences attendant on the writers in English could be traced to the English language, that they had adopted for the creative use.

To say QED for the thesis advanced here is rash since it is not substantiated. Nor is it the purpose of this article to substantiate it here; the concerns of the Seminar on Nativism mentioned earlier ought to suggest the thesis posited here. Be it as this may, the argument that this article advances is 'directly' derived from this thesis. That is, many of the difficulties encountered in the translation of postcolonial native writers into English could be said to point to areas of experience and to implicit native attitudes and assumptions that are intimate to native culture and are not accessible to the English language not because of its inadequacy but because of the radical cultural differences of the native experience. This said, I would next go on to discuss some of the difficulties a translator of native text would normally encounter and the translational strategies that he would normally evolve to overcome these difficulties. It must be noted that these strategies, in the ultimate analysis, are meant to bring the reader as close as possible to the experience of the native text through the available communicative resources of the English language. The degree to which these strategies succeed depends on several factors such as the context in which they are attempted, the discretion and ability of the translator and, of course, on the resources of the English language to negotiate the cultural barriers.

Normally the translator treads the difficult task of presenting the English reader with an idiomatic text without straining his linguistic feel and without at the same time losing the identity and authenticity of the source text. His task becomes particularly difficult when the source text is dense in socio-cultural context, using dialect and is steeped in mythological references or folk beliefs. In dealing with such a difficult situation, a translator normally opts for an excessively source-directed translation and this might result in a book that the foreign reader would find too difficult to understand. If the translator does not like such an outcome, he might throw overboard socio-cultural baggage of the original and opt for an entirely target-directed translation. Both the options are in the extreme and negate the objective of translation. Instead the translator could balance the two approaches and succeed in avoiding the perils of exclusive commitment to either one. That is, the translator could be scrupulously source-directed in places where the original is culture-specific (making a judicious use of the 'outwork' such as footnotes and glosses), while attempting target-directed translation in other places. In the process of presenting a source-directed translation one could keep loan translations, loan creations, collocational deviations and semantic shifts to the minimum to save the translation from becoming unintelligible to the foreign reader. Preserving the native flavour would involve a complex array of translational strategies especially when faced with native mannerisms, gestures, speech rhythms, modes of address, terms of endearment, etc. In any event the translator's success depends largely on his efforts at retaining the original flavour without hurting the linguistic sensibilities of the users of English. But this is a difficult thing to achieve. There are bound to be distances and gaps between the original and the translated version. It would be interesting to see how these gaps are tackled by the Indian English writers, for it is these gaps which would determine the extent of their rootedness.

The translator, however, might adopt different strategies (different from those when he aims at non-native English reader) when he addresses the native readers of other regional languages. That is, if he is translating a Telugu source text for the benefit of Indian readers of other regional languages he might deem it unnecessary to provide a glossary because they share a socio-cultural, political and historical past and present and negotiating the translated version without the props of 'outwork' is not difficult for them.

English translators of Indian literatures, unlike those of the other Western literatures, are yoking two disparate things (that is, trying to convey the Indian socio-cultural experience in an alien language) and as such will do well to guard against the pitfalls of extreme positions. They will probably do well to limit themselves to translating for their compatriots in other regions in India rather than aspire to address the international readership. When they do attempt to do the latter, their choice of the source text could be such that it does not demand too much sacrifice either of the pace of the target language or of the ethos of the source text. Such a choice is possible.

WORKS CITED

Ashcroft, Bill et al., *The Empire Writes Back: Theory and Practice in Post-Colonial Literatures.* London: Routledge, 1989.

Bush, Peter, "It Doesn't Sound Like English." *Times Literary Supplement* 6 Sep. 1996: 11.

Holmstrom, Lakshmi, "Issues in Translation." *Kavya Bharathi.* Translation Issue 9 (1997) 1-10.

Menon, Sadanand, "The Truth Governs Writing." *The Hindu* 5 July 1998: IX.

Ranga Rao, "Perfect Translation, a Mirage." *The Hindu* 4 Dec. 1994: XXII.

Tharu, Susie and K. Lalitha, *Women Writing in India: The Twentieth Century* 2. London: Pandora, 1993.

Trivedi, Harish, "How Original! An Aspect of Post-Colonial Translation." *Indian Review of Books* 5.1, 16 Sep. 1995: 31-2.

4

'First World' Within the 'Third World': The Universalist Fallacy in Criticism

K. PURUSHOTHAM and N.S. RAHUL

Reflecting on the Third World criticism, Aijaz Ahmad wrote the essay "Three Worlds Theory: End of a Debate", which is included in his latest book, *In Theory*. The book also has two important critiques on Edward Said and Frederick Jameson who have written extensively on the Third World Theory. The epithet in Ahmad's essay, "End of a Debate," is rather uncalled for, however comprehensive the essay might be since a healthy debate can never be ended unless in a dogmatic situation, and Ahmad's essay is, not dogmatic. What surprised us most was that the 'ending' of a debate had been proposed by a person like Aijaz Ahmad who writes from the Marxist position. Nevertheless, Ahmad's critique of Edward Said and Frederick Jameson on the Third World discourse is sound and quite convincing.

Though written in the high culture of the metropolitan style, Ahmad's work on the Third World discourse is seminal in understanding the nature of the Third World discourse which is dominantly being constructed by the West. Therefore, it is a natural corollary that the Western construction of the Third World discourse needs to be checked and resisted. The present paper is a modest attempt in this direction aiming at examining: (a) the inappropriateness and the inadequacy of the application of the tripartite division—the First World, the Second World and the Third World to the literary discourses; (b) the vested interest of the west in applying the universalist paradigm to the Third World literature, and (c) the canonicity and the self-canonicity of the Third World writers. The focus of this paper is on the aspect of the prevalence, of the 'First World' in the Third World literary criticism.

II

In the post-cold war era; in an era in which the cold war was 'won' by the U.S.A.; in an era in which the socialist block not only lost the cold war to the West, but crumbled down irrecoverably, the context of the tripartite division of the world is likely to sound obsolete. The Second World—the socialist block—having become, or having been made extinct, there remained only two 'Worlds' much talked about now: the First World and the Third World. These two 'Worlds,' however, are being 'merged' into one in the name of the much talked about globalisation and the liberalisation, therefore, worn out terms in the Third World today. The Third World is being recolonised once again at a faster pace. What is not to be ignored in this context is that the 'First World' within the Third World is a party to the recolonisation, and is a willing partner in the enterprise of the so-called globalisation. While the implications of the 'joint venture' of the globalisation are worth studying by economists and political scientists, it would be interesting to note the possible fall-out of what we have called, the 'joint venture of the globalisation' in the domain of the Third World literatures and literary criticisms. Before that, the following section deals with the *raison de etre* of—or the politics involved in the tripartite division, and the design behind its perpetuation by the West.

III

The tripartite division is purely political in nature; the necessity and the *modus operandi* of the division is dealt with in its historical perspective by Aijaz Ahmad in his work, *In Theory*. The criteria applied to the tripartite division was based on the mode of the economy and the nature of the polity in each country. The capitalist West as the First World, the socialist block as the Second World, and the non-aligned, the underdeveloped (the former colonies) countries as the Third World have been posited as enemies one against the other. However, whether the division sounds rational, and serves political purpose or not, our contention is that the division does not necessarily reflect—the essential ethos of the countries; the typology of the governments; the relations of the means of production and of the people in each country of the three worlds. For instance, the Second World, the so-called socialist block, was not socialistic as they were projected to be. All the 'socialist' governments had been the biggest entrepreneurs, owning the largest properties. Apart from this, the socialist governments—of the then U.S.S.R., China and the East European countries—had been equally imperialistic as the West has been.

Coming to the First World, it is not altogether free from the characteristics of the Third World. The backwardness and the race and the gender-based exploitation in the First World is as predominant as it is in the Third World. Similarly, within the Third World, there are the ruling classes that are at one with the First World in their typology. In other words, some of the characteristics of the Third World can be seen in the First World, and *vice versa*. It can be argued that the Third World features, namely the backwardness and the exploitation based on caste, class, race, gender and religion—within the Third World get submerged in the tripartite division. Therefore, it is necessary to conceive the tripartite division in the light as to how the 'Third World' in the First World and the Third World within the Third World get submerged in the division, and it is precisely for this design (or, the hidden agenda) of the submergence that both the First World and the Third World are interested in continuing and perpetuating the tripartite division. The tripartite division is markedly deceptive in that it hides the essential *oneness* or unity of the three worlds, and it is in this light that the popularity of the present globalisation and liberalisation—or, to use a single word, recolonisation—needs to be understood. The essential unity of the three worlds can be seen in the literary discourses that are particularly constructed by the First World—the 'First

World' in both the First and the Third Worlds. The following section would look into this aspect.

IV

As far as literature is concerned, the unity among the three worlds can be seen in the universalist paradigm presently prevalent in the Third World literatures and in the literary criticisms. This trend is particularly invisible in the domain of the Indian Writing in English. The Western approach to the Indian literature has been, similar to what Macaulay had termed the mission of colonisation: to civilise the savages. The mission of 'civilising the savages' has been carried out in the form of universalising the Third World literatures, identifying some of the features in the Third World literatures similar to that of their own. 'Civilising the savages' has been necessitated, the First World would feel, because the Third World countries always look backward; they are 'barbaric' and 'fanatic'; and the backwardness and the fanaticism are, interprets Edward Said, invariably associated in the 'First World' with Islam, for example, which is why the 'civilising' task! The *modus operandi* of this is accomplished through the application of the universalist paradigm to the literary criticism in various forms.

The First and the most important form of the universalist paradigm is appropriating the Third World writings and the writers themselves. The Third World writings, especially of the English ones, are interpreted applying the universalist mode of literary criticism. Some of the dominant aspects of the universalist paradigms are the eternal quest for the self—*Bildungsroman* and *Kunstleroman*—the themes of expatriation and colonialism, post colonialism, the themes of existentialism, absurdity, the human nature and the predicament of modern man and so many others. The First World locates, or 'detects' these themes in the Third World texts in order to universalise the Third World texts and to preempt the specificities that the Third World texts may deal with.

The quest for the self is a very convenient way of universalising the Third World texts. The best example of this is the (mis)reading of Mulk Raj Anand's classic, *The Untouchable.* This novel has been variously interpreted while reading the esoteric universalist meanings into it. The protagonist in the novel, Bakha, has been interpreted as an existential one; as an archetypal figure; and as one who is in quest for the truth. This is what has been termed as the application of the universalist paradigms to the Third World texts most of which are actually located in a particular space and time addressing themselves *to the specific* problems typical of only the Third World countries.

The Untouchable, for example, *is specifically* about the evils of the caste system, or to be more precise, the problem of, as the title itself is indicative of, the untouchability which is a unique problem prevailing only in India, and nowhere else on the globe. Now, interpreting *The Untouchable* applying the universalist paradigm—as an archetypal, existential or as a novel of quest for truth—is essentially a First Worldist project of appropriating the Third World texts by constructing the universalist critical discourse; of sidetracking the problems that are characteristic of the Third World countries; of canonising the Third World texts and the writers.

While canonising a Third World text like *The Untouchable* through the critical discourses is one aspect, canonising the writers themselves making them adopt the Western literary forms and build into their texts a world view that would be acceptable to the West is another one. Canonisation of the writers generally takes place through the overt means of (re)warding the writers with various prizes—at the state, national and international levels—like, among others, the Sahitya Academy Award, Nobel Prize and the Booker Prize. The fact that most of the Nobel prizes for literature during the last decade (only, and never, or very seldom, before that) had been won by the Third World writers requires to be conceived from the perspective of canonisation.

Apart from canonising the texts through the universalist criticism and the writers with awards, there is another aspect of canonisation that can be categorised as the self-canonisation, which however, is a resultant factor of the latter—canonising the writers. The best examples of the self-canonisation by means of adopting the Western literary form is Vikram Seth's *The Golden Gate* (1986). Vikram Seth, now an author of the biggest novel, and the recipient of the highest amount of advance towards the publication of his *A Suitable Boy* (1993), made his mark as a writer with the publication of *The Golden Gate*. Apart from the theme, the characters and the characterisation, what is far more interesting and important is the form in which it was written: it is a novel in verse. It is in the sonnet form containing only sonnets throughout. Whether there can be a novel in verse form in the Third World context is worth debating elsewhere. Seth's adoption of the sonnet form—a form which is so closely associated with the British literature—ignoring the richest Indian indigenous folk literary forms can be considered as an example of self-canonisation. Such a self-canonisation would not only 'certify' the First Worldist claim that their literature is superior, but it belittles the rich tradition of the indigenous literary forms.

The example of the self-canonisation in the form of building the First Worldist world view into the Third World is Salman Rushdie's *Satanic Verses*. Unlike Vikram Seth, Rushdie is acclaimed for having 'indigenised' the literary form by adopting the oral modes of narration.[1] Besides the literary forms he used, Rushdie's novel have been examined tracing on his First Worldist construction of the gender, the class and the religion.[2] Of these studies, his construction of religion in *Satanic Verses*— which forced him in the 'self' exile because of (can it be said?) his anti-Third Worldist worldview—is important in the present context. *Satanic Verses* is not a universalist novel; whether Rushdie intended it or not, the novel addresses itself to a specific aspect of the Islam. But, views Anuradha Needham:

> Rushdie had misjudged his audiences and willingly *offered* himself up for *Western appreciation*—they conceded that Rushdie had provided a fruitful internal critique that could eventually lead to reform through debate and *critical scrutiny of Islam*.[3]

The western mission of 'civilising the savages' can be seen in the self-canonised Rushdie who provided them 'a fruitful internal critique' leading to the 'scrutiny' and the reformation, of Islam.

The colonialist discourse is another form of resisting and opposing the indigeneity, though the coloniality happens to be one of the problems the Third World countries face. The best example that can be cited for the over emphasis on colonialism undermining the indigenous problems is G.N. Devy's much talked about work, *After Amnesia* in which Devy views that the colonial period is like amnesia during which the Indian critical discourse had been impaired. But, what is ignored in this mode of interpretation is the deliberate and motivated sidetracking of the much more potential indigenous amnesia, the Brahminical cultural construction, that is, which not only impaired but never allowed the gender and caste based creative and critical writings to grow. *After Amnesia* is obliquely silent on this aspect of amnesia.

Another influence of colonialism on the social front is that whatever the liberation struggles such as feminist and 'dalit ones' take place in the Third World countries, they are considered the Western Projects, which is why, argues Anuradha Needham, "without larger structural changes [...] 'third' world texts cannot be adequately or appropriately studied in a 'first' world context; boundaries, for the most part, will not get crossed."[4]

The essential unity between the West and the Westernised Third World, thus assumes the forms of applying the universalist paradigms of criticism of the Third World writers and their worldviews; and constructing colonialist discourse—all aimed at ignoring and dismissing the true third worldist writings. The following section would, then, look into the defence and the legitimisation of the universalist paradigms of aesthetics by the Western discourses.

V

The reason why the universalist paradigms, like the archetypes, get legitimised and sound convincing is, to quote Northrope Frye:

> In an instant world of communication, there is no reason for cultural lag or for a difference between sophisticated writers in large centres and naive writers in smaller ones. A world like ours produces a single *international style* of which all existing literatures are regional development. This international style is [...] a way of seeing and thinking in a world controlled by uniform patterns of technology and the regional development is a way of *escaping from the uniformity.*[5]

Interpreting the Third World texts and the ones that conform to the norm of 'a single international style,' which is appropriating the text and the author, is an effective way of canonising the Third World text and its author.

Another mode of legitimisation of both canonisation and self-canonisation is the attribution of the dubious distinction of liberal humanism which entails that all human beings belong to the one big family called the humanity. The liberal humanism is not only silent on, but would strongly resist the true Third Worldist approach of creative writing and criticism if they deal with the institutional exploitation based on caste, class, race and gender; the typology of the politicians; the politics of recolonisation; and so many other specific problems that characterise the Third World countries (however, it should be said in this context that as far as the Indian literature is concerned, all the English writings do not necessarily represent these Third Worldist problems, but the vernacular writings are rich in representing them). The Western liberal humanism that opposes the spatio-temporal specificities is a Western form of cultural imperialism.

Yet another basis on which the West legitimises their universalist discourse is based on the literary aesthetics. The true Third World writings which address themselves essentially to the local problems, tend to be realistic and social rather than individualistic. Because, they represent the community life and the larger socio-political problems, rather than the individual problems. In such cases where the Third World writings characterise the social life and realism, the Western universalist critics are likely to dismiss the texts as aesthetically in poor taste. Writing on this, Helen Tiffin views, "an orthodoxy has developed which dismisses realist writers as inherently inferior to those with more overtly metaphysical interest."[6] In this regard, the Third Worldist approach would be to question the very definition of the aesthetics, as did Chinua Achebe:

> [...] the trouble with what we have written so far is that it has concentrated too much on society and not sufficiently on individual characters, and as a result it has lacked 'true' aesthetic proportions. I wondered when this *truth* became so self-evident and who decided that (unlike the other self-evident truth) this one should apply to black as well as white.[7]

Achebe raises an important question regarding the rationality of applying the Western literary and critical aesthetic paradigms to the Third World writings. The level of the 'true' aesthetic proportions to be represented depends on not only how one defines what *true* aesthetics is, but also on the validity of giving universal currency to the so-called *true* aesthetics.

In conclusion, it may be said that the First Worldist 'mission' of the universalisation of the literary criticism, which has, of late assumed the latest *avataar* of postcolonialism requires to be delegitimised in order to de-canonise it, and the Third World texts have to be read contextualising the spatio-temporal specificities.

NOTES

1. Though Rushdie uses oral modes of narration such as episodic, fragmentary and discursive, his narrative is, it can be argued, not so oral in nature in view of the complexity involved in the narrative.
2. See my article, "Rushdie's Images of Bharateeya Nari in *Midnight's Children," Kakatiya Journal of English Studies* (1993), and Aijaz Ahmad's long essay on Rushdie in *In Theory.*
3. Anuradha Dingwaney Needham, "At the receiving End: Reading 'Third' World texts in a 'First' World context," *Women's Quarterly* 28, 3 & 4 (1990): 92. Emphasis ours.
4. Needham 98.

5. Northrope Frye, "Across the River and Out of the Trees," *Divisions on a Ground: Essays on Canadian Culture* (Toronto: Anands: 1982) 31-2. Emphasis ours.
6. Helen Tiffin, "Commonwealth Literature and Comparative Methodology," *World Literature Written in English* 23 (1984) 28.
7. Chinua Achebe, "Where Angels Fear to Tread," *African Writers on African Writing,* ed. G.D. Killam (London: Heinemann, 1973) 6.

WORKS CITED

Ahmad, Aijaz. *In Theory: Classes, Nations, Literatures.* New Delhi: OUP, 1992.

Said, Edward. *Orientalism.* New York: Pantheon, 1978.

Mulk Raj Anand. *The Untouchable.* London: Laurence & Wishert, 1935.

Robertson, R.T. "*Untouchable* as an Archetypal Novel" and S. Laxmana Murthy, "Bakha: An Existential analysis." *Kakatiya Journal of English Studies* 11.1 (1997).

Devy, G.N. *After Amnesia: Tradition and Change in Indian Literary Criticism.* Bombay: Orient Longman, 1992.

5

On the Political Semiotics of Othello's Otherness: Rallying Round Postcolonial Aesthetics

PRASENJIT MAITI

OTHELLO: . . . .
I have done the state some service, and they know't.
No more of that. I pray you, in your letters,
When you shall these unlucky deeds relate,
Speak of me as I am; nothing extenuate,
Nor set down aught in malice: then must you speak
Of one that loved not wisely but too well;
Of one not easily jealous, but being wrought
Perplex'd in the extreme [...]
And say besides, that in Aleppo once,
Where a malignant and a turban'd Turk
Beat a Venetian and traduced the state,
I took by the throat the circumcised dog,
And smote him, thus.

(*Othello*, Act V, Scene 2)

This paper seeks to identify the otherness in Shakespeare's *Othello*[1] when in contrast with Desdemona as a mainstream white actor enabled with a certain role performance in the carnival of mainstream identities. I will try to establish in the process that Othello is the 'other' on the marginality of being one who has to constantly negotiate certain role performance like Desdemona's or even Iago's that are iconized as the white self of the narrative as against the black margin, the border of permissible interface with the otherness of the other.

I

What we have to appreciate here is the fact that Othello has always remained the outsider, the stranger whose modalities of interaction cannot be addressed by white narrative. The outsider has a grammar of his own but its syntax cannot relate to the syntactical realities of the white narrative. This is not to suggest, however, that we are so naïve as to be unable to reach beyond the binaries of the text. Othello-Desdemona or even Othello-Iago are dichotomies that have to be interrogated outside the margin of meanings, away from the hegemony institutionalized by the signifier and signified.

So Othello as the outsider is the other who is a spectral point of reference in the context of hospitality. He is not hospitably accommodated within the range of possibilities of the text. It is as if Othello has a countertext all his own whose ethos is yet to be explored while reading the colonial and postcolonial Shakespeares.

Jacques Derrida's hospitality critique argues that any manner of interaction, to be ontologically relevant, has to be essentially informed by a necessitating *spectrality* that would ordinarily require two principal layers i.e. the guest and the host. We would well here to remember that hospitality as a 'dynamic' category of analysis has to be equally shared by the guest as well as the host. Othello as the guest is the unknown spectre, the 'ghost,' who has to be effectively accommodated by the host. Such hospitality is to be accorded entirely on the terms of the guest and not otherwise. But this has not exactly been the case in the play.

So hospitality is really about *openness* and free play of the signifier terms of discourse and their signified meanings, associative cues, semiotics and the like. There is an aspect of 'mystery' and suddenness about the guest that can occasionally be irksome and even disquieting, but such organic specifics have to be duly negotiated by the host to piece together a functional symbiosis.

But why does the host go out of his/her way at all to cohere an ensemble of mutuality with the guest?[2] The explanation lies in the fact that there are possibilities the host would be able, at some point or the other, to benefit from in ways more than one from this relationship. This is not to suggest, however, that benefits are unilateral so far as hospitality is concerned. Moreover, we would not be able to talk in terms of moves and countermoves in the spectral domain of hospitality simply because the latter is all about a *different* reality comprising altogether *different* terms of discourse that are rather (skewed and) incongruous in domains like statecraft and the art of politics.

Hospitality is actually all about accepting the *otherness* of the *other* and providing *openness* to others. This implies that the 'other' is an unknown actor who has to be entirely accommodated on his/her own terms of discourse. The host cannot afford to control the sovereignty or the regime of 'otherness' of the other. This would in its turn tend to ensure an equity of sorts between the guest and the host. This equity is efficacious in sustaining networks of trust[3] between the actors that ultimately tend to facilitate better interélite understanding. But this does not happen in the play.

II

A politico-scientific reading of the play would indicate that Othello is a potential threat to the Establishment, an ambitious counterélitist actor who aspires for even more political powers. I mean real and effective powers of course, and the text emerges as more meaningful if we initially examine the problematics of Othello as structured primarily by the centre-periphery tension and underpinned by different aspects of legitimacy as a fundamental political concern.

Tom R. Tyler has explained that the "discussion of legitimacy has been framed by the perspective of legal authorities, highlighting the balance that they must strike between controlling the public and being sensitive to the public's views. Legal authorities must restrict the activities of those over whom they exercise power, but at the same time their effectiveness depends ultimately on their ability to secure voluntary public compliance with their directives."[4]

A peripheral actor has moved toward the centrality of politics dominated by the powers-that-be. This is the intentionality of Othello's power and it would ultimately (almost) subvert the white bases of power. But this cannot be allowed to happen. Hence Othello's power suggesting that he is organically unable to translate his accepted career as a soldier into the career (not-yet-accepted by the white mainstream) of a statesman. Othello's vertical social mobility is arrested in the process. Foucault says:

> It is only if we grasp these techniques of power and demonstrate the economic advantage or political utility that derives from them in a given context for specific reasons, that we can understand how these mechanisms come to be effectively incorporated into the social whole.[5]

We have to pay special attention to his final speech that culminates in his suicide.[6] The Moor would like the State to 'recognize' him objectively; his achievements and failures should be assessed in a disinterested manner. So the dialectics of *Othello* is now apparent by now. The State's apparatus has repeatedly used the military skill of Othello in incidents like the impending attack on Cyprus by the Turks. But this State can display only indifference when the Moor is being increasingly marginalized in the polyphony of Venice's political carnival.[7] This is polyphony all right, but without the heteroglossia of identities.

This is remarkable as any analysis of subaltern actors in history cannot really afford to do without the aspect of organic identities that emerge from the battlegrounds and politics of everyday life. But we somehow do not find the presence of many voices either in the Moor or in his immediate sociopolitical background. Othello appears to be a flat character bereft of interesting angularities. His are dynamics without the exciting possibilities of further postcolonial critiquing and exploration.

But we may still discover aspects in *Othello* that are insightful if we persist in our technique of separating actors from their institutions and processes of contemporaneous politics. This ensures that compulsions and imperatives of politics are analysed within frameworks like 'actors and institutions' and 'actors in institutions.'

We have to also keep in mind the relative autonomy of the State while negotiating Othello. The Moor is at first an actor about to interact with the ensemble of institutions we ordinarily address as the matrix of sociopolitical configurations when he is *tricked* into committing a capital crime attracting capital punishment. This is murder of the first degree and it has a certain absolute quality about it. It also indicates the point of no return for the extended arm of the law about to retaliate and ensure the prevalence of justice.

But how can we afford to discuss justice when we have not yet resolved the basic problem of tension between the mainstream and the without, the narrative of a hegemonic text and its readerly interpretations? Can we treat the Moor as an actor without a lineage? It is true that Othello cannot realise political power in terms of his genealogy but there is yet another reality outside the reality of descent. This is the reality of praxes as obtainable in a given context of the material conditions of being. Jeffrey Reimen, for example, has analysed:

> The social contractarians realised that people do not normally see their political duties as self-imposed, much less as having been agreed to. If political obligations were to be understood as issuing from an agreed made by those subject to them, it had to be an agreement inscribed in the tendency of their reasoning itself, not an actual signing on the dotter line.[8]

III

Glocal informants that happen to address contemporary postcolonial narratives of power and history or even power in history generally tend to hinge on a strategy, namely 'what is global is local and what is local is global.'[9] This strategy is effective as its priorities comprise apparently wayward and antipodal hyper-realities like territoriality, xenophobia and multiculturalism underpinned by alienation, insecurity and an absence of confidence in organic constructions that are all about the material conditions of life. We have to appreciate that *Othello* is an exemplar of all such benchmarks of analysis.

Alienation or even deidentification can result in a loss of legitimacy,[10] ontologically speaking, "[...] participation in a social system requires human beings to make their own contributions, and it leads to human beings' distinguishing themselves from one another and behaving exclusively for one another; because they must produce their own contributions themselves, they must motivate themselves. When they cooperate one must clarify, despite all natural similarity, who has made which contribution [...] however, that concerns not distinct forms of interpenetration but the fact that greater interpenetration requires more inclusion and more (reciprocal) exclusion. The resulting problem is solved by the 'individualization' of persons."[11] The above concerns would be interrogated after we negotiate, delimit and define the politics of appropriating the other (as in *Othello*), the principal concern of this paper.

Appropriation can be considered to be a function of dispossessing actors in a 'carnival' informed by 'polyphony.'[12] Is this not also indicative of the problem of interaction between civil societies[13] and literary spaces and grand narratives as systems of hegemonizing, majoritarian politics? Here is what Steven Lukes says:

> To use the vocabulary of power in the context of social relationships is to speak of human agents, separately or together, in groups or organizations, through action or inaction, significantly affecting the thoughts and actions of others (specifically, in a manner contrary to their interests).[14]

The next enquiry happens to be: how to problematise a given literary space within a defined politics of ascriptions and identities?[15] Can this be done with the aid of complicity, entrapment[16] and consent as local tactics and global strategies?

IV

We can hypothesise here that language as control can logically lead to conviction in signifier words and signified meanings as an ideology, building up the apparatuses of a polity in the process. So we discover a hegemony of the terms of discourse even within postcolonial, protest literatures, when 'the Empire writes back,' supposedly![17]

> Every human being at every stage of history or pre-history is born into a society and from his earliest years is moulded by that society. The language which he speaks is not an individual inheritance, but a social acquisition from the group in which he grows up.[18]

A certain politics of reversed attribution can be discerned in the process: the periphery interfaces with the centre, resists it in an indigenous idiom, even tries to dislocate it—but the periphery is ultimately rejected, its essence displaced and its perversions co-opted and appropriated by the colonial centre.[19] R.G. Collingwood avers:

> An inquiry into the nature of historical thinking is among the tasks which philosophy may legitimately undertake [...] at particular periods of history, particular philosophical problems are, as it were, in season, and claim the special attention of a philosopher anxious to be of service to his age. In part, the problems of philosophy are unchanging; in part, they vary from age to age [...].[20]

While we are not quite convinced with the treatment of history as a mere collection of the so-called grand narratives, we are also not entirely in consonance with the politics-from-below point of view that tends to examine history as an absolute discourse in terms of black and white. We cannot possibly afford to discuss our categories of analysis in straitjacketed terms, subaltern or the elite. We do not feel comfortable with such 'absolute' categories and would rather prefer to interrogate these in order to explore other in-between areas of research.

This is why we do not want to look at the subaltern as something that was without any further 'paraphernalia' of identity. There must have been intra-subaltern strife and tension, problems of sustaining a workable stock of *social capital* within the subaltern classes themselves.

V

Organically evolved institutions have a greater chance to succeed in the hands of their subaltern end-users as there is a general sense of identity attending on these structures growing out of a sense of social and cultural acceptance and understanding. But what if nothing like this happens, and the people are left with institutions they do not really know how to handle and interact with? The result is a general gap in communicating with the structures, as in *Othello,* that are supposed to represent legitimacy and hegemony, and it can lead either to resentment or indifference towards the kind of politico-legal-cultural ensemble that institutions generally tend to signify.[21]

Gayatri Chakravorty Spivak has argued:

> They [the 'Subaltern Studies' group] *must* ask, 'Can the subaltern speak?' Here we are within [Michel] Foucault's own discipline of history and with people who acknowledge his influence. Their project is to rethink Indian colonial historiography from the perspective of the discontinuous chain of peasant insurgencies during the colonial occupation. This is indeed the problem of 'the permission to narrate' discussed by Said (1984). [...] Within the effaced itinerary of the subaltern subject, the track of sexual difference is doubly effected. The question is not of female participation in insurgency, or other ground rules of the sexual division of labour, for both of which there is 'evidence.' It is, rather, that, both, as object of colonialist historiography and as subject of insurgency, the ideological construction of gender keeps the male dominant. If, in the context of colonial production, the subaltern has no history and cannot speak, the subaltern as female is even more deeply in shadow.[22]

Spivak adds:

> In subaltern studies, because of the violence of imperialist epistemic, racial, and disciplinary inscription, a project understood in essentialist terms must traffic in a radical textual practice of differences. The object of the group's investigation, in the use not even of the people as such but of the floating buffer zone of the regional elite-subaltern, is a *deviation* from an *ideal*—the people or subaltern—which is itself defined as indifference from the elite. It is toward this structure that the research is oriented, a predicament rather different from the self-diagnosed transparency of the first-world radical intellectual. What taxonomy can fix such a space? Whether or not they themselves perceive it—in fact [Ranajit] Guha sees his definition of 'the people' within the master slave dialectic—their text articulates the difficult task of rewriting its own conditions of impossibility as the conditions of its possibility.[23]

So everything else is really a matter of interrogation: how does one perceive the world around one, how would one actually like to react to this given order of reality? This leads us to the ethos of 'high' or dominant politics, and the kind of language (and its discourse) that would be commonly entailed in the framework of such politics.

VI

What we have to understand at this point is the reality of institutions: their usefulness, efficacy and role in nation building and identity formation. This is a somewhat functional approach all right, but it also explains the importance of these structured interfaces for societal interaction and coherence.

Ashis Nandy has contended:

> It should be obvious that this way of looking at social intervention and culpability dissolves the crude dichotomy between the study of the elites and the study of the masses or, for that matter, between elitism and mass-line. Following traditional wisdom, I like to believe that the story of the prince can never be told without telling the story of the

> pauper, and that the cause of the pauper can never be independent of the cause of the prince [...]. As Frantz Fanon recognized, the suffering of the victims cannot but be the sickness of their oppressors and the intranslatability between two sets of life experiences is complete once the rules of translation are identified.[24]

The construct of the subaltern in the context of *Othello* tends to be 'absolute' rather than a relative category of discourse. It certainly has to do with disempowerment in a very fundamental, ontologic sense. Othello cannot apparently envisage his destiny, cannot think and is not even allowed to act within his 'other' terms of discourse.

So we conclude that *Othello* as the other has been doubly relegated to the margin of margin—he is first marginalized as the politico-social other and then as the ontologic other. Such subversion of the Moor's identity has extended across a comprehensive landscape cohered by power/knowledge, a framework of ethos as well as values and a remarkable ensemble structured by hegemony, legitimacy and the politics of ideology; Othello's identity has been transtextualized as the other in the process. Furthermore, we frequently find disquieting parallels of Othello in other postcolonial contexts and in other histories; herein lie both the applicability of our organon as well as the roadmap for further innovative research in this area.

NOTES AND REFERENCES

1. *Othello, The Moor of Venice.* Produced in 1604; printed (in quarto) in 1622. Original plot by Giambattista Giraldi Cinthio (1504-73).
2. Not noticed again in the play.
3. Cf. The concept of *social capital* in present-day social sciences. See Prasenjit Maiti, "Neo-Institutionalism for Making Democracy Work," *The West Bengal Political Science Review* 2.1&2 (Jan.-Dec. 1999) 93-98.
4. Tom R. Tyler, "What Do People Want from Legal Authorities?" *Why People Obey the Law* (New Haven/London: Yale UP, 1990) 71. Also see John Rawls, "The Obligation to Obey the Law," *Morality and the Law,* ed. Robert M. Baird and Stuart E. Rosenbaum (Buffalo/New York: Prometheus Books, 1988) 125-39.

5. Quoted from Michel Foucault. See C. Gordon, ed., *Power/ Knowledge: Selected Interviews and Other Writings 1972-1977* (Brighton: Harvester Press, 1980) 101. As cited in Barry Smart, *Foucault, Marxism and Critique* (London/Boston: Routledge and Kegan Paul, 1985) 84.
6. As cited above.
7. Cf. The career of police officers in India after they 'successfully' fought against urban guerrilla terrorism in West Bengal during the Naxalite Movement (late 1960s to early 1970s) or against secessionist insurgency in Punjab during the Khalistan Movement (1980s). The State has habitually failed to recognize its agents of coercion after violence has been curbed and the law and order situation brought under control. This is supposed to be a specificity of 'good' governance! Pranab Bardhan is of the opinion that India inherited at Independence (1947)—and even chose to retain—the apparatuses of the Colonial State, including the police, army, judiciary, legal system as well as much-vaunted civil service largely unaltered. See Bardhan, "The State against Society: The Great Divide in Indian Social Science Discourse," *Nationalism, Democracy and Development: State and Politics in India,* ed. Sugata Bose and Ayesha Jalal (New Delhi: Oxford UP, 1997) 186.
8. Reiman, *Justice and Modern Moral Philosophy* (New Haven/ London: Yale UP, 1990) 27.
9. Rajni Kothari, on the contrary, writes: "The struggle towards an alternative conception of thought and action has to face the challenge of reformulating and restructuring the dialectic between the locality and the globe. The earlier catch phrase used to be 'Think globally and live locally.' But the new situation is characterized by the radically different perception about the possibility of extending on a universal scale the existing global patterns of living. These global patterns are no longer believed to be extendable in a universal sense." See Kothari, *State against Democracy: In Search of Humane Governance* (Delhi: Ajanta, 1989) 9.
10. "Legitimacy [...] constitutes the difference between authority and power: Authority is [...] legitimately exercis[ing] power." See James S. Coleman, *Foundations of Social Theory* (Cambridge/ Massachusetts/London: Harvard UP, 1994) 470.
11. See Niklas Luhmann, *Social Systems*, trans. John Bednarz, Jr., et al (Stanford, California: Stanford UP, 1995) 220-21. I am grateful to Marcelo da Costa Pinto Neves, Guest Professor at the Institute of Federalism, University of Fribourg, Switzerland for having kindly pointed this out.

12. Certain tropes employed in this paper have been inspired by Mikhail Bakhtin, Francis Fukuyama, Immanuel Wallerstein, Jacques Derrida, Noam Chomsky and Samuel P. Huntington among others without, however, cluttering up the text with notes and references.
13. I thank Professor Lidija R. Basta Fleiner, Director of the International Research and Consultation Centre of the Institute of Federalism, Fribourg for this insight.
14. Steven Lukes, *Power: A Radical View* (London/Basingstoke: Macmillan, 1981) 54. Also see Barry Smart, *Michel Foucault* (Chichester, Sussex: Ellis Horwood, 1985).
15. See, for instance, Benedict Anderson, *Imagined Communities: Reflections on the Origin and Spread of Nationalism* (London: Verso, 1986); Partha Chatterjee, *The Nation and Its Fragments* (Delhi: Oxford UP, 1997) 3-13; Charles Tilly, ed., *The Formation of National States in Western Europe* (Princeton: Princeton UP, 1975); and Tilly, "War Making and State Making as Organised Crime," *Bringing the State Back In,* ed. Peter Evans, Dietrich Rueschemeyer and Theda Skocpol (Cambridge: Cambridge UP, 1985) 169-91.
16. Cf. Partha Chatterjee, *Nationalist Thought and the Colonial World: A Derivative Discourse?* (Delhi: Oxford UP, 1986) 36-53. Also see Bernard S. Cohn, "The Command of Language and the Language of Command," *Subaltern Studies: Writings on South Asian History and Society,* vol. 4, ed. Ranajit Guha (Delhi: Oxford UP, 1985) 276-329.
17. See Bill Ashcroft, Gareth Griffiths and Helen Tiffin, *The Empire Writes Back: Theory and Practice in Post-Colonial Literatures* (London/New York: Routledge, 1989).
18. See Edward Hallett Carr, *What is History*? (Harmondsworth, Middlesex: Penguin, 1990) 31. Also see R.G. Collingwood, *The Idea of History* (London: Oxford UP, 1946) 231.
19. See Homi Bhabha, ed., *Nation and Narration* (London/New York: Routledge, 199).
20. R.G. Collingwood, *The Idea of History* (London: Oxford UP, 1946) 231.
21. "From an institutional perspective, democratic governance involves improving the processes by which a society formulates ends, seeks to achieve them efficiently, elaborates and overturns its conceits, and weaves an understanding of the good life by experiencing its pursuit [...]. Democratic governance involves creating identities and preferences that define what is appropriate, right, desirable, and acceptable, the rule by which citizens and officials are constituted. It involves creating and limiting capabilities for action." See James G. March and Johan P. Olsen, *Democratic Governance* (New York/London: The Free Press, 1995) 246.

22. Gayatri Chakravorty Spivak, "Can the Subaltern Speak?" *The Post-Colonial Studies Reader*, ed. Bill Ashcroft, Gareth Griffiths and Helen Tiffin (London/New York: Routledge, 1995) 24-28, original emphasis.
23. Spivak 27.
24. Ashis Nandy, "Cultural Frames for Social Transformation: A Credo," *The Post-Colonial Studies Reader*, ed. Bill Ashcroft, Gareth Griffiths and Helen Tiffin (London/New York: Routledge, 1995) 264.

6

Jane Eyre and Jean Rhys: 'Gendering the Subaltern'

RAMA KUNDU

The contrast between the hegemonic concepts of universalism and objectivity and the decentred approaches that underscore the binaries of postcolonial theories and postulates is perhaps best brought out with references to the respective discourses on feminism. Whereas feminist discourse within the hegemonic social-cultural system of imperial structures has upheld the cause of female self-determination in the metropolitan context, it has often paradoxically effaced or ignored the identity of the 'third world woman.' On the other hand, feminist discourse within the 'third world' had to grapple with a complex challenge that subtly combined imperialism with androcentrism and patriarchal domination. The contrast gets sharply focalised in Jean Rhys's *Wide Sargasso Sea* (1966) which fractures the text of Charlotte Brontë's *Jane Eyre* (1847) and instills completely new meanings into the old tale, as Rhys interrogates its exclusivist assumptions about the racial Other and explores the issue of female identity from the shifted perspective of the frontier or periphery.

Spivak has rightly argued that in spite of the conventional feminist study of *Jane Eyre* as an allegorical account of female independence in the context of nineteenth century Britain, actually Jane's struggle for assertion and fulfilment involve and overshadow the effacement of the other girl in the novel—the creole wife of Rochester. Bertha Mason, the half-caste from

Jamaica whom Rochester is supposed to have married under mysterious circumstances serves "to render indeterminate the boundary between human and animal and thereby weaken her entitlement under the spirit if not the letter of the Law" (Spivak, "Women's Texts" 249). She has been fixed up in the role of 'the madwoman in the attic'; and her story, if she has one, remains untold. In contrast to her, Jane, the 'pure' British girl, achieves her entitlement as a natural claim. Jane's struggle for independence reflects the central concern of the novel—the predicament of women in nineteenth century England; it explores the possibility of the women's liberation from roles of subservience to the male. But this discourse excludes the woman who represents the racial Other; the question of racial difference remains inscribed in her untold story. This cult of Western feminism which remained firmly entrenched in the mindset of the imperial West over the centuries has been interrogated and rejected by Jean Rhys in *Wide Sargasso Sea,* her last and most significant novel. It shows how in the postcolonial context feminism could be detached from its complicity with imperialist discourses—the "allegories of empire,"[1] nurtured by chauvinist national and colonial culture that upheld colonial masculinity.

In *Jane Eyre* Bertha Mason is no longer a woman, nor even a human. She is reduced to the bestial and rendered almost invisible and inaudible-like "the trope of blackness in Western discourse [that] has signified absence at least since Plato" (Gates 315). Yet she is despised and feared by those who are visible and have a voice. Indeed this dangerous racial Other has not been uncommon in canonical works of English literature. The threatening or destructive Other appears as the Moor in *Othello* (1602), the Jew in *The Merchant of Venice* (1596), Man Friday in *Robinson Crusoe* (1719), Heathcliff in *Wuthering Heights* (1847), in the colonial stories of Kipling, Conrad, Forster, etc.

"Those particularly violent centuries in the history of the world now known as the era of Western colonization" (Young 121) governed the Western discourse of colonialism and determined its uniformist attitude towards the alterities of race, colour or ethnic origin. Their concept of universal human identity was necessarily a historical construct constituted by the exclusion, marginalisation and oppression of racial others. Standards of objectivity, academic authority, or 'intrinsic superiority' were always directed against them. In the case of the woman, again, it was the doubled otherness. The woman as the racial other suffered from "double colonization" under imperial condition. She was "the forgotten casualty of both imperial ideology, and native and foreign hierarchies" (Gandhi 83). In Western literature black women have been "doubly effaced" (Bennet & Royle 161) and silenced both as black and female.

The case of the creole woman represents an even deeper alienation and effacement. It seems to be tripled otherness; she is marginalized thrice over, being the other of the other of the other. Any simple and reductive notion of otherness, therefore, could be misleading in such a case. The question of identity also becomes extremely complex as well as urgent since she presents the highly problematic situation of one who belongs neither to the centre nor to the periphery.

Jean Rhys explores this problematic issue of creole (woman's) identity in *Wide Sargasso* Sea—a novel that engages with the white colonial discourse, and at the same time expresses an embedded colonial consciousness resulting in a subversive discourse which displaces the monolithic and oppressive constitution of identity through an assertion of racial otherness. After nearly one hundred and twenty years Rhys brings into focus the marginalized and effaced racial other of Brontë's novel by rewriting it in the Caribbean context. She presents a re-reading, or what Said would have called "contrapuntal reading" (Said 78) of *Jane Eyre*; and the re-reading produces a remarkable case of re-writing the canon as a means of subverting it. It is not just replacing one text with another. Rhys reconstructs the canonical text by dismantling it through an alternate perspective.

A canon, as the writers of *The Empire Writes Back* contest, is not a body of texts *per se*, but rather a set of reading practices which are inherent in prevailing institutional structures (Ashcroft et al 195). The process of literary decolonisation, therefore, involves a radical dismantling, subversion and appropriation of those reading practices which were dictated by dominant European codes and discourses. A major concern of postcolonial writing is to interrogate the assumptions of the colonial discourse by which Europe maintained its cultural hegemony over vast regions of the non-European world. Thus the re-reading and re-writing of the European historical and fictional records emerge as a vital and inescapable task at the heart of the postcolonial literary enterprise. Ashcroft, Griffiths and Tiffin even go as for as to stress that "these subversive manoeuvres rather than the construction of *essentially* national or regional alternatives, are the characteristic features of the postcolonial text" (Ashcroft et al 196). It has been, indeed, common enough for postcolonial writers to rewrite canonical works. It is also true that "most [such] rewritings are predicated on a hostile relationship to the canonical work and are motivated by a desire to dislodge relationship to the canonical work and are motivated by a desire to dislodge the canon" (Casteel 1999). Subversion of the canon through intertext thus becomes a typical postcolonial preoccupation. *The Tempest,* for example, has been subject to many alternative readings throughout the postcolonial world, including Alme Cesaire's reworking of the play in the African context and George Lamming's similar effort in *The Pleasures of Exile* and *Water With Berries* in the Caribbean context.

Caribbean fiction in particular appears to have reexamined history through the fractured glass of the canon which the Caribbean writers have carefully broken up and remade with their own 'difference.' The Caribbean history had witnessed an almost unprecedented act of genocide before the modern Caribbean began. George Lamming finely sums up this history with an exquisite bitterness in his Toronto lecture (1986) on the "Frontiers of Caribbean Literature." Within twenty-five to thirty years of Columbus's arrival the aboriginal population—the Arawaks and Caribs were almost totally destroyed. For a hundred years after this many European powers had moved into the region and fought each other. Territories were conquered, settled; little peasant holdings began with white people. Then came sugar, and along with the "monster" came large labour force, plantation society, slavery, and later indentured labour. Europe, Africa, Asia entered, clashed and intermixed in the islands. Ethnic conflicts violence, oppression, alienation, merciless exploitation and terrible reprisals became a common historical experience.

This ruthless and complex history, as Lamming points out, is not very prominent in official texts of history. One of the functions of the novel in the Caribbean, according to Lamming, is to serve as a form of social history. "The novelist thus becomes one of the more serious historians" (Lamming 5). Among the many attempts to re-create West Indian history in fiction may be cited, besides Walcott's *Omeros* (1990), several novels by DeLisser (1878-1944), Ada Quayle's *The Mistress* (1957), Orland Paterson's *Die the Long Day* (1972), and Jean Rhys's *Wide Sargasso Sea.*

Wide Sargasso Sea has been acknowledged as a "groundbreaking analysis of the imperialism at the heart of British culture" (Carr 20). At the same time both Naipaul and Wally Look Lai (who was the first to discuss *Wide Sargasso Sea* as a Caribbean novel in 1968) had suggested that Rhys's writing should be understood in the light of her colonial origins (Carr 14), and that Dominca had coloured her temperament and outlook. The novel actually foregrounds the dialectic between place and displacement which has been at the centre of all postcolonial societies and literatures. Displacement generates the crisis in self-image which goes beyond the usual categories of social alienation such as master/slave, free-bonded, ruler/ruled, and includes the free settler as well. "The free settler also shows clear signs of alienation, and manifests a tendency to seek an alternative differentiated identity" (Ashcroft et al 9). Removed far away from the centre the white settler in the Caribbean had undergone this experience of alienation. As Kenneth Ramchand explains, "the problem with the white West Indians was that they had gone native; they were no longer quite English, nor even quite European" (Ramchand 32).

It is against this historical background that Rhys's subversion of the canonical text and her creole heroine's anguished search for identity can be properly understood. Wally Look Lai has defined the encounter between Rochester and his creole wife as "more than an encounter between two people: it is an encounter between two worlds." Indeed, Jean Rhys projects the disastrous encounter between the two worlds—the centre and the periphery—across the great cultural-ideological-psycho-cartographical divide symbolized by the 'wide Sargasso sea.'

For an adequate response to *Wide Sargasso Sea* remembering *Jane Eyre* is essential because Rhys invites the reader to consider the same novel—the same personae and storyline—from a different ideological perspective, i.e. the postcolonial rejection of the colonial norms and its self-assertion over the colonizer's teachings and 'programming.' Here the British text has been undermined by and intertwined with the Caribbean tale consistently and elaborately. The focus shifts from the British girl's dignity-individuality-self-respect to the unnoticed tragedy of the other woman from Jamaica. In Brontë's novel the lunatic Caribbean woman seems to have no past; she is fixed in the moment. She is also dehumanised into a fearsome savage, a growling hyena in clothes. She is viewed through Rochester's eyes, and neither Jane nor the reader finds it difficulty to sympathise with Rochester who is made out to be a victim rather than the victimizer: he finds his wife a coarse, impure and depraved, wholly alien to him, a cunning and malignant lunatic causing him hideous and shameful agonies.

In Rhys's novel this creole woman gets the chance to narrate her own story; the "subaltern" "speaks"[2] for herself. Rhys humanises the 'mad woman,' and gives her a voice, a past, a name, and finally an identity. Accordingly, the scene too, but for the last part, shifts from England to the Caribbean isles across the 'wide Sargasso Sea.' Rhys places Brontë's faceless, pastless, rootless lunatic in her island, both spatially and historically. It is a beautiful place that nurtures a multi-ethnic society, and carries the legacy of a history that combines imperialism, racism and sexism. Yet it is only by remembering her personal past in the *chronotope* of the island that the heroine can get back her identity which she has lost in course of her traumatic marriage with an outsider and the forced deportation.

The narration here signifies a process of remembering on the part of the narrator. The mad creole woman from Jamaica, imprisoned in the attic of an English country-mansion, desperately tries to re-construct her past by groping down memory lane. Friendless, alone, cut off from society, uprooted from the wild naturescape of her home island, and confined in a cold, narrow cell in an alien land, she tries, to salvage her past bit by bit as far back as she can remember. She has lost her sense of time and comprehension of reality. But she is obviously not at ease; she feels restless with a sense of urgency stirring within her. She then realises the challenge of the situation—that she "must *remember*" before all is lost: "Quickly, while I can, I must remember" (*WSS* 44).

It is by a painful attempt at "remember"-ing that the narrator slowly recaptures *her story* of a dismembered life in fragments; how a woman's identity underwent steady dislocation through systematic assaults by scheming male relatives—husband and half-brother—and finally through transplantation from her native place to a distant unknown land across the 'wide Sargasso sea.'

The narrator is engaged here in an act of "deprogramming."[3] Her urgency to remember may be considered in the light of the rise of cultural nationalism that has left considerable impact on much of postcolonial literature across the globe, and specially in West Indies and Africa, as "a conscious attempt to restore the cultural heritage by initiating a process of deprogramming, as a systematic remedial measure" (Ray 104) against the colonizer's systematic programme to destroy the heritage and deflate the cultural values of the colonized.

Thus the narrator finds it important to remember that her name is not Bertha, as she is called by her British husband, and that names matter: "Names matter, like when he wouldn't call me Antoinette, and I was Antoinette drifting out of the window with her scents, her pretty clothes and her looking glass" (*WSS* 147). It is a fine way of suggesting the sensitive girl's reaction to the deprivation of her original identity through the superimposition of another image by her imperial husband who now controls her life. She also misses Antoinette's look (self-image) which would have shown her real face and remind her that she was not a born lunatic to whom a noble English gentleman had been married by trickery but that she was a fine sensitive girl who had once lived in and loved a lush green island separated from England by thousands of nautical miles until she was "broken up,"[4] uprooted and shipped off to England. Since then she has been kept locked in this ugly room without a looking glass. This drab, dull life—where she is dislocated, isolated, and branded as a lunatic—has eventually undermined her grip on past and future, memory and hope; only yesterday and tomorrow remain. As the past recedes from the narrator's consciousness she also fails to relate to an adequate self-image.

Significantly, during this period she is not allowed access to a looking glass. The mirror image has been, indeed, carefully built into a motif in the text. Antoinette's search for identity is effectively reflected in this motif—a search that, after repeated frustrations, attains success. "Long ago when I was a child," Antoinette faintly remembers, "and very lonely I tried to kiss her" (the image in the glass). It was a failed attempt at reaching out since in the sheer loneliness of her childhood there was no one else to reach out, and relate to. Later, when still a child, she had an epiphanic moment of self-recognition in a flash of the Coulibri fire, when with a desperate longing to stay on ("Not to leave [...]. Not to go, not") she ran to Tia, the black child who was her only playmate. Tia threw a stone: "I looked at her [...] we stared at each other, blood on my face, tears on hers. It was as if I saw myself. Like in a looking glass" (*WSS* 38).

But the trauma of her painful marriage and the subsequent attic-prison get the better of her, and she loses the memory of the glimpse of self-knowledge she had once attained. In the absence of a mirror during this period she feels lost and does not know how to relate herself to the world around her. "There is no looking glass here and I don't know what I am like now" (*WSS* 147). By taking the mirror (i.e. an appropriate self-knowledge) away, they have robber her of '*everything*.' "Now

[that] they have taken *everything* away" she finds no answer to her obsessive self-questionings: "What am I doing in this place and who am I" (*WSS* 147).

Rhys achieves a superb stylistic feat in evoking the intonation of a sad, tired, befuddled mind to recapture an amnesia patient's halting, distressed interior monologue. The image of fire (so deeply rooted in her memory of the Caribbs) works as a reviver—first slow, then suddenly strong—in her struggle with forgetfulness. In the bitter cold of England she watches the coal-fire every morning and creeps close to watch the flame which sets her wondering—"Why have I been brought here? For what reason? [...]. What is it that I must do?" (*WSS* 146). But she cannot remember and the fire dies. Then one day the sight of her old dress lying on the floor like a spreading fire—a dress she used to wear during her last days on the island—suddenly brings the past flooding back into her memory like the rushing sea-waves along the island's coasts. "Nights and days and days and nights, hundreds of them slipping through my fingers. But that does not matter. Time has no meaning. But something that you can touch and hold like my red dress, that has a meaning" (*WSS* 151). In a desperate effort to connect her dislocated life with some "meaning" she clutches the dress of the colour of "fire and sunset," "the colour of fire and sunset," "the colour of flamboyant flowers"; and she recalls the old saying of the island: "If you are buried under a flamboyant tree your soul is lifted up when it flowers" (*WSS* 151). Then the past resurges, first in the form of smell. Rhys uses a rich poetic style to describe this process of resurgence. It is, as it were, all the smells of the garden of her childhood have come back. "The scent that came from the dress was very faint at first, then it grew stronger. The smell of vetivert and frangipani, of cinnamon and dust and lime trees when they are flowering. The smell of the sun and the smell of the rain" (*WSS* 151). She also recalls a sound—the ship's siren hooting good-bye to the island for ever. This sudden resurfacing of the moment of parting from Sandi and the island, Sandi's last "life-and-death kiss" benumbs her with its associated pain, and the dress slips through her hands onto the floor where it creates the optical illusion of a spreading fire. These successive memories of smell, touch, sound and colour help her mind back onto the track of self-recognition which is automatically followed by the psychic release:

> It was as if the fire had spread across the room. It was beautiful and it reminded me of something I must do. I will remember I thought. I will remember quite soon now (*WSS* 153).

The climax of this process is reached with Antoinette's third and last dream which ends in the declaration of deprogramming and self-recognition—"I know now" (*WSS* 153). In the dream she retraces the course from confusion to clarity, from present to past, and correspondingly from the attic downstairs step by step. "They think [...]. I don't remember, but I do" (*WSS* 153).[5] Before the final release she has to go through another flash of terror, when she has a glimpse of herself as they see her: "It was then that I saw her—the ghost." She sees herself as reflected in the polished British hall-mirror. She turns away in terror from her ugly insane image as projected by the imperial discourse and seeks assurance from none else than Christophine, her childhood *da* (nurse), the blackest woman of the islands who, if at all alive, must be thousands of miles away at the moment. Yet Antoinette is helped. It is, as if in an answer to her call for help, that a fire starts. The candle she had dropped in her moment of fear has already started a fire. And a wall of fire comes up to protect her from the man who called her Bertha. Also the reddened fire-scape around her seems to recapture her lost past in its entirety: "all my life was in it." She sees the flowers in the garden of her childhood, the 'tree of life' in flames, all the ferns and bushes, all the domestic articles; even the green parrot that died in the Coulibri estate fire now reappears in this vision crying out '*qui est la*'—and finally the pool at Coulibri. A pool is also a mirror—a reflecting surface. Tia, the small black friend of her childhood, appears in this mirror and seems to beckon to her. At this moment the man who 'hated' her calls 'Berth.' She winces at the smart caused by this continued attempt at programming, and with a loud call "Tia" she jumps. Just as the bird answers the question *'qui est la'* (who is there?) by asserting its indigenous identity—*'Che Coco Che Coco,'*[6] so Antoinette, who has at last achieved her identification with Tia and not Bertha, makes her emphatic declaration of the discovery through her final scream.

However, it is through a tortuous and very painful route that she finally arrives at the truth. Because basically her very situation as a creole girl in a colony made her alienated and vulnerable. Even as a child, the daughter of a creole mother and a British father—a plantation owner and ex-slaverunner, now dead—Antoinette had known desertion, despise and poverty. In her secluded childhood she had imbibed a deep sense of insecurity which was aggravated by her domestic situation and intensified by the social climate of the colony that generated impersonal hatred for the creole. The story of the Cosways may be seen in relation to the same violence ridden historical-social process that operated in various ways throughout the Caribbs and set the ethnic groups against one another. The lonely girl grew up in an unstable world where the father had died, relatives-friends-associates had deserted, the garden had gone wild, the house was crumbing. Then the only remaining horse was found dead one morning; the dear old house was burnt down one night by an angry mob; and the fire, by killing Antoinette's little invalid brother and the pet bird, drove her mother mad. When Antoinette came back after a few years in the convent following the Coulibri fire, both her mother and stepfather had died, and Aunt Cora, her only loving relative was on death-bed. It was in this orphaned state that she was partly enticed, and partly forced into marriage with a British fortune-seeker, arranged by her half-brother in exchange for her entire property. The marriage proved disastrous eventually and it was only to be expected. The shadowy knowledge of her mother's last days, when the helpless mad woman, left by her husband in the hands of paid people, was sexually exploited by all and sundry, was enough to cripple the child psychologically. The terrified child grew up a sad girl and her husband, who married her as part of a design, found it easy to "break her up." As the target of his imperialist-patriarchal-racist assault she was shattered quickly and completely. The anonymity of Antoiette's British husband helped him emerge as a role—the representative of a common type of imperial adventurers who were instrumental in the ruling power's exploitative 'programming' of the colony, often leading to disintegrating impact on the colonized.

Antoinette makes an anguished summation of her situation in a moment of agony: "A white cockroach [...]. That's what they call all of us who were here before their own people in Africa sold them to the slave-traders. And I've heard English women call us white niggers. So [...] I often wonder who I am and where is my country and where do I belong" (*WSS* 85). Christophine too fails to define her *doudou's* socio-cultural position: "She is not *beke* like you," she tells Antoinette's husband, "but she is *béké,* and not like us either" (*WSS* 128). Her English husband also finds her an alien. His racism takes the better of him and he finds the girl as despicable and incomprehensible as the strange island, both of which he hates. Though she is considered beautiful by any casual observer, her British husband finds her repellent on racist grounds. Even during the honeymoon he feels annoyance seething within him: "Long, sad, dark alien eyes. Creole of pure English descent she may be, but they are not English or European either" (*WSS* 56). The marriage was a cynical scheme from the word go and the 'otherness' continues to repel him as is evidence by his mutterings: "I did not love her [...] she was a stranger to me [...] who did not think or feel as I did" (*WSS* 78). He cannot accept her as one of his own kind. And finally on the eve of leaving the Granbois honeymoon house he acknowledges his absolute hatred for this 'other,' embodied by the woman and the place to which she belongs: "I hated the place [...] the mountains and the hills, the rivers and the rain [...] the sunsets [...] beauty [...] magic [...] secret I would never know [...]. Above all I hated her. For she belonged to the magic and the loveliness" (*WSS* 141). The declaration, "I hated," is repeated endlessly the way an annihilating hammer strikes.

That Antoinette walked into this trap of a marriage was due to her peculiar colonial situation. Like the typical creole woman of the islands she was left particularly vulnerable alienated as she was from both outsiders and natives. She seems to perfectly answer Francis Wyndham's description of "the mad creole heiresses[7] in the early nineteenth century, whose dowries were only an additional burden to them: products of an inbred, decadent society resented by the recently freed slaves whose superstitions they shared, they languished in the oppressive beauty of their tropical surroundings ripe for exploitation" (Wyndham 11).

Antoinette's attempt to be merged into some collective identity by means of relating herself to the metropolitan white ends up in devastating frustration. It is only at the end that she sees, in the light of the fire, the entire vista of her life and recognizes her own identity in the form of her childhood friend Tia, and this time she does not fail to respond. The creole woman, under the yoke of racial-sexual-imperial domination, realises that ultimately her identity lies with the black women in the islands and not with the metropolitan whites. She finds it possible to identify with the victims—the Christophines and Tias—because she too has been a victim of the imperialist-androcentric power and ethos which had so ruthlessly victimized slave-girls in the colonies. That situationally she (or her mother) has been no better than those slave girls becomes apparent to Antoinette through suffering. So, when at the end, the dream Tia beckons to her she knows what she has to do and she jumps from the English mansion in order to be merged with the dream Tia at the dream-pool of Coulibri.[8]

That Antoinette can finally attain this fulfilment (destructive through) is due to her emotional involvement with the place. As a newly wed bride she tells her husband: "I love it [the place] than anywhere in the world. As if it were a person. More than a person" (*WSS* 74). This rootedness in the place is evident in her automatic loving response to the natural phenomena with its colour, sound, smell, rains, hills, forests, birds and insects ("Our snakes are not poisonous, of course not" [*WSS* 73]) as well as to the human environment in which the African element remains the strongest component. Christophine stands for this component, and Antoinette loves Christophine while her husband hates her as the "dark voice coming from the darkness" (*WSS* 129), i.e. the other, the stranger. Christophine also appears to represent a collective identity and thus offer a counterpoint to Antoinette in her identity-crisis. Christophine, who smells of all the black women of Antoinette's childhood, stands on her own—self-assured, assuring, positive; she is not vulnerable like her one-time creole mistress and her daughter. In spite of the multiplied indignity of her situation—subjected to economic, racial and sexual harassment-exploitation—she can yet emerge as the strong matriarch who has sons, each by a different father, but who has not allowed any "thief husband" to steal her money. Thus she offers a contrast to Antoinette who falls an easy victim to her scheming husband.

Christophine also represents the goal, the shelter that Antoinette reaches out to. Not only in her lonely childhood, but later on as well, when Antoinette is being systematically "broken up" by her marriage, Christophine is the only one to comfort her, protect her, fight for her. Even before her complete breakdown Antoinette knows—actually she has known it since her childhood—that Christophine is her "only friend" (*WSS* 94). In the days of her terrible agony she can turn only to Christophine for comfort. And in her last dream too she would a cry out only to Christophine for help. Through her intuitive connection with Christophine and identification with Tia Antoinette finally realises where she truly belongs. Rhys finds the creole woman (perhaps from her own experience) an outsider among the metropolitan whites, who can achieve her redemption only through an alliance with and a recognition of identity with the coloured women of ex-slave communities—the worst sufferers in a remote colony. Antoinette's identity crisis thus finally finds a solution, though through the immense sufferings of a shattered life.

Rhys makes a richly evocative use of certain folk-elements in the novel to show how and where Antoinette basically belongs. This is evidenced by the way local beliefs, superstitions, dreams, fire-rituals, dirge-songs recur in the text and create an intricate web of meanings. Even Antoinette's interior monologue is narrated in the tone of the dirge which happens to be a strong element in the folklore of any ex-slave black society—particularly so in the Caribbean[9]—a memory of the age of slavery. As a child, Antoinette had picked up only these sad patois songs and they remained embedded in her adult consciousness. In spite of her white descent she has imbibed the sadness which remained embedded in the psyche of the ancient subjugated race.

The dirge-like tone governing the narration of the baffled, harassed woman desperately trying to reconstruct her past casts the spell of an overwhelming sadness over the short novel. It is in tune with the lonely moaning of the Caribbean Sea lapping the desolate islands, and coheres with the exhausted woman's last-ditch effort to attain identity by means of groping along the darkening passages of extremely painful memories of a half forgotten past.

Even the first and second dreams of Antoinette, which are but one dream rhythmically repeated, carry the echoes of African folklore. In view of the strong African element in the texture of Caribbean culture, the tale of the 'Skull' may be recalled in the context of Rhys's attempt to *locate* her novel in the islands. This is a common tale told and retold in various parts of Africa and it has been perceptively used by Ebun Clark in his paper on the African folkloric interpretation of *Othello*. It is likely that Rhys/ Antoinette had heard the tale from the black attendants in her early childhood. It is about the marriage of a beautiful girl with a handsome stranger from some unknown place who takes her through a deep forest while returning his borrowed limbs and torso to their respective owners one by one, until only the 'Skull' remains. 'Beauty' is scared; she weeps and implores to be allowed to go back to her village, but in vain. She is forcibly taken to the 'House of Skulls' where she meted out untold suffering and death.[10]

In Antoinette's own life this very tale seems to have been reenacted with slight variations. On the eve of three crucial turns in her life Antoinette is visited by the same dream. The second one is an extended repetition of the first while the third is a reversal. An echo of the above-mentioned tale is clearly audible in the first two dreams. The first time she sees it, it is in the night which follows her desertion by Tia, and her mother's excitement over the new visitors to the house. In her childlike innocence she has a hunch that things are going to change. That night she dreams: "I was walking in the forest. Not alone. Someone who hated me was with me. Out of sight. I could hear heavy footsteps coming closer and though I struggled and screamed, I could not move I wake crying" (*WSS* 23). Waking up she tries to feel comforted: "I am safe. I am safe from strangers" (*WSS* 23). The reader knows how ironically pathetic this self-assurance will prove to be within a few years. The second time she has the dream is when the rumour of her impending marriage and the necessity to leave the convent make feel uneasy and scared. This dream is a pre-vision of her fatal marriage and its disastrous conclusion in the attic prison.

> Again I have left the house at Coulibri. It is still night and I am walking towards the forest, following the man who is with me. I follow him, sick with fear [...]. Now we have reached the forest [...]. He turns and looks at me, his face black with hatred, and when I see this I begin to cry. He smiles slyly. 'Not here not yet,' he says, and I follow him, weeping [...] we are no longer in the forest but in an enclosed garden surrounded by a stone wall and the trees are different trees. I do not know them. There are steps leading upwards. It is too dark to see the wall or the steps, but I know they are there [...]. It will be when I go up these steps. At the top [...] 'Here in here,' a strange voice said [...] (*WSS* 50).

This dream, carrying unmistakable echoes of the folk-tale also sums up her unhappy marriage; the essence as well as every detail of this dream are later worked out in reality and that concludes the terrifying journey through the wilderness (sea in this case) and beyond it, terminating at the house of 'Skulls' (meaning cold calculation divorced from tenderness, emotion and love).

Rhys's unique linguistic register also imparts a characteristic regional flavour to the text, and thus helps the reader to *locate* Antoinette in her home island; at the same time it also helps the reader—even a causal one—to perceive the assertive difference of the 'English' of postcolonial writings from the 'Queen's English' of the imperial text. Rhys interweaves standard English—while simplifying it to suit the rhythms of the broken narration—with a good stock of words and phrases of various origins, including pidgin, patois, Spanish, and African which contributes to the special Caribbean flavour of the text. Jean D'Costa observes in this regard:

> The polyglot past has yielded the many language varieties of the present. In Caribbean countries a range of usages known as a creole continuum links the standardized English of educated speakers to the true creole speech of the working class [...]. Caribbean speakers have available to them not only two ranges of vocabulary but two ranges of grammatical expression (D'Costa 808).

Jean Rhys shows daring linguistic realism in this novel by linking character, dialogue and mood to the expression and intonation of the place. Thus she comes to represent what D'Costa defined as the Caribbean writers' and readers' "growing appetite for their own words and their own voices. Nothing less can represent the complexities of these cultures" (D'Costa 809).

With all these elements of Caribbean culture interwoven by means of rich imagination and a deep nostalgia for a particular place on the part of Rhys, the novel emerges as a saga of the islands in a particular time-space continuum, and underscores the rejection of imperial values and asserts the new self-hood of an ex-colony.

NOTES

1. The reference is to Jenny Sharpe's title *Allegories of Empire: The Figure of Woman in the Colonial Text* (Minneapolis: U of Minnesota P, 1993).
2. Gayatri Chakravorty Spivak in her essay "Can the Subaltern Speak" shows how liberal academic feminism could silence the figure of the native woman, the 'gendered subaltern.'

3. M.E. Ray explains: "The idea of deprogramming presupposes an idea of programming which [...] is a necessary construct in a colonial situation. Programming is a systematic intellectual man oeuvre through which the colonizer destroys the cultural heritage and deflates the cultural values of the colonized. This is done by convincing the colonized that they did not have any cultural heritage in the first place and whatever they had in the name of culture was absolutely worthless" (104).
4. "Break her up" recurs like a harsh refrain reminding the reader of the colonizer's cynical scheme to programme the colonized so that the latter gets disintegrated.
5. In Derek Walcott's *Omeros*—his epic search for a "Caribbean anthem"—Philoctete bears an ancestral wound which represents a "tribal sorrow" and Ma Kilman, an Obeah woman, must retrieve racial memory in order to alleviate Philoctete's pain.
6. Coco in Spanish is budgerbiger, a local insect-eating bird; Coco is also a green plant commonly found on tropical shores. 'Coco' is essentially of the place. The bird trusted only Antoinette's creole mother, but not her English husband, who had clipped its wings, and as a result it could not escape the fire. The 'Coco' anecdote is proleptic of Antoinette's final assertion and subsequent death.
7. There is a covert hint in Lee Irwin's article at the possible connection between the male settler's sexual promiscuity, often leading to syphilis, and its resultant impact on their wives, and Daniel's insinuation—"the madness that is in her, and in all these white creoles" (*WSS* 80).
8. Antoinette's mother, however, had sensed this truth in her own fashion long way back. Annette, the beautiful young second wife of an old promiscuous alcoholic planter who had, besides his two wives, "all those women" bore no grudge either to the children of these sexual exploits or their mothers. In a way she provided for them and even arranged for Christmas gifts. Annette's gesture, however, was neither appreciated by the whites nor the coloured except Christophine. Then when abject poverty followed abolition of slavery and Cosway's death, no one lifted a finger. It was only Christophine, a former slave woman, who saw them through the hard times.
9. George Lamming says: "There is a lot of African behaviour in Caribbean society, of which the people practising that behaviour are not themselves aware" (Lamming, "Africa and the Caribbean" 16).

   "Whatever may be identified as cultural differences [...] in the Caribbean [...] their one common experience is the culture of

10. In some versions of the tale the girl is killed in the House of Skulls. In others she is saved by a man of her father's choice who marries her; nevertheless she becomes dumb and half-mad having gone through the trauma.

WORKS CITED

Ashcroft, B., G. Griffiths, and H. Tiffin. *The Empire Writes Back.* New York: Routledge, 1989.

Bennelt, A. and N. Royle. *An Introduction to Literature, Criticism and Theory.* London: Prentice Hall, 1995.

Carr, Helen. *Jean Rhys.* London: Northcote House Publishers, 1996.

Casteel, Sarah Phillips. "Autobiography as Rewriting: Derek Walcott's *Another Life* and *Omeros.*" *The Journal of Commonwealth Literature* 34.2 (1999).

Clark, Ebun. "Othello the Complete Gentleman: An African Folkloric Interpretation." *The Journal of Commonwealth Literature* 25.1 (1990).

D'Costa, Jean. "Language (The Caribbean)." *Encyclopaedia of Postcolonial Literature in English.* New York: Routledge, 1993.

Erwin, Lee. "Like in a Looking-glass." *Novel* (Winter 1989).

Gandhi, Leela. *Postcolonial Theory.* Delhi: Oxford UP, 1999.

Gates, Henry Louis, eds. *Black Literature and Literary Theory.* London: Methuen, 1984.

Gilbert, S. and S. Guber. *The Madwoman in the Attic.* New Heaven: Yale UP, 1979.

Lamming, George. "Concepts of the Caribbean." *Frontiers of Caribbean Literature in English.* Ed. F. Birbalsingh. London: Macmillan, 1996.

——. "Africa and the Caribbean" (Interview). *Frontiers of Caribbean Literature in English.* Ed. F. Birbalsingh. London: Macmillan, 1996.

Look Lai, Wally. "The Road to Thornfield Hall: An Analysis of *Wide Sargasso Sea.*" *New Beacon Reviews: Collection One.* Ed. J.L. Rose. London: New Beacon Books, 1968.

Ramchand, Kenneth. *The West Indian Novel and Its Background.* London: Faber & Faber, 1970.

Ray, Mohit K. "Deprogramming through Cultural Nationalism: Achebe and Ellision." *Revaluations* 2.1 (Summer 1996).

Rhys, Jean. *Wide Sargasso Sea.* New York: Penguin Books, 1977. Cited as *WSS.*

Said, Edward. *Culture and Imperialism.* London: Chatto & Windus, 1993.

Spivak, Gayatri Chakravorty. "Three Women's Texts and a Critique of Imperialism." *Critical Inquiry* 12 (1985) 242-61.

——. "Can the Subaltern Speak." *Marxist Interpretations of Culture.* Ed. C. Nelson and L. Grossberg. Basingstoke: Macmillan, 1988.

Wyndham, Francis. "Introduction." *Wide Sargasso Sea.* New York: Penguin Books, 1977.

Young, Robert. *White Mythologies: Writing History and the West.* London: Routledge, 1990.

7

R. Parthasarathy and Poetry as Postcolonial Discourse

P. MALLIKARJUNA RAO

R. Parthasarathy's *Rough Passage* is a landmark in the history of contemporary Indian Poetry in English for two reasons: Firstly, it depicts his growth as a man and a poet in a postcolonial society; secondly, it sensitively maps the rigours of cultural and linguistic dilemmas he encounters as a poet and as such offers a paradigm of the predicament of Indian English poets.

Perhaps, only Michael Madhusudhan Dutt can be considered his poetic ancestor as they both share bi-lingualism and the dilemma of linguistic choice for their poetic communication. Dutt switched to Bengali from English after he was advised by Bankimchandra Chatterjee.

The problems of linguistic choice and the cultural dilemmas that Parthasarathy is preoccupied with are not only peculiar to him; in fact they are precisely the issues a writer encounters in a postcolonial situation. To comprehend fully the larger implications of these problems one has to understand and examine the relation between language and culture.

The principal strategy adopted by the Imperialist forces to subjugate the natives is to culturally reorient them. The hegemonistic nature of the rulers' culture plays havoc with the psyche of the natives. So the biggest weapon 'unleashed' by the Imperialist forces against the 'collective defiance' of the natives is the 'Cultural bomb.' As N'gugi observes "the effect of a cultural bomb is to annihilate a peoples' belief in their names, in their languages, in their environment, in their heritage of struggle, in their unity, in their capacities and ultimately in themselves" (N'gugi 1992: 3).

There is an organic relation between language and culture. Language is both a product of culture and a transmitter of culture. Language has a dual character. It is both a means of communication and also a carrier of culture. Culture of a community embodies its moral, ethical and aesthetic values. It is precisely these values which bestow upon a people their identity and particularity. These values are carried by language from one generation to another. N'gugi rightly observes: "Language as culture is the collective memory of a people's experience in a history. Culture is almost indistinguishable from language that makes possible its genesis, growth, banking, articulations and indeed its communication from one generation to the next" (N'gugi 1992: 15).

According to him language as culture has three important aspects:

(a) Culture is a product of history.

(b) Language as culture is "an image-forming agent" in the mind of a child. We perceive the world through these images and relate ourselves to it through these images: "Language as culture is thus mediating between me and my own self; between my own self and other selves; between me and nature. Language is mediating in my very being" (N'gugi 1992: 15).

(c) Culture transmits these images of the world and reality through the spoken and the written language. (N'gugi 1992: 15).

Thus language and culture act as mutual carriers:

> Language carries culture and culture carries particularly through orature and literature the entire body of values by which we come to perceive ourselves and our place in the world (N'gugi 1992: 16).

By adopting the language of the rulers the colonised adopt their images of the world and perceive it through them. Consequently there occurs a dissociation in the mind of the colonised between him and his environment that leads to cultural alienation. Thus the relation between language and culture is quite complex. We shall examine in this paper how Parthasarathy comes to terms with the issues of language and culture in his *Rough Passage* (1977).

During the early years of his life (1944-'51) Parthasarathy was at Don Bosco; that is when English became a part of his life. Little did he realize then the 'exorbitant price' he was going to pay later. The English education made so deep an impression on him that he was very uneasy in India. "And exposed as I was to English ideas and attitudes, I became hypercritical of everything Indian. Indian society was, I felt, deeply neurotic, its feet chained to a grossly exaggerated past. There was, again, something terribly wrong with the Indian character itself. Spiritually bankrupt and powerless to absorb the shocks of twentieth century, India was a 'nation of sleep-walkers,' its people sick in the mind and helpless. The nation had, I kept telling myself, lost its will to live" (R. Parthasarathy 1982: 66). How is such a conception of India very different from that of the colonialist historian like James Mill? Gripped in the fever of 'Colonialitis' (his own phrase), he wanted to make England his home and become "in fact English, in every sense of that word." As the mists of euphoria cleared, he suddenly confronted the yawning gulf existing between his culture and the British Culture. The result was the painful awareness of his real identity. This subterranean cultural conflict manifested itself in the linguistic choice he encountered. These cultural turmoils are sensitively portrayed in his *Rough Passage.*

Rough Passage is a series of poems which should be read as parts of a single poem. It is the central theme which provides the connecting link between them. This long poem is divided into three parts corresponding with the three phases of the poet's evolution namely: Exile, Trial and Home Coming.

There are eight poems in 'Exile' and the section begins in an introspective mood. After thirty years of his life the poet takes a close look at himself because by then "mud will have settled." He finds himself different by then as he has already experienced the cultural trauma. He articulates the conflict between the twin inheritances of English and Tamil not in explicit terms but through "the subtleties and modulations" of his images and metaphors. One of the important verbal strategies that he employs for a forceful depiction of his theme is the creation of a persona. This enables him to depict his return to his cultural inheritance in very personal terms of a man returning to his bride.

"The affair with the English Language had been prolonged and tempestuous. It is over now and I have, as the phrase goes, settled down with Tamil. She is still a shy, obstinate bride, but, like all brides, she will, I am sure, come round. The relationship will then, perhaps mature into love" (Parthasarathy 1977: 71).

These many years
You warmed yourself at her hands.
The luminous pebbles of her body
Stayed your feet, else you had overflowed

the banks, never reached shore...
All night your hand has rested
on her left breast.

In the morning when she is gone
you will be alone like the stone benches
in the park, and would have forgotten
her whispers in the noises of the city. (15-16)

The image of the hand resting on the left breast is highly evocative and sets off multiple implications. Hand on the breast has not only erotic implications but also suggests a sense of security if it is conceived as a child's arm resting on the mother's breast as suggested by Rosaly Puthuceary. This "dual vision of mother and lover discloses the nature of his attachment to Tamil" (16).

He captures the harrowing sense of loneliness and alienation in the image of the stone benches in the park which with their coldness and loneliness stand in striking contrast to the warmth of his lover.

The second poem of the section is also significant as it suggests the subterranean cultural renewal taking place in him.

In a basement flat, conversation
Filled the night, while Ravi Shankar
Cigarette stubs, empty bottles of stout
and crisps provided the necessary pauses. (17)

Ravi Shankar, a cultural symbol, suggests the nostalgia for home, a quality characterstic of all exiles. Parthasarathy is disillusioned with England where his colonial dreams are rudely shattered. Once the euphoria wears out, the poet stands starkly exposed to the cultural choices he has to make. He is possessed by an over-powering urge to return to his roots.

Yen learn roots are deep
that language is a tree, loses colour
under another sky.

The bark disappears with the snow
and branches become hoarse. (17)

He becomes acutely conscious of his complexion, his true identity, as against the adopted.

Once again his dreams and new expectations crash on the hard rocks of reality. Returning home, he is disappointed. Things are not bright and rosy as he imagines. Inland the Western culture has taken its toll.

Inland, an old civilization
hissed in the alleys and wells. (24)

The native culture and civilization are driven into the lanes, by-lines and alleys and the alien culture flaunts itself on the highways. It no longer holds a sway on the lives of the people. Parthasarathy powerfully captures the changed atmosphere in the following metaphor:

The hourglass of the Tamil mind
is replaced by the exact chronometer of Europe...

There is no fight left in the old beast.
Time has plucked her teeth...

So the poet, disappointed, asks in exasperation

What have I come
here for from a thousand miles? (24)

Nevertheless, his identification with the Western inheritance does not cease and despite his efforts he cannot extricate himself from the snares of Western culture. He brings out the helplessness and desperation involved in this enterprise in the following lines:

Your breasts,
Sharp with desire, hurt my fingers.

Feelings beggar description
shiver in dark alleys of the mind,
hungry and alone. (26)

He finds the British inheritance so strongly ingrained in him that he cannot easily dispense with it. However, his resolution to return to his cultural mooring grows stronger in the wake of his realisation that he had already wasted many years of his life in "whoring after English Gods." So he decides now to give "quality to the other half" of his life.

In 'Trial,' the second section, there are 15 poems which are marked by unmitigated passion. The poet explores his growth and his relation with his cultural inheritance through the images of love. He identifies Tamil as his lover and depicts his relation with it in passionate terms and this lends an immediacy to his experience.

It is night alone helps
to achieve a lucid exclusiveness.
Time that had dimmed

your singular form
by its harsh light now makes
recognition possible

through the opaque lens.

Touch brings the body into focus
restores colour to inert hands,

till the skin takes over
erasing angularities, and the four walls
turn on a strand of hair. (37)

Soon he elevates his love from the narrow confines of private and personal experience by referring to Anupama Devi of Belur and the erotic sculpture of Konark. He emphasises its primeval nature and relates it to his cultural inheritance.

Our bodies scrape home
for passions, older
than the stones of Konark. (38)

According to Puthuceary "The correlation between his passion for his inherited culture and sex, brings to a climax the exploration. By comparing his passions to the stones of Konark [...] the poet captures the primeval nature of the protagonist's love and his umbilical ties with his cultural inheritance (19).

The poet feels reassured now that his affair with the alien inheritance is over. So he now puts aside the past.

in a corner, an umbrella
now poor in the ribs. (39)

However, he is aware that past is something which he cannot totally dispense with or escape from even though its hold on him is tenuous. The umbrella, that is the British inheritance, which he found useful to him once, is today weak in the wake of his cultural renewal. Nevertheless, it impinges on his consciousness. So he says:

Curled around me
are not the familiar arms,
but an octopus past, blurring
the plate-glass of my days. (43)

He reconciles to this fact helplessly and learns to look at it positively.

My past is an unperfect stone:
the flaws show. I polish
the stone, sharpen the lustre to a point. (45)

The title of the third section "Home coming" shows promise. In this section he has a dialogue with his Tamil past. He deplores the degeneration the language has suffered "reeling down the plush corridors" of the cinema and brings out its impoverishment very vividly in the metaphor of the bull, a traditional image of strength and power.

The bull, Nammalvar took by the horns,
is today an unrecognizable carcass,
quick with the fleas of Kodambakkam, (50)

Tamil, which was lofty and magnificent during the period of Tamil Bhakthi poet Nammalvar, has lost all its vigour today and is reduced to a shadow. So he feels that living in Tamilnadu where Tamil has suffered at the hands of time "is to be conscious everyday of impotence." The poem on Vaiki inspired by A.K. Ramanujan's "River" pictures the deterioration of the Tamil culture. He now wonders whether he should turn to English, and asks, "How long can foreign poets provide the staple of your lines?" So he resolves to turn to Tamil.

Scrape the bottom of your past.
Ransack the cupboard
For skeletons of your Brahmin childhood

[...] you may then,
perhaps, strike out a line for yourself
from the iron of life's ordinariness. (50)

But it won't take him very long to realise that Tamil which is "wrenched from its sleep" in *Kural* is not very useful to him. So he wonders:

I fear I have bungled again.
That last refinement of speech
terrifies me. The balloon

of poetry has grown red in the face
with repeated blowing. For scriptures
I therefore recommend

The humble newspaper: I find
My prayers occasionally answered there. (63)

He realises the futility of using ancient Tamil for poetic purposes. So, he accepts Tamil of newspapers for his creative needs. Parthasarathy feels that that the problem of Tamil poet today is "to invent afresh an idiom free from the stylistic and prosodic conventions of a language with a two-thousand-year-old history" (Parthasarathy 1982:72).

So, he reconciles to the present state of affairs and is content to live with what little he could achieve. His ambition to turn to his Tamil past does not succeed fully. Initially he tries to retrieve its glorious past but soon realizes its futility and learns that wisdom lies in adapting himself to the present.

Hereafter, I should be content
I think, to go through life
with the small change of uncertainties. (63)

The result of these efforts is Sundari poem which though written in English has Tamil flavour. Parthasarathy says "[...] I have tried to reach out to a sense of the profoundly Indian—of course, not consciously—often with its complex of family relationships not easily accessible in English, as in 'And so it eventually happened' (Parthasarathy 1982 : 72).

Still the cultural problem remains unresolved. He cannot disown his British past nor can embrace the Tamil inheritance in its present state. In the second section "Trial" he aptly articulates this ambivalence.

A year ago I held these rails, your arms,
and climbed the stairs (all marble to my palms)
of your flesh and bone

towards some dark sphere.
It wasn't the first time I'd been a tenant
there. Other stairs and rails

have guided me, always
with the chill promise of a home. *Only*
the heart isn't hospitable anywhere. (44)
(emphasis added)

Thus, the choice is never made though Parthasarathy has written a few poems in Tamil. It is a problem which defies an easy solution. In fact a resolution of this issue leads him to the poetic dead-end. Commenting on this predicament he observes, "Since there is a choice between one or the other language, the need for a decision becomes inevitable. The decision itself may be postponed or, even if taken, never implemented. But the need is there all the same. The situation, I dare say, is an unenviable one. For me the situation itself is the poetry" (Parthasarathy 1982: 73).

N'gugi's suggestion that one should return to one's own language is not easy and feasible. There is a certain inevitability about this inheritance even in the post-colonial situation. Perhaps, Achebe rightly observes thus:

> "Is it right that a man should abandon his mother-tongue for someone else's? It looks a dreadful betrayal and produces a guilty feeling. But for me there is no other choice. I have been given the language and I intend to use it." (Chinua Achebe 1975: 62)

Parthasarathy too comes out with a similar solution. He observes "One of the basic problems for the poet is to find an adequate, and above all a personal language. In spite of one or two commendable efforts, it has not been possible to extend the resources of the English language or even Indianise it, although it is used with distinction for literacy purposes" (Parthasarathy 1982: 81).

Meena Alexander a fellow Indian poet comes much closer to the truth. In her essay "Exiled by a Dead Script!" she observes:

> In order to make poetry in India with English and yet resolutely refuse exile, the language itself must transform. It must contort itself to become mimetic of *muteness their muteness* which is appropriated as the poet's own and so subvert the invisible ideology of the Indian English.

For this language will always remain a colonizing power till those whom it oppresses steal it for themselves, rupture its syntax till it is capable of naming the very structures of oppression" (25).

Will that day ever come as long as we remain imitative of the English?

NOTES AND REFERENCES

1. N'gugi Wa Thingo, *Decolonising the Mind: The Politics of Language in African Literature.* (1986; London: James Curry, 1992).
2. R. Parthasarathy, "Whoring After the English Gods" in Guyamirthanayagam, ed. *Writers in East-West Encounter,* Hong Kong: Macmillan, 1982.
3. R. Parthasarathy, *Rough Passage.* Delhi: O.U.P., 1977.
4. Chinua Achebe, *Morning Yet on Creation Day.* London: Heinemann, 1975.
5. Meena Alexander, "Exiled by a Dead Script" in Chiranten Kulshreshta, ed. *Contemporary Indian English Verse.* New Delhi: Arnold Heinemann, 1980.

8

Bhabani Bhattacharya's *A Dream in Hawaii*: A Study in Postcolonial Spirituality

D. RAMAKRISHNA

Postcolonial writing attempts relocation of the self and retrieval of the native culture from foreign dominance. Whether it is a travelogue of a Western writer of Indian origin or Indian writer aiming to reach out to the Western readership, there is an interaction between the Eastern and Western sensibilities. The degree of cultural amalgamation or conflict depends upon the maturity of the sensibility of the writer. Gayatri Chakravorty Spivak refers to "the specific intellectual" and "the universal intellectual."[1] The question is whether the intellectual—writer of a travelogue, novelist, or philosopher—can rise above the limited sphere of his own specific culture and attain the universal level.

The postcolonial Indian English writers of fiction have been engaged in this intellectual exploration depicting both the specific Indian culture and the hybridization of Indian culture on account of the Western impact. These cultural crosscurrents have been vibrant in the post Independence times, the writers giving literary expression to cultural displacement and discontinuity. As Jahan Ramazani says, "Postcolonialism, is concerned with what has been called 'the location of Culture.'"[2] The "location" may not sometimes be specifically geographical on account of universal values. Cultural reversal and displacement may result in what Spivak calls "the binary opposition, the Western intellectual's longing for all that is not West—the so-called non-West's turn toward the West."[3] It Will be interesting to see this displacement or transfer of literary sensibility in the writings of Indian writers of fiction in English with special reference to Bhabani Bhattacharya's *A Dream in Hawaii* (1978).

I

Ever since Indians began writing in English, the East-West encounter has been a major theme engaging their attention. After India's independence from British rule, the influence of the British and Western institutions and habits continues to be prevalent.

The postcolonial experience dealing with the political social issues has been rendered exquisitely by major novelists like Mulk Raj Anand, R.K. Narayan, Anita Desai, Kamala Markandaya, Nayantara Sahgal, and Bhabani Bhattacharya. Kamala Markandaya looks at the Swami cult affecting the modern Indian society in *A Silence of Desire* (1961) and *Possession* (1963) from a perspective more mundane than Raja Rao's in *The Serpent and the Rope* (1960), R.K. Narayan's *The Guide* (1959) depicts Raju, after his love affair with Rosie and the prison term, initially masquerading as a Swami and finally achieving self-realization.

Bhabani Bhattacharya in *He Who Rides a Tiger* (1955) describes the social and religious hypocrisy resulting from the Bengal famine in the post-Independence India. Due to hunger and ill-treatment, Kalo avenges on society by transforming himself into Mangal Adhikari, the brahmin, and performs a "miracle": a Shiva linga emerging from the ground. By means of this feat, he plays upon the popular credulity to miracles and reaps dividends. His daughter, Lekha, also a victim of society, becomes the Mother of the Sevenfold Bliss and the object of adoration. Bhattacharya attacks the superstitions and rituals corrupting the Hindu society. Kalo says: "While men died of hunger, wealth grew and kindliness dried up religion was more in demand."[4] It is only the veneer of religion since the same people would not bother to 1ook at destitutes dying. The novelist exposes falsehood in religion through the words of Biten: "Food for the soul is produced and sold like food for stomach, and though the ways of the two trades are different, you pay for both with hard cash. The temple is a market and the priest a dealer. People are always ready to pay well for feeding the inner man" (43). The novelist describes people, belief in the Yogis and Mothers. Lekha takes recourse to rituals for solace to overcome the grief caused by Biten. Referring to Lekha's touching the forehead of a sick child with her toe and the death of the child, Orvelle Prescott says: "Mr. Bhattacharya deplores the suffering caused by blind acceptance of the caste system, and yet pities the blind believer."[5] Whether it is the caste system or hunger or superstition, Bhattacharya exposes the binary attitude concerning religion in the postcolonial India.

In Raja Rao's *The Serpent and the Rope* (1960), the real problem for the central character Rama, consequent upon 'his sensual involvement with Madeleine and Savitri, is to attain inner harmony. Man, entangled in the web of *maya*, takes as serpent what is after all a rope. As Rama tells Madeleine, "The Guru brings you the lantern; the road is seen, the long, white road, going with the statutory stars."[6] The search for the Guru and inner harmony, rendered by Raja Rao in highly complex Vedantic and aesthetic terms, can also be seen in the real life experience of the Westerners and the Westernized Indians in the postcolonial times.

Contemporary man, caught in the whirlpool of the dehumanizing life, looks desperately for succour, seeking peace either in drugs or in the proliferating cults. Taking advantage of this situation, self-seeking Mammon-worshippers, Gurus, Maharshis, and Yogis have, launched spiritual movements and established posh "ashrams" to preach instant meditation. As a result of these perversions and ungodly activities, the very meaning of meditation-*dhyana*—as enunciated in the great Hindu scriptures like the Vedas and Bhagavad Gita—is lost on the contemporary man. The concept of Guru, enunciated in the Holy Books, has, taken on such perverted meanings in the popular understanding that Peter Brent says:

> For Indians, particularly those of the middle classes, there are only two directions they can go to prove that they can love, and beloved. One is towards homosexuality, the other towards the Guru—the two not being mutually exclusive.[7]

Referring to the "Swami" in Indian English fiction, K.R. Srinivasa Iyengar says: "Sometimes the Swamy or Sadhu has no more than a decorative role; he is there because Western readers 1ook for him in novels on India."[8] However, whether it is treated seriously by Raja Rao or in sarcastic terms by Bhabani Bhattacharya, the Swamy motif Indian English fiction—between materialism and spirituality.

II

In Bhabani Bhattacharya's *A Dream in Hawaii* (1978), as in Raja Rao's *The Serpent and the Rope* (1960), the quest is that of an academic for spirituality despite his sensual involvements. The binary opposition of the sensual and the spiritual determines character and action. Instead of leaving the reader lost in the web of Advaita philosophy, Bhattacharya brings him closer to the contemporary predicament. Swami Yogananda, following his erotic adventures with his student Devjani at an Indian university, gives up his professorship and dons saffron robes. At the invitation of the East-West Center, he goes to Hawaii to give a course of lectures on Eastern Philosophy—"to present Universal Religion in its Vedantic concept."[9] He is engaged in a relentless quest for "reality behind the appearances which were *maya,* the stuff of illusion." Several disturbed souls like Jennifer, the socialite and Stella the Ph.D. student in Hinduism, caught in "The crisis in a sick society," look up to him for spiritual help. There are others like Professor Walt Gregson, the estranged husband of Stella and Dr. Vincent Swift, the culture-vulture, who question Yogananda's true credentials to spirituality. Yogananda has taught Philosophy for six years in the Indian universities before becoming "Swamy," and at thirty he is "one of India's famed spiritual leaders" (29). He would like to be different from others of his kind and hence he is clean-shaven unlike the bearded sadhus.

In spite of his discourses on *Bhagavad Gita* to a captivated American audience and his attempts at *dhyana*, Yogananda is haunted by disturbing memories of his affair with Devjani at the Indian university and even in Hawaii he looks for her. He utterly fails to achieve the kind of detachment that is prescribed in Chapter VI ("The Yoga of Meditation") of *Bhagavad Gita* as being the essential requisite for prayer. The Lord says:

> So, with his heart serene and fearless,
> Firm in the vow of renunciation,
> Holding the mind from its restless roaming,
> Now let him struggle to reach my openness.[10]

Swami Yogananda, despite his saffron robes, has failed to hold his mind, "from its restless roaming." In the words of the author of the novel, "The process of sublimation had its own rules, he would point to himself. His submerged mind could not be controlled, nature's compulsions could not be denied" (44). Even as Swami Yogananda lays asleep, "he was in the act of making love. That act possessed him" (44).

Ironically, Yogananda's attempts at spiritual experience take place in the enchanting atmosphere of the beautiful island of Hawaii, a pleasure resort of the most materialistic kind. The sight of "the body's bareness" on the Waikiki beach makes him feel "enchanted." The result is spiritual disenchantment for him. The "reality" that he is searching for proves an illusion. The Guru that the disturbed Americans see in him is himself torn by doubt about his own spiritual integrity and he returns to India. While the effect of Swami Yogananda's experience on the reader is one of the comic, what is ultimately significant in Bhattacharya's presentation in *A Dream in Hawaii* is the Kiplingesque awareness that East is East and West is West.

Bhabani Bhattacharya brings out the binary opposition not only in the East-West encounter but also within the East and within the West separately. This multi-dimensional conflict determines the social and spiritual aspects of the postcolonial life. Transference, displacement, and alienation constitute the postcolonial experiences of not only the Indians settled or born abroad, but also of the Indians in India due to the Western impact. The basic conflict in human nature is presented by Bhattacharya in *A Dream in Hawaii* involving movement between realms. The "Movement" may be different from that of the Indians abroad, born or settled there. It is that of the natives like Yogananda experiencing alienation within their own culture due to the cross-currents of emotional and spiritual problems.

In *A Dream in Hawaii*, the shifting of scenes from India to America and in flashback from America to India is like displacement in the postcolonial sense. In India, when Yogananda comes from Rishikesh and lectures in Delhi, the unsophisticated crowd might have applauded him without understanding the profundities involved. But the applause from the American audience is of lost souls in search of a spiritual mirage.

When Swami Yogananda says, "Our Ancient Philosophy is boldly modern in its own way. The West has read that same story in our ancient temple sculptures at Konark, at Khajuraho!" (18). Stella feels, "Within him the East and the West so readily coalesced!" (18). Ironically, this coalescence goes counter to Yogananda's preaching of *dhyana* which leaves him confused. It is not the external East-West conflict but the inner turmoil of his own soul that disturbs Yogananda. This is the basic binary opposition.

Another level of binary opposition is in Stella with her vain spiritual yearnings as Yogananda's disciple and her conflict with her materialistic husband, Walt. While Stella is looking for solace in philosophy, Walt is seeking "correlations of life and literature, part of his study" (21). Walt tells Stella that he would like to "ask the Swami one or two questions in the context of what he calls crisis in a sick society: that is, our American society' (24). As Walt asserts, "The crises we know are beyond his limited range of experience" (27). The disturbances deep within the soul of Yogananda are evident. Stella recalls that as soon as Swami Yogananda is received at the airport, by members of the Indian Association, he inquired about Devjani. In the flashback is given an account of Yogananda's lecture on Eastern Philosophy at the Indian University where Devjani was a student:

> The instructor has an unseemly impulse: To undo the braided hair and let the disheveled mass cascade over her bosom! [...]. An odd wish for; a man trying to explain Vedanti monism! (13)

At the Kennedy Theatre of the University of Hawaii, following the applause at Swami Yogananda's lecture, Stella reflects: "The Swami's relentless quest was directed to the core of reality behind the appearances which were *maya,* the stuff of illusion" (8). The suggestion is which is reality and which is the illusion in Swami Yogananda himself.

Dr. Vincent Swift is introduced to Swami Yogananda by Stella as "our topmost exponent of cultureways" (52). Hawaii is the "unique East-West mix. The strong interculturation" (56). When confronted by Dr. Swift to comment on the celibacy of the Indian yogis, Swami Yogananda is bewildered. As Swift says to Yogananda, "One expects from an alien analyst of our sick ways something more than hackneyed repetitions" (60). Dr. Swift ridicules Yogananda's visit to America to re-enact the visit of Swami Vivekananda:

> Now could it be that Swami Yogananda's mystical experience which made him reborn is relevant to a certain memorable day in the Vivekananda story? A day that is exactly a hundred years old? (62)

Yogananda has come to America to represent Universal Religion in its Vedantic concept. Dr. Swift would like to set up an institute offering practical help to reduce inner tensions—such help drawn best from Indian know-how and wisdom. Dr. Swift would expect Yogananda himself shed a little of the ancient India in him and absorb a little of Modern America. He feels that is the only way to harmonize diverse cultures. "World culture could have no reality unless based on the broadest spectrum of interchange" (144). Such mutually opposed views concerning cultural interaction causes insurmountable obstacles. The binary opposition makes the lofty ideal of "world culture" only a dream. This seems to be the ultimate message of Bhabani Bhattacharya in the novel.

Referring to the ecstasy of the dancers of the Hare Krishna Movement, Stella wonders:

> Our American society with its contradictions! Violence in its most brutal forms rages through the nation and tries to destroy every civilized norm. Yet a great search goes on widening, the search for [...] shall I say, a new world aching to be born? Two contrary ways running parallel. Where will victory be?" (72)

In addition to the other binaries of characters and ideas in the novel, the basic contradiction within the American culture itself is paradoxical: the dualism of violence alongside an impassioned search, "a search rooted in depths of longing for the new world yet to be born" (73), as Stella says. The dualism is also the result of a paradoxical presence of Puritanism and permissiveness in the American society. Another paradox is in the supertechnology hitting at the very roots of traditionalism, resulting in counterculture.

Whatever the vain attempts of an Indian Swami like Yogananda himself torn between contradictions, to cure the "sick society," the binaries within himself and within the postcolonial Indian culture are pitted against the binaries of the American culture in particular and the Western culture in general. Consequently, the opposition remains.

NOTES

1. Gayatri Chakravorty Spivak, *The Post-Colonial Critic: Interviews, Strategies, Dialogues* (New York: Routledge, 1990) 3.
2. Jahan Ramazani, "Metaphor and Postcoloniality: the Poetry of A.K. Ramanujan," *Contemporary Literature* 39.1 (Spring 1998) 28.
3. Spivak 8.
4. Bhabani Bhattacharya, *He Who Rides a Tiger* (New Delhi: Hind Pocket Books, 1955) 113. Page references are given in parentheses after each quotation from the text.
5. Orvelle Prescott, "Books of the Times," *The New York Times* 28 Dec., 1954.

6. Raja Rao, *The Serpent and the Rope* (1960; New Delhi: Oxford UP, 1978) 192.
7. Peter Brent, *Godmen of India* (Harmondsworth: Penguin, 1968) 16.
8. K.R. Srinivasa Iyengar, *Indian Writing in English* (New Delhi: Sterling Publishers,1984) 328.
9. Bhabani Bhattacharya, *A Dream in Hawaii* (New Delhi: Macmillan, 1978) 144. Page references are given in parantheses after each quotation from the text.
10. *The Song of God: Bhagavad Gita*. Trans. Swami Prabhavananda & Christopher Isherwood (New York: The New America Library Inc., 1951) 65.

9

Past and Present in Anita Desai's *Clear Light of Day*

SYED MUJEEBUDDIN

ALL THAT I AM I WILL NOT DENY.
—JOAN OF ARC[1]

The challenge to Raja Rao and Narayan's construction of an "authentic" India, not surprisingly, comes from among the Indian women writers. For, if as Gayatri Chakravorty Spivak points out, "Knowledge is made possible and is sustained by irreducible difference, not identity"[2] then the "different" space that Indian women writers occupy is the site of production of an-other knowledge, specifically, a space that eschews the predication of an Indian identity on Brahminical knowledge and Vedic wisdom and one which bases its portrayals of India foregrounded in its particular difference.

Though mostly from the upper middle-class and relatively free from the kind of encumbrances that dog the women from the poorer strata of Indian society, Indian women writers have nevertheless tried to delineate the double marginalisation[3] that "patriarchal subject-formation and imperialist object-constitution"[4] en-joins upon Indian women. The postcolonial woman writer as Susheila Nasta points out is "not only involved in making herself heard, in changing the architecture of male centred ideologies and languages, or in discovering new forms and language to express her experience, she has also to subvert and demythologise indigenous male writings and traditions which seek to label her."[5]

The strategies that "subvert" and "de-mythologise" are also the means that produce a hybrid discourse and constitute an earnest examination of the idea of the nation. It is a reclamation that moves beyond a simplistic strategy of positing binary oppositions and fosters a space that expresses a "multiplicity of perspectives and literary poetics"[6] and politics.

Significantly, the proclivities of Indian English writing are not satisfactory, as a tradition for the Indian woman writer. Shashi Deshpande hinting at the inadequacy of this "heritage" says, "what all the English writing by Indian writers meant to me was this—I could only tell myself. I don't want to write like this, not like this, nor like this."[7] From Amrita Pritam to Kamala Das women writers in India have rejected the unilateral and homogenous model of "authentic" and "essential" India as inadequate because on the one hand it contains feminine aspiration and on the other fails to give voice to their predicament. They have instead preferred to affirm a solidarity and affiliation with subordinated "others" that cuts across cultures and problematises their association with other minority groups.

Writers like Nayantara Sahgal and Anita Desai venture in their own ways to contextualise the terms of the necessarily hybrid nature of Indian society. Desai's even-tempered and delicately embellished narrative is in many ways the antithesis of Sahgal's committed and volatile tales of political corruption in high places. Yet Sahgal's narrative shares common features with Desai's. Both have emphatically made the point that being Indians they are as hybrid as Indian culture itself. Both view their hybrid upbringing as "enriching"[8] and a "blessing"[9] rather than a weakness. Both eschew essentialist notions of Indian identity and use fictional strategies that are subversive of established narrative traditions in Indian English writing. The compulsive need in these writers to "understand and thereby determine their position as women and as writers in modern

Indian society"[10] is informed by a sense of India as a syncretic and heterogenous entity—not just a naive, empty, assertion of the plurality of India but rather a dynamic problematisation of its heterogeneity through both theme and technique in their fiction.

Anita Desai, writing of the dilemma that Indian women writers today face, tellingly brings home the point that repression need not be political or state enforced, as in the case of a lot of writers who have faced incarceration due to outspoken criticism of repressive regimes. She points out that in a country like India, relatively free from political repression, women writers have had to countenance other kinds of suppression: "So many limitations. So much censorship and self-censorship. Does this not amount to suppression, the suppression of a whole gender?[11] She refers to "the prison house of religion"[12] in Indian society that effectively paralyses and silences the Indian writer. As she points out, "on the two most absorbing themes that we have on earth—the relationship of man and God—there is either silence or if there are words, they are too often false and hypocritical."[13]

She believes that:

> If literature, if art has any purpose then it is to show one, bravely and uncompromisingly, the plain face of truth [...]. Once you have told the truth, you have broken free of society's prisons. You have entered the realm of freedom.[14]

Desai's fiction itself does not have an overtly feminist agenda; but while it does not incorporate a conspicuous attempt at breaking through "society's prison," it certainly does engage with the severe handicaps that Indian society imposes upon its members, specially women. Her *Clear Light of Day* and *In Custody* are novels that are diffuse with this sense of entrapment; characters in both novels attempt to escape "traps, often traps of their own making"[15] but slowly learn that they can still find freedom inside these same traps. Desai shows them as possessing a profound inner strength which allows them to find freedom through a realisation of their individual truth. This new awareness in her protagonists, contextualised in hybrid, eclectic terms that positively inscribe the "plurality and excess"[16] of India, is marked by a certain dissonance reflected in the incongruous spaces that are at variance with the 'texts' urge towards unity and wholeness.

Set against a broad period of time spanning pre-independence India, its traumatic partition, and the early post-independence times, *Clear Light of Day*[17] depicts the private turmoils in the history of the protagonist, Bim's house. Raja's marrying into the Muslim family, Tara's flight from the "trap" of the house and Mira-*masi's* insanity, and later, death run parallel to some of the significant episodes of the history of this period.

However, it is not so much history that is of importance in the novel as the individual's response to her situation in life and the sense that she makes of her environment. The most abiding achievement of the novel is the protagonist Bimla Das, Bim for short; the complexity of her character lies in the fact that she represents, rather contradictorily, both the figure of the mother and the independent woman, who is yet marked by a feeling of frustration at the role of her own choice as guardian of the house. She realises, towards the end of the novel, that what she thinks of as a trap of her own making is not really so, for she realises that this trap was "where her deepest self lived" (182).

Bim forms a sharp contrast to Tara. For Tara to come back to her old home "at intervals of three or five years," (12) is an attempt to retrieve her sense of belonging, which is yet coloured by a sense of guilt. She is haunted by the feeling that she had abandoned her family, when years ago she preferred marriage with the insensitive and bureaucratic Bakul, to the lacklustre snare that "home" for her had become. The characterisation of Tara's personality, at once bashful and sincere, but artless and ingenuous, yet prudent and perceptive is one that would fit the conventional Indian woman. Bim on the other hand has a capacity for cool, impassioned reasoning which comes to the fore in her attempts at self-scrutiny at various moments in the novel.

Their old house described as "a faded old picture in its petrified frame" (5) where "everything goes on and on [...] and never changes" (4) is the pivot on which the story revolves. Set in Old Delhi, the house seems to acquire the torpid quality of the dilapidated city. As Bim says, "Old Delhi does not change. It only decays [...] it is a great cemetery, every house a tomb. Nothing but sleeping graves [...]. Whatever happened, happened long ago [...]" (5).

But an attempt at retrieval of her own past becomes inevitable for Bim when Tara's visit triggers off memories of the turbulent "summer of '47 (43). Bim finds herself flooded by memories of that turbulent period of her youth; her parent's death, Raja's fever, Tara's marriage and Mira-*masi's* death, all come back to Bim with telling clarity. When she remarks "Youth? [...]. I am glad it is over I never wish it back" (43) she unconsciously expresses the trauma that the summer of '47 had brought in for the young Bim, Raja and Tara. As she continues, "Terrible, what it does to one—what it did to us—and one is too young to know how to cope, how to deal with that first terrible flood of life. One just goes under—it sweeps one along—and how many years and years it is before one can stand up, to it, make a stand against it [...]. I never wish it back. I would never be young again for anything" (43).

Desai's sensitive narrative delineates an ironic, discrepant sense of escape; Tara's escape-route is the traditional form, marriage and motherhood, while Bim, spinsterish and childless, is happy staying back home and taking custody of it, but yet "free" in her own way. Desai, here, subtly insinuates that in her flight, Tara is actually moving into another trap. Attempting to escape her domineering brother and sister she enters a relationship in which again she is the dominated. Bakul is depicted as the typical, traditional, Indian husband and Tara the meek wife who admits her weakness and is always being guided by her husband. She finds it a great strain to be always dependent on Bakul:

> She felt she had followed him enough, it had been such an enormous strain, always pushing against her grain. It had drained her of too much strength, now she could only collapse, inevitably collapse (18).

The seemingly insignificant aside, "The dog suddenly pounced upon the flea" (81) with which the scene of the proposal of Tara's marriage draws to a close, actually shores up for the reader the sense that Tara for all her aspirations of freedom is yet being ensnared. Ironically, it is also the scene when Bim is first made conscious of her grey hair. This also signifies the start of her role as the one responsible for the family.

The above scene is followed almost immediately by the episode depicting Bim's disastrous visit to Dr. Biswas's house, incidentally at the historical moment of Mahatma Gandhi's assassination. This visit is marked by her discomfiture and revulsion at both Dr. Biswas's embarrassment at his mother's befuddled monologue on her son's talents and his own weakness in front of his mother. But what really seems to mark the end of her interest in any male relationships is the appalling misunderstanding that Biswas develop of her:

> Now I understand why you do not wish to marry. You have dedicated your life to others—to your sick brother and your aged aunt and your little brother who will be dependent on you all his life. You have sacrificed your own life for them.
>
> Bim's mouth fell open with astonishment at this horrendous speech so solemnly, so leadenly spoken as if engraved for posterity [...]. She [...] hissed slightly in her rage and frustration—at being so mis-understood, so totally misread, then gulped a little with laughter at such grotesque misunderstanding, and her tangled emotions twisted her face and shook her, shook the thought of Biswas out of her. Later she never acknowledged even to herself, that this ridiculous scene had ever taken place (97).

Dr. Biswas's "type-casting" of Bim's concern for her family is itself typical of a masculinist discourse that assigns women the dubiously admirable, sacrificial, noble and virtuous roles. Biswas, in spite of his German education, his love of music, his Brahms and Bach, cannot understand why Bim is so impatient of him and his weak advances. He is blind to Bim's strength of character, her resilient, magnanimous, spirit as is Bakul who thinks that Tara is preferable to Bim, being, "gentler, and more tender" (19).

However, Biswas's pronouncement ("leadenly" spoken "as if engraved for posterity" as the author tells us) does come true. Bim is left holding the house, and a sense of resentment, while Tara and Raja make emphatic escapes. Raja hurts Bim the most by writing her the offensive letter. Yet Bim is not the helpless, neurotic figure that Mira-*masi* is depicted as being, though she does come to perceive of herself as some kind of surrogate mother.

> All these years she had felt herself to be the centre—she had watched them all circling in the air, then returning, landing like birds, folding up their wings and letting down their legs till they touched solid ground. That was what the house had been [...] Bim's domain. They needed her as much as they needed the sound of the pigeons in the verandah and the ritual of the family gathering on the lawn in the evening (153).

Parallels between Bim and the tragic figure of Mira-*masi* are drawn by the novelist and Bim herself several times in the narrative. Bim, for instance, pointing out the significance of the river Jamuna, says: "It's where my ashes will be thrown after I am dead and burnt. It is where Mira-*masi's* ashes were thrown. Then they go down into the sea" (24).

Married and widowed at a young age Mira-*masi* is the poor, relative who can only be a servant in the Das household. Yet the children, alienated from their own mother and father, take to her so much that she becomes their surrogate mother. "Quick, nervy and jumpy—yet to the children she was as constant as a staff, a tree that can be counted on not to pull up its roots and shift in the night. She was the tree that grew in the centre of their lives and in whose shade they lived" (110).

Bim and Mira-*masi* are both portrayed as centres, one following the other, that held the family together. Mira-*masi's* initial hesitancy is replaced by real affection for the children; she comes to feel that "They owned her and yes, she wanted to be owned [...]. She fed them with her own nutrients, she reared them in her own shade, she was the support on which they learned as they grew. She was the tree, she was the soil, she was the earth" (111).

Abandoned by her siblings and faced with Mira-*masi's* death Bim herself comes close to the mental condition that had precipitated Mira-*masi's* death. Yet it is Bim's intellectual resourcefulness, and above all her indomitable spirit that allows her to come to terms and transcend the distress caused by the desertion of her brother and sister. The novel closes on an unmistakably eclectic, hybrid note, T.S. Eliot rubbing shoulders with Mohammed Iqbal. Listening to the old man, Mulk's guru, sing Bim is struck by the thought that though Mulk and his guru are of different ages there was a similarity between them. Bim recalls Eliot's famous lines:

> *Time the destroyer is time the preserver* (182).

This prompts her to think about her "own house and its particular history":

> With her inner eye she saw how her own house and its particular history linked and contained her as well as her whole family with all their separate histories and experiences—not binding them within some dead and airless cell but giving them the soil, in which to send down their roots, and food to make them grow and spread, reach out to new experiences and new lives, but always drawing from the same soil, the same secret darkness. That soil contained all time, past and future, in it. It was dark with time, rich with time. It was where her deepest self lived, and the deepest selves of her sister and brothers and all those who shared that time with her (182).

The novel ends with the guru singing lqbal's words:

> Your world is the world of fish and fowl.
> My world is the cry at dawn...
> In your world I am subjected and constrained, but over my world
> You have dominion. (182-83)

Yet beneath the smooth wholeness of the apparently resolved frictions—as if "plait(ed) [...] into a composed and concentrated whole" (167)—is a certain unease caused by Mira-*masi's* terrible tragedy. The trope of the house metonymically linked with the "soil," ("dark with time, rich with time") the reference to "roots" and the "secret darkness" from which the "deepest self" emerges, the invocation of Eliot's unified sense of time, all these contribute to a creeping sense of the text's complicity with the self-same systems that produced the much-abused image of the nation as "motherland." Given the metonymic nature of the tropes of "earth" and "soil" and given the fact that both Bim and Mira-*masi* are figured as mothers, the novel can be read, at a more mundane level as making a fictional record of a historical transformation of the figuration of the mother as "nation." The figures of Mira-*masi* and Bim are juxtaposed, the one archaic and obsolete "nation" (the deified yet violently abused woman) now giving way to the modern and progressive nation (the "new" woman-self-willed, independent, modern and progressive).

Yet one is forced to reflect on the question that Shirley Chew poses in her perceptive evaluation of the novel: "Where in the totalising systems of Indian and European cultures does she (Mira-*Masi*) fit."[18] The reference to Eliot's poems are as much representative of a continuing neo-colonial hegemony as are Iqbal's poems indicative of an indigenous orthodoxy. Juxtaposed together they highlight Mira-*masi's* inability at articulating her plight for she neither possesses a voice nor the resources that would enable her to gather her fragmented life into a composite whole, as Bim, for example, can do.[19] The novel while outlining its unity, its harmony, and wholeness actually leaves this space of lack—a space of undecidability wherein the revenant figure of Mira-*masi*, "an object constructed and used by others" stands as a silent, tragic, witness to Bim's attempts at drawing her life together.

Between the sites of modernity and orthodoxy is the *colonial* site that Anita Desai locates her text in. This hybrid postcolonial site may well be the new face of Indian English writing; one that can confidently count either English or Urdu literature and culture or both (or any literature and culture) as part of its tradition. "Eclecticism is a natural condition of modern India, says Meenakshi Mukherjee[20] and indeed in Desai's novel, Byron Lawrence and Eliot nestle snugly beside Aurangzeb and Iqbal while the *Thodol Bardol* is compared with *The Waste Land.*

Poised thus at this postcolonial site—the liminal space between the imperialist's epistemic violence and the brutality of an indigenous past—the episode depicting Mira-*masi's* predicament emblematises an indictment of both systems. Thus Eliot's lines, from *The Waste Land.*

Who is the third who walks always beside you?
When I count, there are only you and I together
But when I look ahead up the white road
There is always another one walking beside you
Gliding wrapt in a brown mantle, hooded
I do not know whether a man or a woman—
But who is that on the other side of you? (41)

bear an ironic timbre as they ring though the novel reminding both Bim and the reader of Mira-*masi's* unlaid ghost and the discrepant space that it occupies in the text.

"The desire for unity and order compels the author and the reader to balance the equation that is the texts system" notes Gayatri Chakravorty Spivak. Elucidating the technique of deconstruction she continues, "The deconstructive reader exposes the grammatological structure of the text, that is its 'origin' and its 'end' are given over to language in general [...] by locating the moment in the text which harbours the unbalancing of the equation, the, sleight of hand at the limit of a text which cannot be dismissed simply as a contradiction."[21] However, in the case of *Clear Light of Day,* it is the text itself that locates the "unbalancing moment" and thereby effectively deconstructs its own aspiration towards being a unified whole: this makes it useful to remember J. Hillis Miller's remark that great works of literature, themselves "have anticipated explicitly any deconstruction the critic can achieve."[22]

NOTES

1. Quoted in Betty Friedan, *The Second Stage* (London: Abacus, 1983) 86.
2. Gayatri Chakravorty Spivak, "A Literary Representation of the Subaltern: Mahasveta Devi's *Stanadayini,*" *Subaltern Studies: Writings on South Asian History and Society V* (Delhi: Oxford UP, 1987) 112.
3. Judie Newman, "The Untold Story and the Retold Story: Intertextuality in Postcolonial Women's Fiction," Susheila Nasta, ed. *Motherlands: Black Women's Writing from Africa, the Caribbean and South Asia* (London: Women's Press, 1991) 24.
4. Gayatri Chakravorty Spivak, "The Rani of Sirmur: An Essay in Reading the Archives," *History and Theory* 24.3 (1985) 268.

   Also see Shirley Chew, "Searching Voices: Anita Desai's *Clear Light of Day* and Nayantara Sahgal's *Rich Like Us,* in Susheila Nasta, ed. *Motherlands* 45.
5. Susheila Nasta, "Introduction," *Motherlands* xv.
6. Nasta xvi. Also see, Kathleen McLuskie and Lyn Innes, "Women and African Literature," *Wasafiri* 8: 4.
7. Shashi Deshpande, "The Dilemma of the Woman Writer," *The Literary Criterion* 20.4 (1985) 31.
8. Anita Desai in discussion with Olga Kenyon, *The Writer's Imagination* (U of Bradford Print Unit, 1992) 37.
9. Nayantara Sahgal, "Some Thoughts on the Puzzle of Identity," *The Journal of Commonwealth Literature* 29.1 (1993) 14.
10. Shirley Chew, "Searching Voices," 46.
11. Anita Desai, "A Secret Connivance," *Times Literary Supplement* 4563 (Sep. 14-20, 1990): 976.
12. Desai 976.
13. Desai 976.
14. Desai 976.
15. Desai, *The Writer's Imagination* 41.
16. Desai, "*A Secret Connivance*" 972.
17. Anita Desai, *Clear Light of Day,* (London: Penguin, 1980). All references are to this edition and are cited parenthetically.
18. Chew, "Searching Voices" 52.
19. Chew 52.
20. Meenakshi Mukherjee, "Towards Liberation: Four Recent Novels from India," *Westerly* 28.4 (1983) 68.

21. Spivak "Translator's Preface," *Of Grammatology* (Baltimore: The John Hopkins UP, 1976) xix.
22. J. Hillis Miller, "Deconstructing the Deconstructors," *Diacritics* 5 (1975) 31.

10

The Reverse Patterns of Journey in Anita Desai's *Cry, the Peacock* and *Where Shall We Go This Summer?*

SANJAY KUMAR

Widely acclaimed as a gifted writer and the winner of the Sahitya Akademi Award, Anita Desai continues to spearhead the second generation of Indian English fiction writers that links the established greats like R.K. Narayan, Mulk Raj Anand and Raja Rao and the emerging greats like Salman Rushdie, Vikram Seth and Arundhati Roy. Endowed with a searching psychological insight and capable of writing an intense poetic prose, Anita Desai seems to have sensed the absurdity of human existence and wants it to be communicated to her readers.

Consequently, her novels depict a world of alienation, loneliness and suffering. In Anita Desai's novels it is common to confront characters who suffer from a metaphysical anguish, a matrimonial boredom or a tragic sense of loss. Besides, there are the symbolic journeys which her characters take and which highlight the futility of all human endeavours establishing thus the ultimate absurdity of human life. The present paper also studies such patterns of journey in Anita Desai's *Cry, the Peacock* and *Where Shall We Go This Summer?*, but with a shifted vision. It attempts to establish the subtle reversal of these patterns of journey despite an apparently similar tapestry of these two novels.

Now it is established beyond doubt that much like many other works of Anita Desai, both *Cry, the Peacock* and *Where Shall We Go This Summer?* portray the troubled life of her female protagonists—Maya and Sita respectively. Both Maya and Sita seem to suffer since they have been married to the males who fail to understand the agony of their fractured identities.

In Maya of *Cry, the Peacock* Anita Desai probes the heart of a woman who suffers from a mysterious premonition about the tragic end of her marriage. She is made to believe that either she or her husband would die in the fourth year of their marriage. The ominous prediction also suggests the death to be produced "by unnatural causes."[1] When the novel opens Maya's marriage with Gautama is running in its fourth year and the emotional woman, Maya, is just beginning to reel under the pressure of the prophecy that threatens to shatter her married life.

Maya's fear is aggravated as she fails to relate to Gautama, her husband. Between the husband and the wife there exists a terrible communication gap as both of them seem to live in different worlds. Maya is an instinctive woman of passions and emotions. Gautama, on the other hand, is a philosophical intellectual. Driven by an instinctive nature "Maya expects some emotional and physical satisfaction in married life but both of them are denied her, one by Gautama's cold intellectuality and the other by his age."[2]

Contrary to the expectations of Maya, her husband has a mechanical attitude towards life. There always is an air of detachment about whatever he does. Because of their different mental make-ups Maya and Gautama do not share anything at emotional level. Even on a physical level, they hardly enjoy any spontaneity. In fact so vastly disparate are their ways that they hardly relate to each other at any level. Even when they make love, it is a mechanical, formal ceremony performed in a loveless manner. But even the moments of their such brittle union, the occasions are few and far between. Usually it is an appalling indifference with which Gautama seems to share Maya's passionate overtures.

Engrossed in his busy schedule, Gautama continues to ignore Maya's needs remaining callously immune even to her physical desires. This is how Maya usually suffers the agony of her unfulfilled desires:

> Telling me to go to sleep while he worked at his papers, he did not give another thought to me, to either the soft, willing body or the lonely wanting mind that waited near his bed. (9)

Bitterly disappointed with Gautama, Maya has no one or nothing to turn to. Even when she consciously tries to divert herself from pain, she is not helped by Gautama at all. Once when she suggests Gautama to take her to South as she wants "to see the Kathakali dances," (42) Gautama's response is as lackadaisical and placid as ever:

> If that is your only reason for wanting to go all that way south, I suggest you wait till a Kathakali troupe comes to give a performance in Delhi [...]. (43)

This physical, mental and emotional separation torments Maya who struggles in a pursuit to relate to Gautama. They live in a loveless cage of marriage in which Maya's emotional urges usually get defeated by Gautama's rudely philosophical gibberish. Maya groans under the weight of Gautama's borrowed wisdom as he often quotes from the Gita to prove to her his intellectual superiority. When Maya demands from him his love for her, Gautama resorts to a bewilderingly frigid explanation of a matter that needs tender, emotional treatment:

> Love? Love that is without any ambition, without any desire, without any life except that which keeps it alive burning, yes, that is well. But do you not—mistake attachment for love? And there lies egoism after all. (120)

It looks painfully comic and absurd to be told how to be a 'yogi' or a 'sunnyasi' and to achieve 'detachment' when what one craves for is the conjugal love and emotional fulfilment with a natural, mutual attachment. This stolid and philosophical speech in fact underlines the predicament of not just Maya and Gautama but most of other pairs in Anita Desai's works. Most importantly it is their choice of living on separate planes that denies them a real understanding. Their diversity disjuncts them from each other and condemns them to a lifeless relationship. Maya and Gautama just continue to chase their disparate visions about life. To Maya life is a pulsating, throbbing possibility while for Gautama it is a clear, precise and concrete truth. Maya's approach thus is instinctively passionate while that of Gautama is essentially intellectual. In fact "what is real to her is shadowy to him what are facts and hard realities to him have no interest for her."[3]

To make matters worse, all that Maya ever pines for, perishes quickly. Her life appears to be an endless tale of separation and lovelessness as she begins to lose everything just after her marriage. Once having enjoyed a "princess like, a sumptuous fate of the fantasies of the Arabian Nights the glories and bravado of Indian mythology, long and astounding tales of princes and regal queens" (43), she now seems to face the quick reverses of fortunes. She misses the company of her father, his positive, affectionate attitude but is painfully shocked to see him turn immune to her after her marriage to Gautama. Defeated by human beings she tries to latch on to her pet Tota, but it too dies suddenly.

She plunges deeper into problems as she fails to do or deliver anything meaningful. Her household is run by the servants around leaving her idle and more tuned to developing her neurosis. The lack of activity thus renders her unoccupied and more conducive to mental nervousness and anxieties.

To add to her misery, she happens to be a childless woman, deprived thus of an opportunity of a healthy, spontaneous outlet of her feelings. Her life thus suffers from a terrible eventlessness. Unoccupied, unloved and alone Maya begins to hallucinate the things. The world of her aspirations falls apart around her and she begins to lose her sanity.

A sense of gloom, a threat for an imminent disaster chokes her as already insecure and alienated, she is dogged by the prophecy of an albino astrologer who predicted her husband's or her own death in the fourth year of their married life. It is noteworthy that given a healthy, spontaneous and occupied routine, Maya would have shrugged aside the fears of the prophecy. But the fact that her life seems to be "an endless tedium with nothing significant taking place at any time,"[4] leaves her extremely vulnerable plunging her deep into a life of miserable existence of bizarre fantasies and nightmares.

Exhibiting thus a cruel aloofness towards Maya's apprehension, Gautama aggravates her frustration. He refuses to come out of his cocooned shell of intellectuality and fails to see Maya's growing desperation. Placed on the rake of helpless frustration, Maya's visions become chaotic and her dreams turn nightmarish. Condemned to live a life of physical, emotional and spiritual loneliness, Maya's whole being gets converted in a "hysterical self [...] pining for companionship."[5]

With a remarkable psychological accuracy, Anita Desai demonstrates how Maya lurches to a macabre imagination as her ideal aspiration of a conjugal bliss is met with a terrible reality. In Maya, Anita Desai portrays an unfortunate woman who lives on a borrowed optimism before marriage. This happens because so far "she has led a protected life and has been brought up on fantasies."[6] But now, after her marriage with Gautama she seems to have lost her way. Instead of a compassionate soul she finds in Gautama a symbol of stony wisdom who neither consoles nor convinces her.

Maya's life thus reveals a subtle pattern of the protagonist's journey from a state of expectation to that of disappointment. Finally this disappointment of hers takes her to the final disaster. Nervously crumbling under the weight of her obsession, she grows more and more certain of the prophecy made by an albino astrologer long back. The novelist gives a befitting climax as Maya herself becomes the Nemesis of her own destruction as pushing first Gautama from the balcony one night, she kills herself afterwards.

Cry, the Peacock thus depicts a movement from disappointment and defeat to disaster. The atmosphere of this disaster is carved throughout the novel and when it reaches its climax, somehow satisfies the reader. We are made to experience the origin, the growth and the climax of this novel which seems like a blossoming balloon bursting in the end. This is then a journey from defeat to disaster that Maya, the protagonist is shown to undertake in *Cry, the Peacock*.

Similarly, Anita Desai's *Where Shall We Go This Summer*? too depicts a pattern of disappointment and disaster, but this time the pattern is reversed. In this novel we see Sita, the protagonist, returning almost from the brink of disaster to accept what to her has been the defeat of her life. Like Maya, Sita too is an emotional woman who fails to relate to her husband.

Where Shall We Go This Summer?, "the shortest existential novel,"[7] by Anita Desai is particularly remarkable for its intensity and depth. Sita, the protagonist here suffers since she too, like many other women of Anita Desai, fails to communicate with her husband. In many ways Sita is a reminder of Maya. She too, like Maya, suffers from an existential neurosis. Like Maya again, Sita too is obsessed with a bizarre thought about the impending disaster. Highly sentimental and totally alienated from her husband, Sita, quite like Maya, suffers the pangs of an incoherent and fragmented matrimonial relation. But it is here that the similarities between these two women come to end and what looks more important to the reader is their being different individuals. If Maya is passive and withdraws from action until she pushes Gautama in a hysterical outburst, Sita believes in action right from the beginning.

In fact the novel begins with her deciding, rather obstinately, to stage the most unthinkable adventure of a woman—not delivering the baby that she carries in her womb—at Manori—a utopian land where her late father once produced several minor miracles in his life. Obviously expecting to do the unbelievable, Sita is quick to run herself into trouble and refuses to wait for the tragedy to strike her. Again unlike the childless Maya, she happens to be the mother of four children and carries the fifth one in the novel. Thus she seems to suffer from a surfeit of something which Maya desires so ardently. Moreover, Maya fails to avert the disaster though she tries hard to avoid it whereas Sita successfully negotiates a disaster by taking it by horns.

Maya knows that the disaster is one day going to swallow either Gautama or herself, but rather than doing anything to avert it, she becomes an instrument in its execution. Thus Maya waits for things to happen. She even allows disaster to overwhelm her. But Sita refuses to bow before a decided pattern of life. She surprises one and all as in the normal course, it is absurd for a woman to believe that she can retain her child in her womb and not let it die or be born. Of course, it illustrates Sita's obsessed vision, and her unsettled psyche or a convoluted revenge that she decides to take on her husband and his society. But it also demonstrates her will to fight out the established patterns of human life.

Unlike many other women, Sita is endowed with a peculiar vision and sets herself on a search for self. She always questions the usually unquestioned one. Her cynical but realistic observation cannot be missed out as she summarises the littleness of human existence saying: "They are nothing—nothing but appetite and sex only food, sex and money matter."[8] In Sita, the novelist exhibits the frustration of a woman who is sick at having to repeat the process of delivering a baby in a routine uncomplaining manner. Angered at the callous immunity of her husband, she decides to slap on him as a mark of her subtle, convoluted revenge which is neither to abort nor to deliver the baby she carries. Thus unlike Maya she imposes her wishes on others rather than letting others impose their wishes on her. Her revenge thus, though fantastic and psychic, looks convincing enough.

The relations with the in-laws is another yardstick that determines the difference between Maya and Sita. While Maya craves for the company of her mother and sister-in-law, Sita it seems, does not get along well with them. She "soon finds the atmosphere at home too stifling and her husband buys another flat for them to live separately."[9] But it fails to give her peace as she continues to realise the futility of her life and feels bored with it. Fed up with the repetitive pattern of life and is pained to see "what a farce marriage was, all human relationships were" (144). The chasm between her husband Raman and Sita widens as he fails to comprehend the meaning of her boredom and exclaims "Bored [...]. Why? How? With What?" (144). It is the moment when Sita realises that they both belong to different worlds.

Already dissatisfied, and now totally disillusioned, Sita decides to subtly avenge the futility of human relations. She decides neither to abort nor to deliver the baby she is expecting. When she tells Raman "[...] I don't want to have a baby" (34), he is stunned and thinks that Sita has suggested an abortion as he asks in a surprised tone "What do you mean abortion?" (35). But he goes nonplussed as Sita brushes the idea aside—"Mad! It's all I want! I want to keep it, don't you understand?" (35). Raman can just express his exasperation: "What's up? What is up!"(35), at this bizarre proposition from his wife. Raman is forced to conclude in a bitter chagrin: "You've gone mad" (35). But Sita retorts: "I think [...] what I'm doing is trying to escape from the madness here, escape to a place where it might be possible to be sane again" (35). Sita has set her eyes on Manoli village where once her charismatic father produced miracles like removing women's sterility and curing people of their deadly ailments. Sita believes that Manoli, once being the land of her father's miracles, would not disappoint her as well. With its touch Manoli would help her produce a miracle herself—her not delivering the conceived and developing baby inside her. She seems almost obsessed with the idea of doing the unthinkable—by neither terminating her pregnancy, nor letting her produce a baby, but just by retaining it inside her.

Driven by such a bizarre passion Sita takes her two children Moneka and Karan with her and sets out for Manoli village. Raman can spot this cause and tries to mock away her bravado: "So, you're running away—like the bored runaway wife in—in a film" (36). But Sita stabs her with a glare: "It can happen in real life, Raman," and declares stoutly: "I will go. I am leaving tomorrow. On the island—it'll be different" (36).

Now both in the life of Maya and Sita the disaster seems inevitable. They both know that there is no escape from a tragic fate that awaits them. While Maya foresees the death either of hers or her husband's, Sita reels under the anxiety of having to produce another baby in a hostile world. Another reason why she repels another baby birth is the fact that her relation with her husband is a bored, finished reality where no revival is possible. Like Maya and Gautama, Sita and Raman too make a loveless, estranged couple. Anita Desai summarises the listlessness of their relationship when she portrays the feelings of Raman who, while looking at the face of Sita, thinks:

> It was the face of a woman unloved, a woman rejected. He shook his own head a little, with an equine movement—it was hard to believe now that he had married her, in a romantic whim, not only out of a cavalier's pity for a maiden's distress, but for her fire and beauty. (134)

Thus like *Cry, the Peacock, Where Shall We Go This Summer*? too depicts the tragedy of a fragmented married life. A matrimonial boredom and an alienation mainly of women obviously are the keynote of both these novels. But like all skilled writers, Anita Desai reverses the pattern in her latter work. If *Cry, the Peacock* (1963) moves from disappointment to disaster, *Where Shall We Go This Summer*? (1975) returns from a wild disaster to a normal disappointment. Sita manages the disaster by running into it deliberately. Maya, on the other hand, reels under it and fails to do anything until it envelops her. Consequently then, she is overwhelmed by the tragedy in the end. For Sita the tasting of tragedy beforehand, works as a safety-valve which releases her tensions, relieves her of her darker, tragic, suicidal mood as she returns to embrace her disillusioned self. She thus undertakes a journey from disaster to disappointment while for Maya it is the other way round.

NOTES

1. Anita Desai, *Cry, the Peacock* (1980; New Delhi: Orient Paperbacks, 1988) 30. All the subsequent textual references have been taken from the same edition of the novel, cited hereafter with the page number(s) in parentheses with the text.

2. M. Rajeshwar, "Superstition and Psyche in Anita Desai's *Cry, the Peacock,*" *Feminist English Literature,* ed. Manmohan K. Bhatnagar (New Delhi: Atlantic Publishers, 1999) 241.
3. K.R. Srinivas Iyengar, *Indian Writing in English* (New Delhi: Sterling Publishers, 1985) 466.
4. Rajeshwar 243.
5. S.P. Swain, "Note of Existentialism in the Novels of Anita Desai," *Commonwealth English Literature,* ed. M.K. Bhatnagar (New Delhi: Atlantic Publishers, 1999) 140.
6. Marie Fernandes, "The Outer Weather in Anita Desai's Novels," *Indian English Fiction 1980-90: An Assessment,* eds. Nilufer E. Bharucha and Vilas Sarang (New Delhi: B.R. Publishing Corporation, 1994) 170.
7. Madhusudan Prasad, *Anita Desai: The Novelist* (Allahabad: New Horizon, 1981) 60.
8. Anita Desai, *Where Shall We Go This Summer*? (1982; New Delhi: Orient Paperbacks, 1988) 4. All the subsequent textual references have been taken from the same edition of the novel, cited hereafter with the page number(s) in parentheses with the text.
9. Fernandas 172.

11

Moving the 'Small' to the Centre: *The God of Small Things*— A Study in Style

T. VINODA

To my mind Arundhati Roy's Booker Prize-winning book, *The God of Small Things* breaks the mould of the old novel that engages in entire structures of discourse which intellectuals are fond of. *The God of Small Things,* fittingly titled, is not about big human questions, nor has it appealed to the international community and especially to the Booker jury because it is about such weighty human questions. Interestingly enough Arundhati Roy who steadfastly refused to write about these human questions in her novel, wrote recently an anti-nuke article for *Outlook* (August 3, 1998) that only a writer known for the power of her words can write; many have missed the irony of the faith and conviction that informs the outlook article *vis-a-vis* the completely amoral detachment that tempers the approach of her novel throughout. It must be noted that the novel is a different thing altogether and not to be mistaken for any ideological or theoretical construct. This is precisely the point about the novel.

The novel succeeds with modern readers the world over and with the uncommon, enlightened cultivated readers because, to put it plainly, it has the tone and temper, attitude and chutzpa, profanity and cynicism, frivolity and humor, savvy and sophistication, and innocence and commonsense. The sensibility here is modernist and the novel is in line with the kind of fiction where it is futile to look for a spiritual or moral centre. Prema Nandakumar brackets Vikram Seth, Amitav Ghosh, Upamanyu Chatterjee and, Arundhathi Roy and says: "But these writers, when they comment upon the socio-political scenario exhibit a strange lack of faith in the future. They are depressed by the present and add to it their own desecrations. Comparing them with earlier novelists like Venkataramani and Raja Rao one feels that this is a generation of disillusionment" (*The Hindu,* Sep. 6, 1998 xiv). She is right in perceiving that these writers lack affirmative faith.

It is important, however, to see them as writing a new novel —what goes by the name modernist/post-modernist novel— where formal considerations, experiments with technique and use of language, etc. become more important, often all important. A host of writers beginning with Flaubert, Joyce, Eliot, Mann, Celine, Gide, Robbe-Grillet have laid extraordinarily exclusive emphasis on formal considerations and have written what have come to be described as "writerly" (Barthes 206) works. These writers are chiefly responsible for forming a new taste that is basically free from ideological commitments, be they humanistic or otherwise. After these writers and the tradition that they have established for modern writer, it no longer makes sense to look upon such a work of art as a responsible power, a force for belief, a sacred testament of faith and a means of judgment. Moral relevance of art in a larger sense of the term, is a thing of the past. The modernist code puts all emphasis on sensibility, style, subjective response, and sincerity; the old mode of engaging in moral discriminations is thrown overboard. If anything, cynical laughter, irreverence, and desecration rule high in the modernist writing. Rushdie's sacrilege against Prophet Mahomed in *The Satanic Verses* is only a glaring example of this attitude. Upamanyu Chatterjee's system-busting cynical lying and parody, again, are of a piece. For in the new novel the centre of value has been knocked out and what we find in it are interesting patterns which need not be meaningful in the old sense and which appeal to the new generation the world over. The new novel may be seen as the defeat of humanistic hopes by some, but these writers did not intend it to uphold a humanistic faith. Referring to such writing Saul Bellow has once complained that here the "cult of the 'human' has given way to a large consciousness, one that is less anthropocentric" (cf. his Nobel lecture). The new code of writing negates the old which was nothing if it was not value-centred. Writers like Salman Rushdie, Amitav Ghosh, and now Arundhati Roy are in the tradition of this new novel in their individual ways.

Roy's way of succeeding could be seen in the appeal of her novel to the modernist sensibility whose composition would at once become clear when the novel itself is analyzed. The Booker tribute to the novel hit the nail on the head when it emphasized the novel's "extraordinary linguistic inventiveness." Indeed the novel uses the language in the most unorthodox way and in a way that largely makes for its riveting quality. The earlier Indian writers in English, for the most part, wrote the way the Englishmen did (the linguistic creativity displayed by a Raja Rao or a Desani wasn't the kind of inventiveness that is meant for international audiences and therefore should be discussed in a separate category altogether). Kamala Das aptly says that these writers in India felt responsible towards the language: "We didn't take English lightly. We felt we had to beat the British at their own game [...]. But Arundhati uses English as a plaything. She can spit at correct English" (*Outlook*, Oct. 27, 1997: 125). While this observation largely explains the appeal of Roy's novel, it is likely to be misunderstood.

It is true that Roy takes liberties with the language for creative purposes in the novel, but she does not often meddle with the structure, grammar or the rhythm of the language. In places where she makes use of the speech of the inadequate bilinguals as when someone like K.N.M. Pillai appears—Roy does so (as did Nissim Ezekiel or G.V. Desani) to lend credibility and authenticity to the character. However she does not fetishize it to the point of rendering the novel queer or unintelligible. Fortunately for her, the people she chose to write about are Westernized Syrian Christians. For this reason, to say that the book "reads the way we speak" is stretching things too far. It must be noted that Roy is in Rushdiesque linguistic tradition where the language used is not only legitimate but also shorn of the gravitas of nationhood: the effort here is to internationalise the language. However the most engaging part of her use of language could be seen in the new way that often combines irreverence, humor, and irony for startling effect. This style arrests. What appears as "lush style" and a "tendency to overwrite" or "too much artifice" (*Outlook*, Oct. 27, 1997: 124) in the novel is in reality a deliberate style choice made by the author to suit her aestheticist creed that puts exclusive emphasis on manner. Looking for teleological ends of such a style is like searching for shade in Sahara. In this philosophy of art, working out human possibilities, or affirming faith in human spirit, dignity, nobility or focusing on man's heroic struggles and suffering, or on the pathos of his condition, or on the complex of human emotions, feelings, dreams, etc. take a back seat. This is one reason why the focus of Roy's fictional world is unremittingly on perverts, eccentrics, maniacs and such other diminished men. And the whole thing is touched by amusement, cynicism and parody. This perhaps is the reason why none of the heroic struggles that Arundhati Roy's mother, Mary Roy, puts up in real life find fictional transference, although many people believe she is the prototype of Ammu.

Discussed below is the incidence of features which are foregrounded by virtue of departing, in some way, from general norms of communication by means of the language code; for example, exploitation of regularities of formal patterning (schemes—anaphora, parallelism, antithesis, etc.), or of deviations from the linguistic code (tropes—metaphor, simile, synecdoche, meronomy, irony, oxymoron, paradox, etc.) is freely indulged in the novel by the author.

Schemes are mostly the foregrounded repetition of expression. The text provides plenty of examples in this category:

p.319 "Estha. Baby Kochamma chose. Knowing him to be the more practical of the two. The more tractable.

The more farsighted. The more responsible. 'You go. Good boy.'"

Description of the incest abounds in anaphora:

p.328 "Only that there were tears.

Only that quietness and emptiness fitted together like stacked spoons.

Only that there was a shuffling in the hollows at the base of a Lovely throat.

Only that a hard honey-coloured shoulder had a semicircles of teeth marks on it.

Only that they held each other close, long after it was over.

Only that what they shared that night was not happiness but A hideous grief.

Only that once again they broke the Love Laws."

p.32 "It was lodged there deep inside some fold or furrow, like a mango hair between molars. That couldn't be worried loose."

p.128 "His nipples peeped at Rahel over the top of the boundary wall like a sad St. Bernard's eyes."

The God of Small Things is replete with tropes. Tropes are the foregrounded irregularities of content. They invariably involve selectional restriction rule violations. Metaphors, similes, synecdoche, meronomy, paradox, oxymoron, irony, personification, pun, etc. are pressed into service to bring freshness and novelty to expression and sometimes to reveal shock. Given below are some examples in this category:

p.83 " [...] The coconut trees were sea anemones waving their tentacles [...]."

p.65 "Automobile islands in a river of people."

p.105 "Clean children, like a packet of peppermints."

p.119 "Chacko lay like a beached whale on the narrow hotel bed."

p.33 "(Communism) [...] seeped into Kerala like tea from a tea bag."

p.37 "Rahel's new teeth were waiting inside her gums like words in a pen."

p.4 "Her face was pale and as wrinkled as a dhobi's thumb from being in water for long."

p.128 "His nipples peeped at Rahel over the top of the boundary wall like a sad St. Bernard's eyes."

p.32 "It was lodged there, deep inside some fold or furrow, like a mango hair between molars. That couldn't be worried loose."

p.317 "Four saucers stared back at her."

Figures of speech involving (a) concrete tenors and abstract vehicles, and (b) *vice versa* are found here:

P.9 (a) "Strange insects appeared like ideas in the evenings."

p.328 (b) "Only that quietness and emptiness fitted together like stacked spoons."

p.127 (b) "[...] her childhood fled, flailing its thin arms."

Instances of personification involving an inanimate object or an abstract concept spoken of as though it were endowed with life or with human attributes or feelings are not infrequent. A significant dimension to Arundhati Roy's style lies in the creative use of the selectional-restriction rule violations. The exploration of the panorama by the narrative eye is not inert, but active and imaginative; 'looking at' something means grasping what it 'looks like.'

p.10 "Heaven opened and the water hammered down, reviving the reluctant old well."

p.10 "The grass looked wet green and pleased."

p.29 "[...] her sad, paint-flaking fridge."

p.63 "He watched cloudy children at car windows with yearning marshmallow noses."

The oxymorons, collocational clashes and paradoxes are always functional in the context;

p.28 "Noisy Television silence."

p.239 "mirthless smile"

p.187 "Beautiful Ugly Toads"

p.202 "Green heat"

p.19 "listening with his eyes."

pp.166-67 "she could see the music as it left her violin"

p.35 "jungles, rivers, rice-fields, communists"

p.73 "A lucky leaf that wasn't lucky enough."

For all their startling effect, these collocational clashes are neither arty nor improbable; if anything, they provide us a persuasive insight into the inherently contradictory, ambivalent nature of the small detail of life. This makes for a riveting reading. In this case the novel really lives in its detail which renders it into a superbly crafted "bright book of life."

The novel is a site for puns, innuendoes, alliteration, assonance, etc.

p.69 "Cardamom Kings, Coffee Counts, and Rubber Barons [...]."

p.64 "There was hustle-bustle. And police whistles."

p.90 (Of a bow-legged porter) "Balls-in-Brackets."

p.73 "There's a nipple in the air," Larry McCaslin said to Rahel and laid his palm gently against the suggestion of protest from a chilly nipple through her cotton T-shirt.

p.31 "Baby Kochamma said, 'As ye sow, so shall ye reap.' As though *she* had had and nothing to do with the Sowing and the Reaping."

There are apparently playful expressions like

p.306 "Dark of Heartness tiptoed into the Heart of Darkness."

in the novel which at first give the false impression of contributing nothing to the context, but are in reality loaded with meaning.

Arundhati Roy's work does not generally allude to other writings; however when it does so, she brings to it a sureness of touch:

p.126 "So there it was then, History and Literature enlisted by commerce. Kurtz and Karl Marx joining palms to greet rich guests as they stepped off the boat."

There is no way we can miss the irony and paradox implicit in the scene described here.

Arundhati Roy has a finely tuned sensitivity to the variegated background of the innumerable characters and to each she brings the appropriate register. However the brilliant use of these registers is consistently shot with an impish humour. When, for instance, the hybrid character of Indian Marxism is sought to be described, there is on display an expert use of semantic sets that is amusing:

> The Marxists worked from within the communal divides, never challenging them, never appearing not to. They offered a cocktail revolution. A heady mix of Eastern Marxism and Orthodox Hinduism. Spiked with a shot of democracy (67).

Again when K.N.M. Pillai's misplaced missionary zeal about Communism is dealt with, the novel's narrative adopts a hilarious tone even as it captures the hollow Marxist rhetoric with its brilliant use of the political register appropriate to the leftist pamphleteering. K.N.M. Pillai is shown to lapse into the pamphleteering rhetoric at the slightest provocation. When Chacko casually asks him if their march was a success, he assumes a lofty voice and says:

> "Unless and until demands are met, comrade, we cannot say it is a Success or Non-success." A pamphleteering inflection crept into Comrade Pillai's voice. "Until then, struggle must continue" (276).

The Rhodes scholar and Oxonian Chacko is not spared either from this kind of treatment. The lofty academic tone that Chacko frequently assumes to hector at people is referred to as Oxford Moods by Ammu. He feels called upon to assume this lofty academic tone when, for instance, he explains about the abandoned History House:

> But we can't go in [...] because we've been locked out. And when we look in through the windows, all we see are shadows. And when we try and listen, all we hear is a whispering. And we cannot understand the whispering, because our minds have been invaded by a war. A war that

> we have won and lost. The very worst sort of war. A war that captures dreams and redreams them. A war that has made us adore our conquerors and despise ourselves. (53)

He goes on in this vein and puncturing snide remarks from Ammu are unable to stop this flow of his academic rhetoric. The humour of this situation notwithstanding, the point to be noted here is the academic register pressed into service to lend authenticity to the depiction of such eccentrics. When Baby Kochamma's garden is described again the narrative uses the appropriate Botanical register, but once again the effect sought is comic; Baby Kochamma is another of the novel's collection of freaks.

Another important style feature of Arundhati Roy's novel is the indulgent use of graphological sentences (p. 3 "Not old. Not young. But a viable-die-able age."), and heavy punctuation marks. Capital letters are plenty. Italics are also frequently used for emphasis. Fancy spelling sometimes is used to mark the perception of the children ("infinnate" "Lay-ter") and at other times as substitute for phonetic script to indicate the specific Indian English pronunciation of people like K.N.M. Pillai. "Die-vorced" (130), "Amayrica" (129) and "(Ammu) told her to stoppit and she Stopited" (300). Arundhati Roy coins new usages which also contribute to enlivening the style of her novel: "afternoon-mare" (217) coined after the word, nightmare; "His face grew dark and outdoorsy" (13). In addition, the novel uses Modifier Head type of Noun phrases with complex classifiers which come to readers as something of a surprise even as it seeks to make the style crisp and compact:

p.36 "It had been the What will Sophie Mol think? week."

p.221 "It was a clear-as-glass kiss."

p.145 "A Far More Angry Than Necessary feeling, etc."

p.300 "Ammu's trying not-to-cry mouth."

Arundhati Roy uses graphological style to a telling effect and often succeeds in infusing breathless pace into the style even as she underlines things that are to be taken note of. The following passage describing the man with an artificial leg on the Cochin railway platform is an excellent example of this style:

> (A) Inside it (his unstrapped artificial leg) he stored his ticket. His towel. His stainless-steel tumbler. His smells. His secrets. His love. His madness. His hope. His infinnate joy. His real foot was bare (301).

Style here is brusque and emphatic. Much of this impression comes from her tendency to use very short graphic units, with heavy punctuation. The punctuation here is abnormally emphatic: she disjoins by full-stops constructions which syntactically form part of the same sentence. The punctuation itself has an important stylistic role, as may be seen by a comparison of the first part of the above paragraph, rewritten below with more orthodox punctuation. The first nine sentences in this ten-sentence para can be combined into a single sentence with asyndetic and syndetic co-ordination:

> (B) Inside it he stored his ticket, his towel, his stainless-steel tumbler, his smells, his secrets, his love, his madness, his hope and his infinnate joy. His real foot was bare.

The comparison should reveal that graphological style is not just a question of where the punctuation occurs, but how heavy it is, 'B' differs from its original in terms not of the graphic units alone, but in respect of the weight of punctuation. The full-stop, the 'heaviest' punctuation mark, has the greatest separative force; hence the effect of using full-stops, in 'A' is to emphasize the autonomy of each piece of information, which is thereby asserted with the maximum force.

Semantically speaking the para talks about the way he stuffed his possessions (ticket, towel, stainless-steel tumbler), his personality and his dreams (smells, secrets, love, madness, hope, infinnate joy) into the hollow of his artificial leg unmindful of the barefoot.

The end-focus "His real foot was bare" puts the inanity of existence into focus while what precedes it engages the reader with lexical sets that violate the selectional-restriction rules. While one can understand the lame man stuffing his material possessions into the hollow of his artificial leg, one is shocked into realisation of the pathos involved in the predicament of the man when the narrative voice describes the man stuffing abstract concepts into it. Such a rare mixing of abstract and concrete elements enables the writer to crystallize the felt life through the perceived paradoxes. Thus the end-focus helps in capturing effectively the tragedy of the handicapped individual, *i.e.* suffering getting to be a habit.

The brilliance of Arundhati Roy's sensitive style can be felt everywhere. In the following example, her style combines perspective, nuance and realistic detail of the surroundings in a way that is very engaging:

> Rahel held by Ammu's hand. A mosquito on a leash. A Refugee Stick Insect in Bata Sandals. An Airport Fairy at a railway station. Stamping her feet on the platform, unsettling clouds of Settled station filth. Until Ammu shook her and told her to Stoppit and she Stoppited. Around them the hostling-jostling crowd.
>
> Scurrying hurrying buying selling luggage trundling porter paying children shitting people spitting coming going begging bargaining reservation-checking (300).

The first para here employs capital letters, graphological sentences, metaphorical expressions, coinages ("stoppit/ stoppited") and partial reduplicated compounds (hostling-jostling) to bring freshness and novelty to the expression. And the second para reveals the brisk transaction of life that is taking place on the railway platform. It employs such linguistic devices as alliteration, assonance, rhyme and phonaesthetic lexical sets to evoke and to echo station sounds. Another important feature of this para is that it does away with punctuation marks. The absence of punctuation not only helps building the tempo of activity on the platform but also shows how one activity flows into the other with a breathless speed.

The paradoxes of modern India are captured in the brilliant descriptions of the Hotel Heritage environs. The style employed here reminds us of *The Waste Land* (cf. 126-27).

Humour is the dominant element of this novel. It evokes laughter which is an end in itself. Arundhati Roy does not employ tendency comedy or tendency wit here because she does not conceive her work as a satire. The humour that she employs is a harmless form of the comic. The materials are selected and managed primarily in order to interest, involve and amuse the readers. Wild fancy of the narrator necessitates wild comparisons.

1. "A column of shining black ants walked across a windowsill, their bottoms tilted upwards, like a line of mincing chorus girls in a Busby Berkeley musical." (155)
2. "Jesus in mini." (74)

The novel way adopted in describing the gestures results in pictures of startling vividness.

> Ammu grew tired of their proprietary handling of her. She wanted her body back. It was hers. She shrugged her children off the way a bitch shrugs off her pups when she's had enough of them. (222)

The unconventional, iconoclastic, irreverent analogy employed here is successful in evoking a vivid picture of the scene here.

Humour manifests itself in the delineation of character as well. Baby Kochamma, Pappachi, Mammachi, Margaret Kochamma, Chacko, K.N.M. Pillai, Latha, and so on constitute a cavalcade of such characters. For instance, Chacko, the Rhodes scholar at Oxford, looked like an-untidy beatified porcupine" (241). His ears stuck out on either side of his head like "teapot handles" (41). Lying on a hotel bed he looked like a "beached whale" (119). His Oxford moods, his Read-Aloud Voice, his "Man's Needs" (295), his wrongly buttoned up shirt, untied shoelaces, his Pus-filled diabetic boil on his foot, his love and infatuation for his ex-wife, Margaret Kochamma, his mismanagement of Paradise Pickles and Preserves and a host of other such detail the author chooses individuates him for us even as it evokes laughter. Similarly, Kochu Maria, the "vinegar-hearted, short-tempered midget cook" (15), is"thick wrinkled like rhinoceros in a frilly apron" (201). Rahel is "a mosquito on a leash" (300). The little Estha and Rahel squatting amidst woodshavings at Velutha's workshop are "hunched punctuation marks" (78-79). A man looking like a knot (80) gives Baby Kochamma his red flag to hold and wave it. Dead Ammu, wrapped in a bed sheet is a "Roman senator" (162). Thus the comparisons used are not commonplace but are startlingly unexpected and fresh.

The attitude that tempers the novel is patently urbane, humorous and that which refuses to make distinction between the sacred and the profane, the beautiful and the ugly—all is grist to the style that seeks to make it engagingly real. Example:

> Baby Kochamma lifted her rumpled sari. Rahel studied her baby grandaunt's enormous legs. (Years later during a history lesson being read out in school—*The Emperor Babur had a wheatish complexion and pillar-like thighs*—this scene would flash before her. Baby Kochamma balanced like a big bird over a public pot [...] poor little tiny feet to carry such a load!) Baby Kochamma waited for half of half a moment. Head thrust forward. Silly smile. Bosom swinging low. Melons in a blouse. Bottom up and out. When the gurgling, bubbling sound came, she listened with her eyes. A yellow brook burbled through a mountain pass. (95)

On occasion Arundhati Roy brings in local colour and habitation by using Indian English which helps her capture the patterns of social behaviour which ill-assort with those of the English and the Anglicised Indian Christians. This may be best seen in her portrayal of Comrade K.N.M. Pillai. One of the remarkable creative choices that the novelist appears to have made in writing this novel is to set up an inadequate bilingual, K.N.M. Pillai (though with a Master's degree) for her persona. For when an average Indian expresses himself in English the deviations from the LI variety of English that invariably appear in his speech reveal his socio-linguistic background and allow us a glimpse of his cultural differentiate. This novel would have been less Indian and far less amusing had Arundhati Roy absolutely confined herself to the Westernised Syrian Christian characters whose English approximates the standard British variety.

The Western reader of this novel is bound to find K.N.M. Pillai's family decidedly unEnglish not merely because the speakers are non-Westernised non-Indian Christians but because the attitudes, assumptions and expressions manifest in their speech are distinctly Indian. The episode in which K.N.M. Pillai meets Rahel the first time after she returns to Ayemenem from America dramatises for us the underlying assumptions of the speaker relationships that are typically Indian. The expectations of social behaviour which the English language brings with it are completely upset here. The English language, known for irony and understatement, is yoked in this context to a sensibility that is not given to inwardness and to the exclusive sense of privacy in social interaction. K.N.M. Pillai is unhesitating in asking Rahel the details about her private life:

> p.130 "So!" Comrade Pillai's smile broadened as he turned all his attention like a search light on Rahel [...].
>
> "Mol's husband?" he wanted to know.
> "Hasn't come"
> "Any photos?
> "No"
> "Name?"
> "Larry. Lawrence [...].
> "Any issues?"
> "No" Rahel said. "Still in planning stages, I suppose? Or expecting?"
> "No."
> "One is must. Boy girl. Any one" Comrade Pillai said. "Two is of course your choice."
> 'We're divorced." Rahel hoped to shock him into silence.
> "Die-vorced?" His voice rose to such a high register that it cracked on the question mark. He even pronounced the word as though it were a form of death [...].

> "That is most unfortunate," he said, when he had recovered. For some reason resorting to uncharacteristic, bookish language: "Most unfortunate."

The all-out breezy camaraderie of K.N.M. Pillai and his no holds—barred sociability and his trespassing into Rahel's personal life—all come home directly to the Indian readers while the English should find this approach baffling. Unlike the average Indian, the WASP character is especially noted for self-sufficiency and reticence. To a native English reader, more than the inadequate bilingual speech used here, it is the ruthless wiping out of the distinction between public and private affairs that comes as a shock.

Another important Indian trait that this style lights up in K.N.M. Pillai's character is his exuberant self-dramatisation. His harangues, his penchant for quotations, his extraordinary pride in his son, Lenin, who works for foreign embassies, his admiration for "foreign returnees"—all blend into the moulding of an authentic Indian stereotype. His loud, desultory conversations, his chatty behaviour and demonstrative display of personal feelings in the given situations, all prove to be decidedly un-English. His irrepressible loquacity is all the more remarkable considering the woeful ineptness with which he handles English.

As for the Indianness at the formal level, this novel offers a rich variety of examples in which one can observe innumerable features that are an outcome of inadequate mastery of English or inter-language interference.

(1) The Indian tendency to misuse the English articles could be noted in the language used by K.N.M. Pillai:

p.277 "He is good worker."
p.274 "He is genius."
p.130 "One is must."
p.276 "Design is same. Only difference is in text, I suppose."

All the examples here are to be noted for the absence of the required article 'a' or 'the.'

(2) Some of the most striking examples of the strident intrusion of LI in the English used here could be observed in its "be+verb+ing" constructions even with those verbs which in Standard English do not occur in the progressive aspect:

p.275 "He's standing first in class."

p.273 "What is the news? How is your daughter adjusting."

(3) Another important feature of Indian English is the use of "aunty" and "uncle" as mode of address even in the context of total strangers:

p.274 "Lenin Mon, tell comrade Uncle the one papa taught you. Friends, Romans, Countrymen [...]" Lenin continued his nasal treasure hunt.

"Come on, Mon, it's only our Comrade Uncle [...]."

(4) The regular ordering of declarative sentence elements,— 'subject-verb-object' is changed to 'object-verb-subject' under LI influence:

p.129 "His daughter's daughter is this. In Amayrica, now."

The elaborate kinship relationships that we have in India necessitate specifying British Standard English (BSE) 'grand-daughter' as 'daughter's daughter' or 'son's daughter.'

(5) Again under the influence of Malayalam in K.N.M. Pillai uses 'colour' with 'red' and 'blue' unlike the Anglicised Chacko. It is an instance of redundancy.

p.276 "Prussian Blue," Chacko said

"Prepared from Acetic Acid?"

"Royal Blue," Chacko said [...].

"[...] Same Royal Blue colour, but c. and I.c.?" Chacko nodded.

"[...] This will be red colour, I suppose."

As may be seen in K.N.M. Pillai's response here ("Prepared from Acetic Acid?") Indian English generally manifests itself in such echo questions.

(6) Wrong use of prepositions such as 'send off' for 'send away' (278).

(7) Quantifier which premodifies a Noun-head in a Noun phrase in BSE is made to post-modify the Noun-head under LI influence.

p.276 "this all is in caps, I suppose."

(8) Variant Indian English pronunciation is shown in changed spellings of the words.

p.271 "saar"
p.312 "yooseless goose"
p.134 "one mint" (for "minute")
p.130 "die-vorced" (for "divorced")
p.130 "Amayrica" (for "America")

(9) Besides using Malayalam expletives, modes of address loan-shifts (p. 273 'avalose oondas'; p. 198 'akkara') and loan translations (p. 22 'punnyan kunju' trans., "the little blessed one") Arundhati Roy also puts to creative use typically Indian English words like "issues" (meaning "children"), "double-promotion," etc.

The God of Small Things uses the Indian English idioms, collocations, vocabulary items, syntax and pronunciation to a telling effect. The disparity between what one has learnt to expect from standard English and what one finds manifested in the Indian English here has become a great creative opportunity for the novelist to light up some significant aspects of the common Indian personality. Style here is no longer a mere dress of thought, but is its soul.

WORKS CITED

Barthes, Roland. *SIZ*. Trans. Richard Miller. New York, 1974.

Bellow, Saul. "Nobel Lecture." *The American Review*, 2 (Win, 1978).

Ghose, Sagarika. "English, chutneyfied'." *Outlook* (October 27, 1997) 125-26.

Menon, Venu. "Sleepy Aymanam." *Outlook* (October 27, 1997) 126.

Prema Nandakumar. "From Dean Mahomed to Roy" *The Hindu* (September 6, 1998) XIV.

Roy, Arundhati. *The God of Small Things*. New Delhi, 1997. All the references to this novel are indicated in the text before or after the quotation.

Roy, Arundhati. "The End of Imagination." *Outlook* (August 3, 1998) 62-71.

Suri, Sanjay. "Goddess of the Moment." *Outlook* (October 27, 1997) 118-24.

Vinoda, T. Naveen, G. Rama Reddy and P. Shiv Kumar. "*Drukkonam*: A Discussion on Arundhati Roy's *The God of Small Things*, in-Cable T.V., August 29, 1998.

12

Urban Bias as a Postcolonial Distortion: A Note on Badal Sircar's *Third Theatre*

E. RENUKA and SHAMPA BHATTACHARJEE

As he was attached to the city of Calcutta in more ways than one, Badal Sircar has an intimate feel of the urban conscience of this city and has a profound understanding of the middle class life, and, through almost all his major plays, he is found probing into the Calcutta middle-class mind. In the dramatic form, he accommodates and expresses practically all the major concerns, aspirations and frustrations of the new rootless urban generation. In fact, four of his early plays—*Evam Indrajit* (and, *Indrajit*, acclaimed as the *Waiting for Godot* of the Bengali theatre[1]), *Baki Itihas* (The Other History), *Thringsha Satabdi* (The Thirtieth Century), and *Shesh Nei* (There's No End) which formed a set called the *Calcutta Quartet* and brought him laurels—have a linking urban theme.

And, after writing and directing such plays for the conventional stage for about twenty years during the fifties and sixties, Sircar could look at the roots of the city of Calcutta when he noticed that two cultural trends ran parallel to each other giving rise to a fundamental dichotomy between the urban and rural lives,[2] particularly in the cultural field. With this understanding he had come to realise the existence of two distinct kinds of theatre in rural and urban areas respectively in India. In an attempt to produce plays that can be appreciated by the city and village audiences alike, he wished to attack at the root of this dichotomy by creating a link between the two theatres through his *Third Theatre*—a theatre of synthesis in his own perspective. In fact, he pioneered this new theatre with the avowed aim of awakening the urban audience to an awareness of exploitation in rural India and the rural audience to a sense of its power. He envisaged the *Third Theatre* as one which is neither restricted by the costly, and often immobile, paraphernalia of the conventional proscenium theatre, nor infested by the commerciality and reactionary values of the prevailing folk theatre (Also, he wanted to break the barriers and come closer to the spectators, to "take full advantage" of direct communication that theatre as a live-show offers. He wanted to share with his audience the experience of the joint human action).

However, Sircar is conscious that the dichotomy in the cultural field cannot be removed without a fundamental change in the socio-economic situation, and he has no illusion that it can be done simply through theatre. But he firmly believes that theatre can be one of the many facets of a movement that is vitally needed to bring about the desirable change, and that makes the idea of the *Third Theatre* meaningful to him.[3]

His first major experiment in the direction of the *Third Theatre* was his play *Spartacus*, which tells us the story of the great slave revolt that shook the mighty Roman empire. The second, third and fourth plays—*Michhil* (1974), *Bhoma* (1976) and *Basi Khabar* (1979)—have been staged widely in the widest possible range of situations and environments not only by his own group *Satabdi* but other theatre groups as well. They have been rendered into English and published, their English titles being *Procession, Bhoma* and *Stale News* respectively.[4]

2

With the Santhal insurrection as its apparent theme, the play *Stale News* (1979) delves into the origins of colonialism in India. For evolving this play, Sircar has depended on the work of Suprakash Ray[5] who established that the very presence of the British power in India goaded the Santhals to revolt because their enemies—the landlords and moneylenders—"owed their authority and their existence" to the new arrangement in landed property introduced by the colonial government and the accelerated development of a money economy under its impact. The rising constituted, therefore, a critique not only of a local administration but of colonialism itself.

Also, the play exposes the collaborationist role of the proprietary middle class that was created in India during the British rule. The middle class people—upper and lower—who were interested in absentee landlordism and who were engaged in various professions opened out in consequence of expanding trade by the colonialist—acted as the lackeys of the British and served the colonialist at the war front and also at the cultural front.

It was this class of proprietors, enriched by the plunder of millions of poor peasants, who brought about a cultural resurgence in the city. The mouthpiece was Rammohun Roy (1772-1833). This resurgence has often been mistakenly called the *Indian Renaissance* by the class which were its beneficiaries. According to Ashok Mitra, this so-called *renaissance* bore the indelible stamp of the class among whom it was noticed and it was pre-eminently confined to the city and among these absentee landlords. This renaissance was brought to fruition by an alliance with the ruling power by a class of absentee landlords and *banians*[6] aspiring to be 'junior partners' living away from the village. This *renaissance* did not touch the rural economy of the country at all. The country at large practically did not exist for this *renaissance*.[7]

And, in Sircar's *Stale News*, a member of the CHORUS separates from the rest to 'become' Raja Rammohun Roy addressing ONE:

> RAMMOHUN. 'The peasantry and villagers in the interior are quite ignorant of, and indifferent about [...] the government [...]. Many of those, however, who engage prosperously in commerce, and of those who are secured in the peaceful possession of their estates by the *permanent settlement*, and such as have sufficient intelligence to foresee

the probability of future improvement which presents itself under the British rulers, are not only reconciled to it, *but really view it as a blessing to the country* [...].'

CHORUS. Hoo-oo-oo-ool. (Revolt)

(114-15: emphasis added)

Rammohun Roy was also of the opinion that the European settlers of 'character and capital' would greatly improve the resources of the country, and also the condition of the native inhabitants. According to him, the indigo planters, on the whole, performed 'more good to the generality of the natives' of India, than 'any other class of Europeans.' Hearing him, the CHORUS shouts 'Hool,' and he calls it ('hool') 'a flagrant manifestation of the imprudence of orthodoxy' (113-14). In fact, the indigo planters, according to Radha Kumud Mookerji, a member of the Land Revenue Commission on Bengal, were notorious for their treatment of the native cultivators as slaves and compelled them (cultivators) to grow indigo on any plot pointed out by the planters, and, on failure, oppressed and tortured the cultivators with impunity, and paid them less.[8]

It is to be noted in this context that two cultures, each with a long history and rich traditions, were intensely interested in Bengal during the nineteenth century. The arena of this interaction was the city of Calcutta. The participants in the interaction were the colonial officers, professionals (educators, scholars, doctors and lawyers), businessmen, and missionaries from England and the urban, Western-educated, Hindu upper-caste Bengali elite composed of Brahmins, Kayasthas and Baidyas. And, Rammohun Roy and Bankim Chandra Chatterjee belong to this Bengali elite.

The playwright is worried to find that this middle class continues to adjust itself to, or, is trying to promote, the cultural legacy of the colonialists even during the postcolonial period. Hence the subject of the Santhal rebellion is 'contemporary' to him as the conditions have not changed fundamentally even today. The play relates a historical phenomenon of the nineteenth century to the contemporary bourgeois attitudes prevalent in our country, particularly in relation to everyday calamities and dilemmas.

3

In 1982, Sircar described Calcutta as an "artificial city created in the colonial interests of a foreign nation. A monster city that grew by sucking the blood of a vast rural hinterland which perhaps is the true India. A city of alien culture based on English education, representing, distorting, buying, promoting for sale the real culture of the country."[9]

But, much before that, in 1974 itself, Sircar, through his play, *Procession,* could expose some of the postcolonial problems that haunt the city—the unemployed, frustrated and angry youth, pestering beggars, black marketeers, soaring prices, selfish political leaders, cutthroat religious fanatics, status-quoist administrators and domineering magnates—all living in a marketplace-like society ridden with fake encounter deaths, human degradation and so on. The stress and strain of living is unbearable. Poverty and distress are writ large on the face of the city. The term procession in the play itself emanated from the traumatic postcolonial situation. It stands for screaming youths that suffer from hallucinations. It embodies the agony of the suffering masses at different levels and serves as a metaphor for protest and fighting the evil forces. The play evokes echoes of the past by presenting patriotic cries and slogans like "Death to the British dogs," "Quilt India," and "British Imperialism, leave India!" (19).

However, the exploitation of the vast rural hinterland has not been portrayed in this *Third Theatre play.* There is only a casual mention of a facet of the rural question:

> THREE: The untimely rain left all the rice rotting, our debts with the moneylenders have risen to a Mountain (24).

But the play is said to have been well-received even in the villages, despite its strong urban appeal.

4

The play *Bhoma* exposes the supremacy of the cities over the countryside which is again an important thing passed to us by the British colonialists.

India was converted into a backward agricultural country that can serve as a gigantic market for the British industrial goods. And, the rapid growth of large urban centres like Calcutta in British India was regarded with holy pride and consequently the whole administration unconsciously assumed an urban complexion. And, the *urban complexion* had no difficulty in surviving Independence in 1947 as the new political leadership emerged after 1947 was far more urban-oriented than the population as a whole. Hence, the trend accentuates discrimination against the rural areas.

Through a series of concretes borrowed from this social scenery, Sircar, in *Bhoma*, harshly exposes the spirits of the oppressed rural population against the backdrop of the *grandeur* of the city of Calcutta. He shows us how the hungry villagers' "red blood blossoms into white jasmines of rice" on the plates of the city-dwellers, twice everyday (76). The playwright was enraged by the fact that the urban community despite its own problems of distribution of food, generation of electricity and transportation could be so totally indifferent to the impoverishment of the villagers. Hence, anger, as Rustom Bharucha puts it, has come to be the driving force of *Bhoma*—a relentless, though rigourously controlled, anger directed against the well-fed, easy-going bourgeoisie of Calcutta.[10]

But Bharucha who, in the beginning, considered *Bhoma* as a play confronting "the dichotomy between urban and rural life in India," was somewhat cautious in making the following final comment on *Bhoma:*

> I can think of no other play in the Bengali theatre that makes an audience question its relation to the *oppressed people* with such emotional power and clarity.[11]

The *oppressed people* include the *Bhomas* coming in groups after groups to Calcutta (86) and living in shanty towns in the suburbs of Sealdah, Tapsia, Bediaganga, Dhapa, Kusumkumari [...] (86), and washing pots and pans in the houses of the city gentry (86), and the pavement-dwellers in *renowned* cities like Calcutta of even this twentieth century (87), and "thousands of beggars, vagrants, and refugees" who live permanently in Sealdah station.[12]

Also, the nationalised banks—

while catering to the needs of the urban elite like the proprietors of the Samson and Blackbird Co. (56-61)—

help

> the *upper class peasants* and landlords like Gadai Mitter *living in the villages* (60-61).

But they (the banks) treat alike

> a small entrepreneur like one of the Mahamaya Co. (56-58), and other poor and middle class people of the city—and— the *poor peasants* and labourers of the *villages*—

in refusing loans to them on flimsy excuses.

Thus the urban-rural dichotomy, in the final analysis, turns out to be matter that takes into account the realities of class alignments. That is why Bharucha aptly uses the term *the oppressed* in his final opinion about the play and sees similarity between Sircar's *Third Theatre* and the *Theater of the Oppressed* of Augusto Boal.[13] Bharucha might have detected that the playwright, without serious consideration, had set up in *Bhoma* a false dichotomy between the urban and rural life.

The analysis of an economist who uses the term *urban bias* for *urban-rural dichotomy*, in a similar context, is quite appropriate to be cited here. According to him, a better utilisation of rural community's resources or a more equal distribution of the agricultural produce is impeded by a number of *distortions* of a combined economic, political and social character, and these *distortions* or *biases* can be summarised under the following eight headings: the urban bias, the foreign bias, the bureaucratic bias, the capital bias, the production bias, the landlord bias, the rice bias and the private bias. He emphasises the necessity to confront the central dynamics of the society as a whole instead of eliminating one or two of the most powerful biases. He adds:

> [...] the use of the expression urban bias in no way means that the consistent *class character* of the policies should be

> overlooked. The neo-populist versions of the urban-bias concept currently in vogue even in World Bank rhetoric can be highly misleading, and may serve to obscure the fact *that basic contradiction is not between rural and urban residents but between classes—both in the countryside and in the Cities.*[14]

Even when Sircar says that—

> *Bhoma* is not a play aiming at entertaining the well-dressed front row audiences in a lush theatre. I am sure that those who do that kind of theatre will not touch my play anyway—[15]

he appears to have noticed that *Bhoma* has latent class leanings.

And, the other two plays *Stale News* and *Procession* too, relying on juxtapositions, illuminate the contradictions and disparities of the socio-economic situations examined in the plays. Thus his principle of rural-urban dichotomy turns to vague, sometime clear, class distinctions in practice.

Also, Sircar has come to find that his *Third Theatre* is "not really trying to make a synthesis" of the indigenous rural theatre and the urban theatre but is actually "directed towards evolving *a new theatre, an alternative theatre.*"[16] He has got himself into a fix and is unable to give his theatre a new name. But he has come to notice that his new theatre can truly visualise its *raison d'etre* on the streets.[17] And, it has truly come to be known as *Sircar's Street Theatre.*[18]

5

Mention must be made of Sircar's *Shukhpathe Bharater Itihas* (Indian History Made Easy), written after *Michhil* (Procession), wherein we are made to feel the continuing ethos of colonialism in India. In this play, a destitute woman who carries the Union Jack is shown, at the end, with a huge dollar sign pinned on the back of her sari.

Thus the three plays *Stale News, Procession* and *Bhoma,* originally written to meet the demands of the *Third Theatre* movement, along with *Shukhpathe Bharater Itihas,* have emanated from the traumatic postcolonial situation. Implicit in the *themes* of these plays is an appraisal of the colonial experience itself. Criticism of colonialism is the common *theme* of all these four plays which can be grouped and christened the *Colonialism quartet* of Badal Sircar. The new quartet lays bare the negative legacy of colonialism while his Calcutta quartet just presents the urban scene. Sircar's coming out of the proscenium theatre itself is an indication of his anticolonial approach because the Bengali proscenium theatre is an offshoot of the cultural subservience of a colonised people.

The socialist leader Ram Manohar Lohia had launched a movement in the 1960's *(Lohiaesque)* for the removal of the statues of the British Viceroys and generals from public places in India, whereas Sircar's new quartet asks the people to demolish the colonial culture that still pervades our society.

NOTES

1. Rustom Bharucha, *Rehearsals of Revolution: The Political Theatre of Bengal* (Calcutta: Seagull, 1983) 188.
2. Badal Sircar, *The Changing Language of Theatre* (New Delhi: ICCR, 1982) 31.
3. Badal Sircar, *The Third Theatre* (Calcutta: 1978/1983) 3.
4. Badal Sircar, *Three Plays: Procession, Bhoma, Stale News* (Calcutta: Seagull Books, 1983). Subsequent page references indicated in parentheses are to this edition.
5. Suprakash Ray, *Bharater Krishak-bidroha O Ganatanty~Samgram* 1 (Calcutta, 1966).
6. A *banian* is a native personal assistant to an English employee of the East India Company, who managed his transactions with the people of the country.
7. Ashok Mitra, "Fifteen Decades of Agrarian Changes in Bengal," *Essays in Honour of Professor S.C. Sarkar* (New Delhi: PPH, 1976) 401.
8. Ashok Mitra 397.
9. Badal Sircar, "A Letter from Badal Sircar," *The Drama Review* 26.2 (Summer 1982) 51.
10. Bharucha 174.
11. Bharucha 181.
12. Bharucha 180.
13. The Brazilian dramaturge, in his work *Theatre of the Oppressed* (New York: Urizen Books, 1979), says that the theatre may not be

"revolutionary" in itself but it is, potentially, "a rehearsal of revolution."

14. Stefan de Vylder, *Agriculture in Chains: A Case Study In Contradictions and Constraints* (London: Zed Press, 1982) 35 (emphasis added).
15. Sircar, *Three Plays* 4 & 45.
16. Badal Sircar, "Towards Third Theatre," interview with Arvind Korba, *The Deccan Chronicle* 6 Aug. 1986: MS 3.
17. Vinay Varma, "Street-Plays have a big role," *The Indian Express* 10 Aug. 1985: 7.
18. Vimal Rai Bhatnagar, "Street Theatre is Streets Apart," *Weekend Review* (March 17-23, 1987) 7.

13

DOULOTI AS A NATIONAL ALLEGORY

JAIDEV

For its action, *Douloti* (1985) one of Mahasveta Devi's Palamu novellas, keeps itself confined to Palamu district.[1] Most of its chief characters are quite ignorant of India the nation-state. Even those few of the *bandhuas* who do remember 1947 remember it for the freedom it brought to their caste-superiors. 'When you people got your independence—' is these slaves' characteristic remark and indeed most valid response to 1947.

Predictably enough, the upper-caste characters in *Douloti* are fully aware of 1947, the nation, and the new opportunities for profit that exist for them now, in post-1947 India. The novella does not grudge India or her upper castes and classes, their independence, but, being about the prevalence of slavery in post-colonial India as it is, it is at pains to demonstrate that both the nation and independence have remained in the service of the so-called Great Indians.

Mahasveta makes Douloti's 27 years a parable of post-colonial India,[2] a parable addressed to whatever/whoever professes to be the nation. Syphilis-ridden, *Douloti* dies coughing out blood in the night leading on to 15 August 1975—over the map of India. This bloody end is the sole reward she gets for 14 years of merciless exploitation in the Misras brothel. The long term of labour has yielded over 40,000 rupees but all this money has been neatly expropriated by her owners, though she was secured only for 300-odd rupees. There is no doubt whatsoever that her blood is on the independent nation.

The novella is Douloti's story—but its protagonists are innumerable Doulotis and Ganoris spread all over the nation. This drive towards national allegory explains the firm, informed authorial intrusion half-way in the narrative:

> *This bonded labour system prevails all over India.* In Andhra the people of Matangi, Jaggali, Malajangam, Mahar and other castes become Gothi. In Bihar Chamar, Nagesia, Parhaiya, Dusad become Kamiya or Seokiya. In Gujarat the Chalwaris, Naliyas, Thoris and others become Halpati. In Karnataka the low of birth become Jeetho, in Madhya Pradesh Haroyaha. In Orissa Gothi and in Rajasthan Sagri. The Chetty rayats of Tamil Nadu keep Bhumidases. In Uttar Pradesh the Bhumidas is called Maat or Khandit-Mundit or Sanjayat. The Bhumidases of the Laccadive Islands are Nadapu.

Bonded labourers are thus known by different names in different regions.

The system is slavery, and the outcastes, the harijans happen to be its victims. (*Imaginary Maps*, 61-62)

***

The facts of Douloti's existence are easy to catalogue, and they speak for themselves. Born in 1948 she is carried away openly from her village home in 1962 by a brahmin brothel-owner from a nearby town who 'incredibly' promises to marry her. The man at once offers her to Latia Sahib, an influential government contractor with a seemingly unending sexual urge for harijan girls. After Latia discards Douloti, she is passed on to another contractor, a Singh Sahib. He keeps her for over two years.

Singh's departure coincides with Paramanand Misra's sudden death. The brothel now passes on to his son, who introduces new management policies here. Unlike his 'kind' father, Baijnath Misra believes in making a fast buck. He compels each girl to take dozens of customers every night—irrespective of what such an overloading would do to them. He is a better economist and sees that it is more profitable to reduce their rates and take more customers than to have fewer customers paying more money. Of course, the girls turn into old, rickety things very fast, but then, thanks to a good drought, the 'old cows' get easily replaced.

It is thus that even though she is only in her mid-twenties, Douloti looks like an emaciated, sick, old creature. She is discharged only when she cannot attract even one-rupee customers; she is dying, of course.

When Douloti's father, Ganori Nagesia's oversight leads to the death of a bullock, Munavar yokes Ganori himself to the paddy cart. He collapses under the weight, and although he survives, his back is permanently broken. Hence his popular name Tedha Nagesia. Hence also Munavar's ready release of him from bondage for three hundred rupees.

The novella duplicates Ganori Nagesia's career in his daughter. Both are *bandhua* slaves. His pointless release turns his daughter into a bonded prostitute. The system is illegal, but is practised in broad daylight and offers lavish returns to *bandhua* owners.

The novella does not permit the reader the consolation that the *bandhua* system is restricted to the countryside only. Bono, a Seora harijan, thinks he is going to be free as a worker in Dhanbad colliery. But once there, he realizes that he is now the labour-contractor's *bandhua.* The contract labour is fleeced by everyone, the shopkeeper, the moneylender, the post office staff, and the contractor's goons.

Relating his experiences at Dhanbad, Bono says, 'Government-*Union*-contractor-slum landlord-shopkeeper-post office, each is the other's friend' (*Imaginary Map*s, 24). This is a neat description of how exploitation creates a whole intricate circuit of vested interests.

To talk of Douloti is also to talk of numerous other characters both high and low. The 85 page-long novella is epical and contains almost an equal number of identifiable characters, besides many unnamed choral figures, whose narratives intersect Douloti's. Each such character has a narrative of his or her own;

it exists in dear outlines so that the reader can easily fill in the details. For example, Somni, a fellow-prostitute, tells Douloti how she was brought to the brothel to repay by her earning the loan her husband had taken in the village. Somni, however, is trapped in the brothel: She cannot go back home because she has already borne Latia Sahib three sons. They are beggars, and she has no money. She is allowed to leave the brothel when she is a mere skeleton, and a deranged one at that. By that time, she has lost her beggar-sons, too.

Douloti is certainly important in her own right, important as a tragically blighted life, but she is even more important as the site on which a whole variety of 'the Great Indian Meaning'—mythological, historical, socio-cultural, class, casteist and gender—converges as a set of operative, oppressive forces. It is in their astonishing range that these forces turn *Douloti* into a national allegory, or, rather, an elaborate chargesheet against the nation.

A number of the high characters openly, brazenly project themselves as affiliated to gods. They include Parmanand Misra alias Sankatnarayan; the priest Hanuman Misra; Parmanand's assistant, the bawd Rampiari, and another brothel-owner named Kishanji. Munavar—which in Persian means the bright, the dazzling—calls himself a cream-white creation of God. This band of predators flaunt their divine pedigree, projecting the predicament of the *bandhuas* as something divinely ordained, ordained right at the moment of their birth. Who can blame the victims if they have got the whole oppressive mythology introjected?

History as memory reinforces this vicious mythology. Prior to Independence, the local prince fleeced village harijans to indulge in gambling! Post-colonial India has seen the abolition of princely regimes but has ironically multiplied the number of unofficial, uncrowned princes, including the District Collector and local police. Internal colonizers have been flourishing all along.

The Great Indians are starkly imaged in Munavar, as he yokes Ganori to his cart, flourishing the whip. Like Munavar, the

Misra brothel-owners keep indiscriminately loading upon the bodies of their prostitutes customer after customer, until the girls are mere wrecks or die. The image they use for the girls is lorries or trucks. They must be loaded to the full, must keep plying non-stop, must ply as fast as they can.

It is not that things have not changed since 1947. Only exploitation as a system has not faced any extensive, sustained threat. If anything, it has grown more and more sophisticated and repressive. In the 1962 elections, Munavar names his candidate—and he wins. In the next elections, though, he has raised a private army of goons for election duty. In the town during the 1960s, Parmanand Misra does not altogether neglect the health of his *bandhua randis*, but his successor, during the next decade treats them as trucks deserving no maintenance simply because it is better to discard the creaking ones and obtain new ones. During the 1960s Kishanji is benevolent to his 'fleet' of prostitutes but in the 1970s he takes to selling off women and children in markets far away: the new line involves fewer hassles. In a parallel development, the state-owned collieries stop recruiting regular labour and instead entrust the task of supplying labour to contractors who treat the workers as *bandhuas* and maintain discipline with the help of professional goons. This history is the underbelly of the development story that passes for official post-colonial history.

Mahasveta introduces over a dozen *bandhua randis* at the Misras' brothel. Each is similarly trapped here, and yet they are all distinct individual beings, each with her distinct past and in some cases at least, with a distinct set of aspirations. Kalawati died in the brothel—because she was not allowed to recover from abortion by Latia Sahib. Douloti is luckier than her in that while she is bleeding following abortion, the Indo-China conflict keeps Latia Sahib busy on a different front. Somni's tragedy has already been mentioned. Revti and Gohumani have equally poignant tales of their own. Then, there is Jhalo with her black magic who bullies Rampiari into sharing her secret savings with the prostitutes. She is determined to see to it that unlike herself and her *bandhua* husband back in the village, their daughter does not become a *bandhua*. None of the prostitutes is capable of defying the structure of exploitation. Even so, they are not identical either in their individual consciousness or capacity for rebellion. Mahasveta does not expect a revolution to begin in the brothel, but she carefully makes us see that the victims are not mere types.

A similar characterization strategy is seen at work with regard to the male *bandhuas* in Seora. Ganori Nagesia cannot ever question or think of changing what he assumes to be God's law. Old Bhuneswar has turned into a cynical quietist after a lifetime of exposure to the landlordly ways. Bono, however, is always willing to try new, liberatory ways. On the other hand, we have Mohan Dusadh, an intensely superstitious fatalist. In the same way, even the high-caste characters are not painted in the same colour even when they go all out to curb dissent. Munavar's son does not approve of the father's crude feudal ways. Kishan is more 'enlightened' and more in tune with time than the Misras. Mahasveta does not deny her various characters their individual slants, although, of course, these exist within the severe constraints of their location within the structure.

Munavar, Latia, Kishanji, the Misras, the labour-contractor in Dhanbad, the official machinery, the priests, the Deputy Collector, etc.—all constitute the Great Indian Meaning in practice. This Meaning ropes in all kinds of motifs, ranging from Lord Rama's treatment of Shambhuk to Mahatma Gandhi's 'deservedly'[3] violent end, to legitimize an ideology in which those who are weak or marginal not only have no means of escape but are actually expected to be grateful to their exploiters. This Meaning arguably perverts whatever motifs it picks up from mythology or history, but its perversions are more the norm than aberrations. In any case, they work!

Resistance develops to the Great Indian Meaning but alas, in spite of New Delhi, Patna, or social research centres. It develops, simply because it is in the nature of injustice to give rise to resistance, although side by side the ever more effective means of repression are also fashioned out by those favouring the status-quo. Not only does the arrival of the Naxalites on the scene bring in a great number of police, para-military and military forces, but even the contractors and landlords raise their private armies.

In a scene far, far superior to the ending of *Untouchable*, the statements of *bandhua randis* at the Misra brothel are solicited by Father Bomfuller, a missionary collecting facts about bonded labour for submission to the Government of India. The priest is accompanied by four concerned persons.

Father Bomfuller is appalled to learn how an initial investment of three-hundred-and-fifty rupees has generated a profit of over 40,000 rupees to the Misras without there being any prospect of freedom for Douloti. Now follow several exchanges between his four companions.

The Gandhian Puran Chand recommends peaceful fasting to transform the hearts of evil-doers. When Bono asks him if he would have resorted only to such fasting if the honour of his own female relatives was at stake, Puran Chand dismisses the question saying that the women of his caste are never dishonoured. Mohan Srivastava cannot shed his faith in the constitutionally elected governments. He hopes that the governments would act and eradicate social evils.

The most crucial characters in the brothel scene are Prasad Mahato and Bono. Prasad Mahato is a harijan himself, and his encounter with Douloti and other *bandhua randis* alters him permanently. Realizing the futility of peaceful demonstrations and of rattling off appeals to government departments, he goes underground and forms the Palamu Bonded Labour Liberation Front in 1971 with active support from the Naxalites.

All his life, Bono has been a free-floater, an escape artist of sorts, escaping *bandhua* slavery but otherwise not at all able to act except in an improvisatory manner. All along, though, he has been reflecting, learning, and clarifying things to himself. In some ways he is the true protagonist: for he keeps learning and changing, learning to change and to act. He learns from the outsiders how big is the community of *bandhuas,* and he informs them, including Mohan Srivastava the teacher, that while the harijans do borrow money from money lending rajputs for marriage or other social ceremonies, the reason for their inability to pay back the debts lies in their not having any land of their own. The point is that Bono develops into a thinking being with the help of others to whom, in turn, he imparts several ground lessons.

Something similar can be imagined taking place between the Naxalites and Prasad Mahato. Prasad is wanted by the police, and is of course involved in radical activities. Still, he is clear that the battle has to be fought on several fronts. He knows that although nothing can be changed by the laws alone, it is nevertheless important to fight for just laws. If the laws are just, then their radical action will be for their implementation, and thus look more credible. If just laws are enacted, then more Mohan Srivastavas will come out in support of the radical groups.

Of all those present in the brothel scene, it is Prasad and Bono who most feel Douloti's suffering. Bono understands the language of her fingers as these gently caress his calloused feet. In spite of having lived some thirteen years in this hard place, she behaves towards him as a near kin. Hardly any words are exchanged between them, but they each understand the other. It is difficult to convey in words the impact of the poignant, mute interaction between Douloti and Bono. I can only say that it is one of the most tragic, sheer lyrical and utterly unforgettable moments in world literature.

A seemingly minor detail in the brothel scene deserves attention. In spite of his correct belief that the police and the state government are on his side, Baijnath Misra does feel scared as soon as Father Bomfuller mentions the Government in New Delhi. The moral is that if only they develop a social conscience and resolve to enforce justice, the Government and the police could effectively end so much of oppression. Mahasveta does not have any illusions about the nation-state or its so-called democratic apparatus, but she does not wish to carelessly dismiss these. She also feels that although Srivastava is distant from

Douloti both in caste and class terms, it is better to have a Mohan Srivastava than no Mohan Srivastava, even perhaps a Father Bomfuller than no Father Bomfuller. Mahasveta knows how limited such moral supporters or fact-gatherers usually are, but she does not believe in a rigid, exclusionary agenda according to which one is either totally on one's side or else is an enemy.

The above statement should not be interpreted as indicative of condescension on her part. Mohan Srivastava does not join radical politics, but he does risk his security by helping Prasad Mahato rather than the police; and in doing so, he willingly 'loses' the official reward! A tiny act this, but then each tiny act helps. Bono, who offers his services to Prasad, is much too old for any real action. Still Prasad welcomes him. He too will be contributing his tiny share to the movement.

The organic intellectual emerges from within the oppressed group. One becomes an organic intellectual with the help of experience, observation, reflection. Prasad Mahato proves to be as willing to learn from and collaborate with the sympathetic outsiders as he is to impart them his ground-based wisdom.

The most important moral *Douloti*, like several of Mahasveta's tales, holds out is this: all those who fight on behalf of the victims fight equally, if not more, on behalf of their own conscience. The Naxalites are deservedly the heroes of post-colonial India, because their conscience responds to it as a human collectivity. Their sacrifices are sacrifices offered in the hope that this nation can be civilized, made to learn the basic lessons in human decency.

***

In a rejoinder to Fredric Jameson's thesis about Third-World texts all of which he says should be read as national allegories,[4] Aijaz Ahmad has asserted that collectivities in the specific sense of classes and social formations are as relevant categories in postcolonial societies as they are in the First or the Second World. Ahmad's rejoinder is actually more sharply against the currently dominant post-modernist and post-structuralist positions according to which nation and nationalism are imaginary, obsolete, or irrelevant categories, are 'mere myths of origin and [...] essentialist coercive totalizations' (Ahmad, 1993: 12). Ahmad, like Edward Said,[5] does not see the nation as an irrelevant category—but does not allow it to eclipse the more basic categories like class and relations of production, either. Nations have often been coercive but there is nothing to stop them from being progressive or revolutionary (Ahmad 11).

The term national allegory is not gratuitous, although it makes more sense if we remember the following: 1. It is universal in application rather than restricted only to Third World texts; 2. Not all texts are national allegories, although in many texts the nation intrudes through astonishingly transformed motifs and patterns; 3. National allegories are not necessarily xenophobic, chauvinistic or issued out as character certificates for the nation; 4. They, more often than not, do proceed along the specific lines of class, caste, gender, and region,[6] and as such can effectively subject the nation to merciless scrutiny, put it on trial, as it were, instead of reifying or fetishizing it as something beyond interrogation; 5. Where they score heavily over sociology or history is in the fact that they are often successful in complexifying issues like caste, gender and class by suggesting that even the similar victims of a system need not manifest an identical level of consciousness or of capacity for praxis; 6. It is not at all necessary for national allegories to resort to that kind of rhetoric which takes the form of: 'Ask not what your country can do for you.'

One has to be wary of many an arrogant post-structuralist exercise in debunking the nation, aimed at wishing away the Third-World nationalism on the ground its origins or its having been hijacked by a flawed nationalist bourgeosie. Whenever or however we might have turned into a nation, indeed whenever or for whatever sinister purpose we might have been inspired to turn into a nation, the nation-state today is a realized fact, albeit admittedly a badly realized fact acutely in need of redefinition and negotiation right at the conceptual level. The postmodernist globalism that seeks to render nation irrelevant is too much in complicity with a multinational consumerism in which the rights of the consumer are the lone consideration, not those of the citizen.[7] As such, that globalism is utterly unresponsive to all such chunks of humanity as are not market-worthy. Honestly, one sees very little evidence in practice of the First World having truly outgrown its nationalist habits of the heart. Given a crisis, it can anyway always resurrect nationalism if that would help even the so-called multinational corporations. Post-structuralist theory, like any theory for that matter, might be quite out of step with the way things really are. Mahasveta Devi depicts realities which are often the obverse of the conditions that sustain such theoretical globalism. Very comfortably-placed intelligent people can work the nation-state to their maximum advantage and then 'forget' it for the sake of going global; their preferred range notwithstanding, the nation-state continues to exist and work for them. Mahasveta's harijans and tribals are often ignorant of India or 1947, but the blows that continue to batter and cripple them generation after generation are administered by the nation-state; the nation again continues to exist. Theory, to that extent, is no magic wand with which historically generated realities can be exercised.

In any case, our national victims can hardly appeal to global corporations or agencies to protect them. Their local communities are of no help to them, as seen from the landlord, the police, the forest officers, the priests, and so on. They get no justice from Patna. Even New Delhi sides with the oppressors. Still, all these oppressors are specific, concrete enough to protest against, to wage a struggle against. Most specifically, how many countries beyond India would be able to even comprehend the concept or mechanism involved in the practice of owning *bandhua randis*? Even if these were explained to them, how many multinational corporations would oppose the practice when such people have no status whatsoever as consumers? Even if some international groups decide to take up their cause, the remedies still have to be routed through the nation-state. Mahasveta Devi has realism enough to concentrate on the concrete, instead of generalizing the issue to such an extent that its hard outlines get all but totally blurred. The fact that *Douloti* ends with its focus on the Indian map should be enough to prove how terrible but still how specific India remains for her Doulotis and Ganori Nagesias.

Mahasveta Devi sees no practical use of abandoning national terms of discourse. She is insistent that her tales are parables of India, national allegories along the collective lines of class, caste, gender and tribe. She is against being termed either merely a Bengali writer or a writer of subaltern fiction. She insists that she is an Indian writer.[8]

Douloti also allows us to infer another strong logic behind Mahasveta's 'obsession' with the nation. This reason is of different order. The novella can be read as a plea for that nation to be defined by the victims rather than by the ruling, parasitic groups. The nation as a concept is not to be dumped, it is only to be saved from the self-styled Bharat Bhagya Vidhatas. There is no doubt that much vision, much imagination and intelligence, much over determination has made the nation as we have it today: after all, all kinds of significances from Lord Ram down to Mahatma Gandhi, from predestination to efficient management policies, from fear of hell to fear of police have contributed to the vicious, repressive entity that the nation is today. Let the victims' alternative vision, imagination, intelligence, and culture—all their resources and potential energy which are not allowed expression or realization—be given a try. To put it more correctly, the novella is a plea for a radical change at the structural level so that the alternative vision is able to fashion out a more decent, less asymmetrical India.

Let me refer in brief to one of the core motifs present throughout the novella, namely *mamatva*, maternal, protective regard. This motif is invariably associated with the victims, both male and female. Bono's hands kill the rapist-goon in Dhanbad, because the goon arouses no *mamatva* in him, because he does not appear to be any mother's son. Later, as Bono is being held captive in the house of the ruthless landlord, he finds that Munavar arouses no soft feelings in him, that Munavar, too, does not strike as any mother's son. Latia Sahib rapes Douloti repeatedly every night, and while the girl faints, he keeps, devouring her, making grunting noises like a pig. Later Douloti wonders if the man has a heart at all. In contrast, she goes very maternal while caressing Bono's calloused feet, in the brothel scene. It is her unrealized maternal affection that similarly makes her donate part of her secret savings so Somni can buy some bread for her beggar-children. One has only to contrast such low characters as Douloti and Bono with the landlord Munavar's enormous wife, who quite candidly says that she cannot identify with anyone except herself, anyone in this case including her son and his wife. *Mamatva* is a value, although in the given order it doesn't have any; this is Mahasveta's way of reinforcing her call for an alternative structure, a structure in which *mamatva*, together with the tender poetry it generates, would have value!

The female farm-labourers reaping the wheat crop in Munavar's farm break into a short collective song whenever they think of Bono:

> In the wheat farm has landed
> a pretty yellow bird
> and inside, its beak is so red, so red!
>
> (Section I; my translation)

Taken as such, the lines touch us by their delicate lyricism. However, they are themselves framed between two contextual details. The first relates to the reason why they suddenly start singing: they dare not talk about Bono's flight from bondage but his daring nevertheless occupies their thoughts. Bono stands for daring as well as freedom. The other detail follows the song and shows the women's young children each 'picking up wheat grains one at a time—quite like the birds' (*Imaginary Maps*, 22). The tenderness for the birds is an extension of the women's tenderness, their *matritva*, for their own brood. Bono is the bird in the children; being himself capable of *mamatva*, he becomes the recipient of *mamatva*.

Motherhood, maternal solicitude for one's children being extended to free, sweet little birds, memory of Bono the rebel leading to a song about the free bird whose delightful sight seems to get doubled in the children's—all these details interfuse around the song, which, in its own right, is an authentic proof of the villagers' culture-making, creative capacity.

***

This is not exactly the occasion to discuss the literary features of *Douloti,* but since the *mamatva* motif has taken us into its form, there is perhaps no harm in noting that in its superb control of sympathy and distance, in its use of parody, caricature and 'alienation effects,' and in its sensational swerves between stylistic registers, the novella is a highly self-conscious text. While it is true that Mahasveta always prioritizes her urgent human themes over form and technique, one ought not to assume that she is indifferent to the latter. For *Douloti* is brilliant in its subversive parodies, its careful use of motifs such as freedom, lack of freedom, and the freedom to deny others all freedom; fairy tale versus reality; hands and burdens; its sharp contrasts as between Douloti's and Latia's expressions of naturalness; and its images of birds and beasts as well as of carts and trucks; and also in its narrational swerves and principled indirection. Consider, for example, the narrator's apparently casual but very deliberate, loaded statement at the beginning of section VII that her story is not really about Bono's and Prasad Mahato's transformation into radical beings or about how Mohan Srivastava would help Prasad, not the police. The novella ends with a shattered Mohan Srivastava facing Douloti's corpse on the national map, and the narrator wondering what he will do now. From this end-perspective, though, we realize the significance of the earlier, casually tendered information about Bono, Prasad and Mohan. In that bit of information, the last question stands already answered. There is nothing casual about her casual interventions or flash-forwards. If anything, these are a 'formal' expression of her regard, her *mamatva,* for the redeemable characters: she is not the one to deny them their 'whole' stories, even if the ending cannot quite accommodate them.

I should like to conclude this essay be referring to the seven insets in *Douloti,* each stylized, formally isolated from the main narrative, each an apparent case of alienation technique. These insets demonstrate her careful discrimination between the three distinct kinds of voices in the narrative, namely the exploiter's, the victims' and the narrator's. The reason why the narrator decides to foreground her own voice in this way is that Douloti as the narrator's performance is acutely concerned with two all important questions: does a non-dalit writer have the right to tell a dalit story? and if yes, then how does she go about it?[9]

There are two inset speeches allowed to Parmanand Misra and Munavar Chandela. Parmanand projects himself as a modern Sankatnarayan, and Munavar harps shamelessly on his innate, god-given kindness (*dayaluta* and *daya*). Both marshal gods to their side. Their rhetoric is mythical, self-justificatory, and patriarchal, aimed at forcing the victims into abject surrender to their wishes.

In complete contrast to the terms of discourse evident in these two 'high' and pompous speeches, there are four songs, the first a two line verse from Ganori to his 'imagined', apparently superior but actually unsympathetic and unimaginative, bespectacled interlocutor, and the next two directly sung by the harijan women. The fourth is a song delivered by the narrator to introduce Parmanand's *bandhua randis*. It comes in response, comes as an informed response, to Douloti's query regarding the status of the other inmates here. It is addressed as much to the audience/listeners/readers as to Douloti, and is in the form of the narrator's anguished but knowledgeable response to the refrain: 'Whose *maats* are all these young girls here?' It has none of the flush supernatural bombast that dominates the brothel-owner's emancipatory rhetoric. It reinforces the exact parallel between Munavar the landlord and Parmanand the brothel owner. More importantly, the song includes details from Himalayan regions where *bandhua* are called *maats*. Such an informed perspective is not possible to the girls or even to Rampiari. The song thus extends the range of reference for the otherwise specific, localized story.

If this song prepares the way for national allegory, the other intervention by the narrator—in hard, factual prose—makes the reader grasp the logic of the nation-wide phenomenon. The kind of perspective and analytic skill seen in it are offered to the reader as a necessary bit of social instruction.

To the reader, I repeat. For the intervention comes in the wake of the narrator's fierce rebuttal of what the social scientists dole out as the neat, well-footnoted explanations of the *bandhua* practice. The narrator sums up their whole approach: they come to research the phenomenon and end up laying the blame on the victims themselves. She is caustic towards the methodological sleight-of-hand used by social researchers who 'would tour the district for statistics and then conclude that all these sections had become bonded labourers only because of hassles connected with marriage and religious rituals, thus carefully avoiding any mention of the fact that all those whom the landlords made their slaves were invariably small farmers.'

Having countered this motivated social research, the narrator now offers the following inset intervention. Its tone is blistering, dangerous; it remains unfinished in a most ominous way:

> All such scholars need Government support and the Government needs the support of landlords! Land-owning-moneylenders are a neo-landlord caste—and this caste has been created by the Government of Independent India. This government needs the support of land-owning-moneylenders, for what are Bhilai and Bokaro and Jamshedpur after all? Nothing, their contribution is really nothing to the Government purse. The Government exchequer is sustained by agriculture land, and that land has landlords for its real rulers! These princes and rulers of agriculture and land need free labour and free land, that's why they come out like warriors and turn people into bonded slaves and servants and labourers. But really uncovering and propagating such facts is illegal, because [...].
>
> (my translation)

The unfinished passage supplies a larger structural perspective to the specific patterns of exploitation in evidence in Palamu. It is also the most unambiguous indictment of the

Government for its complicity with, and encouragement of, the neo-princes and neo-rulers. Finally, the last, unfinished sentence posits a conscientious, truth-telling writer against the entire state apparatus. The abrupt termination of her sentence offers a kind of irony Mahasveta absolutely loves: apparently stopping her radical, subversive outburst because it is illegal, but really stopping not until she has performed a total demystification of the nation-state. If such seething demystifications strike some critics as unaesthetic, well, that only shows how necessary it is for us to modify our aesthetics.

What this hard-hitting inset reveals is a macro-perspective, an understanding of the structural logic, which is not available to the harijan characters for self-evident reasons. For less acceptable reasons, that kind of a perspective is often not available to the literate, supposedly knowledgeable sections of our privileged population, either. The inset is nothing less than a rebuke to them. This perspective is offered in the hope that they would review their location *vis-a-vis* both the nation and its victims. It is offered in the hope that they will undergo the necessary, humanizing change of heart and develop some ethical responsibility, some love for the victims.[10] That is how, one may argue, Mahasveta justifies her own position as an interpreter of, a spokesperson for, her *bandhua* friends. The effort is to be of some use to them, not just because it is a good cause, but because this is the only way for her to justify herself. The need is her own even before it is theirs.

Mahasveta Devi is the most disturbing writer India has ever produced. She is also our most necessary writer, simply because she lashes us out of complacence in the way conscience is supposed to do. It is important to remember that she is not only a writer. There is no division between the artist who creates and the person who suffers, works for ensuring justice to the sections who have long been victims, among others, of an appalling national ingratitude. Both her life and her fiction demonstrate beyond question the possibility of a non-dalit, middle-class person to earn the right to write the dalit. But there is no easy route to such a right. It is not even claimed as a right; nor is it earned by dissolving one's own identity as a non-dalit or a middle-class person. One remains what one is: and then one acts in every possible way to legitimize one's existence as a decent, socially conscientious, thinking being. The rest takes care of itself, for any efforts to preserve conscience leads one away from one's cosy class, hurries one down to the victims, pushes one against the numerous structures of torture that are the badges of identity for our nation. There is, in short, no disjunction between Mahasveta's art and her activism. For her art is intervention, an act of retrieving the corpses from beneath the apparently charming-looking national spots as well as of visualizing a better, more humane nation. To cling to any dehistoricized, universalist formalism while reading Mahasveta is only to highlight one's own Nero-like location rather than to say something sensible about her art.

NOTES

1. Mahasveta Devi, *Imaginary Maps* (Calcutta: Thema, 1993) 61-62. Cf. Mahasveta Devi: "The Palamu I have depicted in my stories [...] is a mirror of tribal India; and I have named the village Seora. But there are such villages everywhere in Palamu [...]. Douloti is still true, and true for the rest of India [...]. Decolonization has not reached the poor. That is why these things happen. Women are just merchandise commodities [...]. For the flesh trade all you have to invest is two saris, a bit of food, some trinkets, and a bit of money for the parents. Poverty, poverty, poverty," *Imaginary Maps*, pp. iv, xiii-xiv. Also cf. *Palamu*: 'any number of terms exist for the *bandhuas*-sevakie, kamia, harwaha, charvaha, etc. Such is the custom that they remain in lifelong debt.

   Of these, the lot of dharmaru *bandhuas* is the most pitiable. Palamu is a place where anything goes. In itself Palamu is a microcosm of India.' In *Douloti* (Hindi), 117.

   Also cf. Mahasveta: 'Using Palamu as an example, I have revealed again and again the exact shape of India's land owning system and feudal class divisions.' *Bhumika, Rudali* (Calcutta: Dey's Publishing, 1993) 5.
2. *Douloti* is available in both Hindi and English translations. The Hindi translation, by Dilip Kumar Banerjee, is included in a collection of three of Mahasveta Devi's Palamu tales entitled *Douloti* (New Delhi: Radhakrishna, 1987), pp. 9-95; the English translation, by Gayatri Chakravorty Spivak, is titled "Douloti the Bountiful" and

is included in Mahasveta Devi, *Imaginary Maps* (Calcutta: Thema, 1993) 19-95. I find the Hindi translation the more reliable, but for quotations in this paper have mostly adapted Spivak's. I have italicized all those words in quotations which I have substituted in place of Spivak's.

3. Hanuman Mishra, the priest in the nearby town, is categorical that although Gandhi was 'a truly great soul,' his deeds were foul: "He went to the infidel country England, and in Africa during the Boer War he also carried infidel corpses [...]. He died so terribly because he made these mistakes. He did not get a house in old age, *nor was* served by his son or cared for by his wife [...]. Caste differences, untouchability—these are God's rules" (*Imaginary Maps,* 39).
4. Fredric Jameson, "Third World Literature in the Era of Multinational Capitalism," *Social Text* 15 (Fall 1986): Aijaz Ahmad, "Jameson's Rhetoric of Otherness and the 'National Allegory'" (1987), rpt. in Ahmad, *In Theory: Classes, Nations, Literatures* (London: Verso, 1993) 95, 122, esp. 102, 107, 110, 112-20; see also Ahmad's remarks in "Introduction: Literature Among the Signs of Our Time," 11-12.
5. See Edward Said, *Culture and Imperialism* (London: Chatto & Windus, 1992) 256.
6. Cf. Gayatri C. Spivak on "'Standayini': Here the representation of India is by way of the subaltern as metaphor." Breast-giver: for author, reader, teacher, subaltern, historian [...], in Mahasveta Devi, *Breast Stories,* trans. Spivak (Calcutta: Seagull, 1997) 79. Also cf. Mahasveta Devi: "'Standayini' is a parable of India after decolonization." Unpublished intervention, Subaltern Studies Conference, Calcutta, Jan. 9, 1986, quoted in *Breast Stories,* 78.
7. I am indebted to Javeed Alam for this insight.
8. 'Mahasveta Devi: In Conversation with Amar Mitra and Sabyasachi Deb,' *Indian Literature* 179 (May-June 1997) 163.
9. These questions trouble a great many concerned but non-dalit citizens. Gayatri C. Spivak argues that there is nothing wrong at all in a non-dalit speaking on behalf of the subalterns—since unlike their ontology, which belongs to themselves, their epistemology might often be accessible only to a specialist. I feel ambivalent, indeed quite skeptical, about this otherwise very attractive distinction. See my 'This Fiction is Injurious to Illusions,' *Indian Review of Books* (16 June-15 July 1997) 3.
10. The most poignant expression of this hope is in *Pterodactyl, Puran Sahay and Pirtha.* Cf. Puran: To build (the communication-point with the tribals) you must love beyond reason for a long time. For a few thousand years we haven't loved them, respected them [...]. Only love, excruciating, explosive love can still dedicate us to this

work when the century's sun is in the Western sky, otherwise this aggressive civilization will have to pay a terrible price, look at history, the aggressive civilization has destroyed itself in the name of progress, each time. 'In *imaginary Maps* 197. Gayatri C. Spivak's useful term for this love is ethical responding—a two way road; 206.

14

RECOVERY OF THE SUBORDINATE SELF: POSTCOLONIAL PROBLEMATICS IN *DEVIL ON THE CROSS*, *JAGUA NANA* AND *SULA*

ASHOK K. MOHAPATRA

Over the past few years postcoloniality has emerged as a site of theoretical and creative engagement with the nature of the identity of the subordinate self, the mode of its counter-discourse and the possibility of its recovery in a state of equitable power-relation, where the strong do not dominate, oppress and exploit the weak. Postcolonial literary theories render the prospect of such recovery doubtful. The intricate quibbling over post-colonial/postcolonial (Mishra & Hodge 1991) and the argument (McClintock 1992) that post-colonialism brings back all over again the ghost of colonialism and the whole range of its oppressive binaries like self-other, metropolis-colony and centre-periphery are a case in point. Added to these is Aijaz Ahmad's argument that 'Third-Worldism,' the vanguard of postcolonial movement, is itself effected through the mediation of metropolitan pedagogy (Ahmad 45). Should one then lose one's heart? Certainly not.

There is nonetheless some hope since the metropolitan academy does acknowledge the presence of oppositional voices from marginal locations, and indeed, this acknowledgement of the presence of the Other is a precondition for "reciprocal recognition," a Hegelian process through which the subordinate self finds a scope to define its identity and its marginal location. Fanon elucidates this process thus:

> Man is human only to the extent to which he tries to impose his existence on another man in order to be recognized by him [...]. It is on that another being, on recognition of that other being that his human worth and reality depend (Fanon 216-17).

The subordinate self desires to have an ideal dialectical interlocking with the Other. But this desire is fraught with the danger that the state of mutual recognition is likely to be supplanted by a unidirectional recognition, where the dominant Other gets the upper hand, and the subordinate self loses its voice and the right to define itself. But then the subordinate self does challenge, interrogate and write back to the Other through a radical gesture of self-acknowledgement, notwithstanding the futility of this exercise. Even if it resigns to a state of silence, or dies, it still gestures towards the ideal condition of reciprocal recognition, in which at least the possibility of its recovery obtains.

In this paper I would like to discuss three separate modes of self-acknowledgement in three novels, namely *Devil on the Cross* by Ngugi wa Thiong'o, *Jagua Nana* by Cyprian Ekwensi and *Sula* by Toni Morrison. The three female protagonists of these novels exemplify them. These novels have little in common in terms of themes, focuses, narrative structure and individual beliefs as well as imperatives of the authors. Morrison is a "black woman writer"—so she prefers to be called—from America, while Ngugi and Ekwensi are from Nigeria and Kenya respectively. The divergence of their novels makes up for a highly variegated terrain where the gesture of postcoloniality is played out in varying forms and with varying implications. Their postcoloniality is predicated, among others, on the questions they pose to the novelistic traditions within which they emerge.

Ngugi wrote *Devil on the Cross* in the Gikuyu language sometime between 31 December 1977 and 12 December 1978, during the period of his detention without trial in Kimati

Maximum Security Prison. This novel was purported on the one hand as a corrective to the image of Africa in colonial writings and on the other hand a curative to the post-independence mind-set of the Kenyan comprador bourgeoisie. On being asked to write a book in 1967 on the social life of the European settlers in Kenya, Ngugi discovered that the views, assumptions and fantasies of colonial settlers about the country had remained as deeply entrenched in Kenyan literature as ever. This country figured as a "vast erotic dream land" in the works of Karen Blixen and as a winter-free landscape of eternal leisure and physical pleasure in those of Gerald Henley (Ngugi, *Detained* 29-31). The full-throated celebration of care-free settler life had erased the history of colonial brutality and the voice of the oppressed. Christianity served mostly as a palliative to the oppressed and was promoted in collusion with colonial rule, a culture of unquestioning submission to authority. Ngugi reacted against all these and revived a very vivid sense of history of the Gikuyu people in his novels. He used folklore, legends, myths and prophesies to not only narrativize the local history, but also reinterpret biblical myths and symbols to interrogate the imperialist history.

Jacinta Warringa evolves within the disgraceful history of post-independence Kenya to empower herself. Born in 1953, during the worst period of colonial oppression, she is separated from her parents, who are sent away to jail. She grows up to be seduced by her uncle and then to be forced into prostitution. She is impregnated by a 'Rich Old Man' from Ngorika, who later deserts her. She attempts suicide, but fails. Later she takes up a secretarial job in a multinational company in Nairobi, but she is given the sack for refusing sexual favours to her boss Kihara. After wading through many difficulties, she becomes an automobile engineer and attains economic independence as well as respectability. In fact it is through Jacinta that Ngugi envisions the new Kenyan woman who breaks the colonial stereotype of a woman, whose only job is to "make bed and spread her legs in the market of love" (*DC* 218). In the climax of the novel, Warringa kills the father of her fiancé on the day of their wedding as the prospective father-in-law turns out to be the same old man who had once impregnated and deserted her. Warringa's murder of the old man is a decisive gesture of self-assertion. This is corroborated by the fact that she chooses to dress herself in the traditional Gikuyu costume at this fateful moment. It is the moment of Warringa's reprisal as an agent of postcolonial history, and she is prepared to face the consequences of her action.

In the *Prison Diary*, Ngugi admits that he had with him, during the period of detention, the photograph of his daughter Njooki, which means someone who has come back from the dead. About the same time Warringa took shape in the toilet papers which Ngugi used for writing the novel. Both Njooki and Warringa were conflated in his imagination.

> Njooki, a picture sent through post, and Warringa, a picture created on the rationed toilet paper, have been more than a thousand trumpets silently breaking through the fortified walls of Kimati Maximum Security Prison to assure me that I am not alone; Warringa, by constantly making me conscious of my connection with history, and Njooki, by constantly making me aware that I am now in prison because of Kamirithu and its people (Ngugi, *Detained* 27-28).

Warringa develops as a figural extension of Njooki, and both women are invested with a radical self-consciousness filtered through a sense of history. Besides, Warringa turns her body into a metaphor of resistance through suppression of sexuality as she declares: "these are not times for decorating our bodies with necklaces and perfume [...]. These are times for keeping our bodies and minds in a state of readiness" (*DC* 242).

Ekwensi's *Jagua Nana* deals with female body as a metaphor of sexual subjugation, which a woman must overcome as an act of acknowledgement of independent self-hood. This novel is not polemical like Ngugi's, and Ekwensi had none of Ngugi's revolutionary agenda.

Jagua Nana tells the story of Jagua, an ageing prostitute, who frequents Tropicana, a sleazy night club in Lagos, and roams the streets in search of customers. Despite her casual affairs with many men she holds on to young Freddie. She is fixated on him as if he were her son. And yet she needs him as a husband in future when men will no longer desire her. But Freddie deserts her and marries a young girl.

The story of her life, like those of other prostitutes in African novels, is a sad commentary on the economic, political and moral rot in the post-independence African cities. The urban reality featuring corrupt politicians, corpulent businessmen, contractors and hoodlums finds full expression in this novel as these people form a nexus through sex and money. The colonial legacy of flesh trade thus finds fresh impetus in this environment. The rural woman runs away to the city from the economically ruined countryside and accepts the fate of a subordinate self to be sexually exploited by powerful men. Jagua revels in her sensuality under the male voyeuristic gaze and flaunts her anatomical assets to influence men of rank and power. But this power of hers is a gloss over the fact that she comes into being only as a body in the eye of the male voyeurism before a mirror. This amounts to her collusion with the male gazer to reduce herself to an object of desire. There are several instances of her gazing at herself in the mirror in the presence of a man (*JN* 5 & 111). But she overcomes this state of bondage and also the son-fixation through maternity, and thus exonerates herself from the stigma of barrenness. Although the baby boy she gives birth to does not survive, his name Nnochi has a significance to Jagua's life. It means 'replacement.' In fact, her old life gets replaced by a new one in her native place. She looks "fresh and sweet [...] and completely one with Ogabu forest" (*JN* 192). She reintegrates herself with her community, women of Onitsha. This thought fills her with a dream of self-sufficiency and liberty. She thus dreams at the end of the novel with her mother and Rosa, a friend for company. She also wonders "how good" it is "to be dreaming" (*JN* 192). This dream involves neither narcissism nor any fixation. Further, Jagua is now in the company of the women, not men. She thinks about the dream as she dreams and thereby suggests the sense of conscious self-hood which she has attained overcoming sexuality, not suppressing it like Warringa does.

Morrison's Sula neither suppresses nor overcomes sexuality. On the contrary, she adds a subversive dimension to it. Warring and Jagua affirm their belongingness to the community and work out concepts of self-hood in terms of an ideal community—futurist and radical in Warringa's case, and pre-colonial and traditional in case of Jagua. But Sula breaks away from community in pursuit of self-identity.

The portrayal of Sula is in conformity with her critique of Africanism in the Eurocentric literary discourse. As Africanism consists of an "invented Africa" (Morrison, *PD* 7), where race gets naturalized and the black people become reified in terms of fixed notions and myths, to interrogate it within the domain of "invented Africa" becomes ineffectual. One has to break free from this domain, and Sula does it. Unlike Nel and most other characters, Sula remains isolated from the community and subverts not merely whiteness, but also blackness as well as the socio-cultural mores that define it. What Morrison does in her novel is to obliquely affirm communal values of family, neighbourhood and ancestry through an agent of dislocation and rupture, namely Sula.

Besides Sula, many other characters in the novel attempts to seek an essential 'me-ness,' with varying degrees of success. Shadrack, the disbanded soldier from the World War, has a sudden impulse to see his own face in order to get a grip on himself as his present is empty and future uncertain. He does not have a mirror in the prison cell where he has been lodged on charge of vagrancy and drunkenness. He manages to see his reflection in the water of the toilet bowl in his cell. To have a better view of his reflection he blocks the sunlight from falling on the toilet water. His darkness, reflected in the dark toilet water, greets him with its "indisputable presence" (*Sula* 13). He feels assured and cheered, and falls to "the first deep sleep of his new life" (*Sula* 14). This is the epiphanic moment of his self-acknowledgement as being dark in the abominable darkness of the toilet. His self-definition in his own terms is thus possible, although it is shot through with mordant irony.

Elsewhere, during her younger years Nel comes back home to Medallion with her mother from New Orleans, where she has visited her grandmother. The new experience of journey by train, the thrill and fear of having seen unknown world and people, all suggest to her a new sense of self-identity. On an impulse she gets out of bed, lights a lamp and looks at her face in the mirror while whispering: "I'm me. I'm not their daughter. I'm not Nel. I'm me. Me" (*Sula* 28). Linden Peach writes in the connection: "Nel's 'me'ness develops only after seeing her mother Helene's experience of being black in the larger white community" (Peach 43). But the knowledge of this essential self-identity is accompanied by a terrible burden of existential loneliness which she cannot bear. She soon lapses into conjugal relationship and allows herself to be defined by Jude, her husband, and seeks her worth within the framework of unidirectional recognition. The narrator says playfully: "She did not have a neck until Jude remarked on it, or that her smile was anything but spreading of her lips until he saw it was a small miracle" (*Sula* 84).

Sula is stronger than Nel. She spurns the community and questions marriage, the social institutions which legitimize the subordination of women. She holds on tenaciously to be loneliness of her essential self-hood as she boldly declares to Nel: "But my lonely is mine [...] your lonely is somebody else's" (*Sula* 143). Even if she died, she would die "like one of those red-woods," and not as a "stump," and would proudly say: "I sure did live in this world [...]. I got me" (*Sula* 143). Sula is also stronger than Shadrack because, unlike him, she refuses to be burdened by the oppressive stasis of blackness. While making love to Ajax she ruminates:

> If I take a chamois and rub real hard on [...] the ledge of your cheek bone, some of the black will disappear. It will flake away into the chamois and underneath there will be a gold leaf. I can see it shinning through the black. I can know it is there [...]. If I take a nail file or Eva's old paring knife

> [...] and scrape away at the gold, it will fall away and there will be alabaster [...]. Then I can take a chisel and small tap hammer and tap away at the alabaster [...] and through the breaks I will see the loam, fertile and free of pebbles and twigs [...]. (*Sula* 130)

Here, in Sula's perspective, blackness mutates into gold, which in turn gives way to white alabaster. Even the white alabaster breaks and dissolves into loam that signifies absence of colour and form, but suggests the presence of a fertile and regenerative force in decay and decomposition. It is through mutation, dissolution, formlessness and death that Sula strikes a radical gesture of self-acknowledgement. She dies in the end. But through her death she alerts us to the possibility of the ideal condition of reciprocal recognition and the recovery of the subordinate self.

In conclusion it may be said that within the parameters of post-coloniality, the subordinate self seeks the ways and means in some texts to create a condition of 'mutual recognition' in order to recover an identity, which is not so much 'hybridized' (a la Homi Bhabha) as monolithic.

WORKS CITED

Ahmad, Aijaz. *In Theory: Classes, Nations, Literatures*. Delhi: Oxford UP, 1996.

Ekwensi, Cyprian. *Jagua Nana*. London: Heinemann, 1987.

Fanon, Frantz. *Black Skin, White Masks*. Trans. Charles Lam Markmann. New York: Grove Weidenfeld, 1967.

McClintock, Anne. "The Angel of Progress: Pitfalls of the Term 'Post-colonialism.'" *Social Text* (Spring 1992) 1-15.

Mishra, Vijay and Bob Hodge. "What is Post(-)colonialism?" *Textual Practice* 5.3 (1991) 399-414.

Morrison, Toni. *Sula*. London: Picador, 1988.

——. *Playing in the Dark: Whiteness and Literary Imagination*. London: Picador, 1992.

Ngugi wa Thiong'o. *Detained: A Writer's Prison Diary*. London: Heinemann, 1981.

——. *Devil on the Cross*. London: Heinemann, 1987.

Peach, Linden. *Modern Novelists: Toni Morrison*. London: Macmillan, 1995.

15

The 'Psychic Arena' in Bessie Head's *A Question of Power*—A Study

R. SARASWATI

Bessie Head's novels are charged with an honesty and power that arise from deep personal experience with the issues explored. Obviously all works of fiction are fashioned in some way from the author's experiences, yet with Bessie Head, life experience plays an unusually large role. The central characters in the three novels, Makhaya (*When Rain Clouds Gather*), Margaret (*Maru*), and Elizabeth (*A Question of Power*), all share some aspects of the author's self and move sequentially closer to her own experience. This progression has a direct bearing on the shape each novel takes.

In Bessie Head's novels as the protagonist strives to resolve his or her inner crisis by an effective engagement with the outer world, a pattern emerges; the interior torments of the character are set in a concrete, historically specific context, they work through the psychological stress created by this disjunction to a reconciliation of the interior and the exterior, the private and the social.

Cherry Wilhelm detects in the novels 'growing stress' on the 'psychic arena', and argues for a sequential movement away from the realism of *Rain Clouds*, through the allegorical mode of *Maru*, to the almost entirely inner, psychic struggle of Elizabeth in *A Question of Power*. Bessie Head becomes progressively more concerned 'with the symbolic and metaphysical significance of personal events.'[1] This is what Arthur Ravenscroft refers to as 'organic growth in both her art and her central concerns.'[2] Accordingly, the interest in each case is with smaller and smaller groups of people, ending with the narrating consciousness of a single protagonist (Despite the fact that *A Question* of *Power* is not narrated in the first person, there is little attempt to disguise the fact that it is Bessie's own life that is under scrutiny).

The stress becomes progressively more interior and also more personal. As the focus narrows from a broader, external one to an inner psychic one, so the issues approximate more closely the personal experiences of the author. The problems which are displayed on a flat Botswana landscape in *Rain Clouds* are embodied by individual characters in *A Question of Power*. Autobiography is the natural end point of this sequence.

Few readers can resist the pathos of the life-story Bessie Head tells:

> I was born on the sixth of July, 1937, in the Pietermaritzhurg Mental Hospital [...]. The reason for my peculiar birth place was that my mother was white, and she had acquired me from a black man. She was judged insane, and committed to the mental hospital while pregnant.[3]

Bessie Head's birth in an unwelcome and unwanted situation and her miserable physical and psychological development, in a country swayed by racists contributed greatly to her tragic existence both in South Africa and Botswana. Her insecure position as a member of the Cape Coloured community of South Africa, with whom she was unwilling to identify herself, drove her to a hectic search for an identity within this chaotic racial spectrum of South Africa. This very insecurity worked in shaping her vision regarding the efficacy of organized political action.

Bessie Head's maternal grandparents came from England and her paternal ones were from South Africa. Since her birth was not ordinary, she avoided any intimacy with either of her grandparents. Bessie Head's mother, who was a white lady, was admitted by her parents to an asylum when she was found to be pregnant by their black stable boy which was considered to be a culpable act according to the Immorality Amendment Act. It was in the asylum that Bessie Head was born. Bessie Head's mother committed suicide when Bessie Head was hardly one year old. Rejected in her formative years by the white community, her brown colour made her a member of the cape-coloured community. She was given to a poor coloured family to be brought up. She could not identify herself with the cape-coloured community. As she described to Cecil Abrahams:

> Here were the people with various shades of brown. Those who looked white, those who looked brown, and those who looked like Indians, and those who looked like Africans. As a new comer to the Cape, I thought I had found the ideal place for my mixed race soul. But I quickly and painfully learned that if you were not fully grounded in the colour brown, you would have to be excluded from the community's business and be ready to endure insult. I know then that I would not find rest in that god-forsaken country.[4]

After working for a short time as a teacher, she started wandering around the country in search of peace and a secure home. She worked as a journalist in Johannesburg for the Golden City Post (1958-1960) writing articles for teenagers in the Home Post Supplement. In 1960, she moved down to Cape Town where she met the man, a newspaper reporter, Harold Head. She married him and gave birth to a child, Howard. Harold was involved in 'Unity Politics' and Bessie was obviously found guilty by association when, on the breaking of her marriage, she applied for a passport to take up a teaching position in Botswana. This request was refused and she had to leave on an exit permit, which prohibits re-entry to the country.

In March 1964, she left the country with her small son for Botswana. It was in Francistown, she began writing, and *When Rain Clouds Gather* appeared in 1969. She moved back to Serowe. It was here that she experienced the onset of mental illness which occurred in the form of sporadic attacks spread over a period of two years. This may have been congenitally induced. Bessie was, throughout her life, acutely conscious of the fragility of her mental balance. *Maru,* her second novel appeared in 1971.

A Question of Power, which appeared in 1973, describes in graphic and disturbing detail the harrowing process of her mental breakdown. At one point in her life (which she records in the novel) she accused Sir Seretse Khama of ritual cannibalism and incest and posted these accusations outside the post of in Scrowe. This marked the real onset of madness and she was taken into psychiatric custody. When she emerged from the hospital, it was with a reconstituted sense of self, a new resolve and a firmer grip on the world. Significantly, *A Question of Power* ends with "a gesture of belonging."[5]

Bessie Head's novels are intensely personal and remarkable. Arthur Ravenscroft has remarked that Head's novels form a trilogy—the journeying into the minds of the protagonists gives them cohesion. He observes that each novel strikes out a new and reshoulders the same burden.[6] Bessie Head tries to solve the problems in the novels in different ways. In each novel, the central issue is the struggle of protagonist to resolve the inner torment at the same time effecting harmony with the outer world. A brief over-view can establish this fact.

In *Rain Clouds,* Makhaya's struggle is to reconcile his material existence with his inner life. His life is conceived to be channeled by his experiences in these two dimensions. He acts in the real world and the world in turn provokes an inner reaction. The two realms are finally brought into accord. With Maru (*Maru*) the stress is more upon the inner self. Yet Maru succeeds in his ideals only when he has brought the outside world into harmony with his inward desires. In *A Question of Power,* the relationship between inner and outer is at its most tenuous. There is virtually no causal connection between reality and Elizabeth's nightmares. At one point in the novel, she questions this disjunction: "How did it all happen here, in so unsuspecting a climate, these silent, tortured, universal questions of power and love; of loss and sacrifice?" (97-98); an increasing interiority of perspective culminates in the cathartic.

The structure of *A Question of Power* is the most subjective of Bessie Head's novels. The entire narrative is filtered through the consciousness of Elizabeth, the main protagonist. Here is a disturbed consciousness; throughout most of the novel she is seen suffering from a nervous breakdown and the narrative is actually a description of events as they unfold within her mind and of the relationship between these internal events and the world outside. The outside world is Motabeng, Botswana, where Elizabeth works as a school teacher and then as member of the local agricultural co-operative. Within Head's narrative design, the social environment and Elizabeth's role in it are presented as periodic interruptions of what is the continuing and dominant reality in the novel.

Of the three novels, *A Question of Power* is the most laboriously written. As Randolph Vigne puts it, "It is a prolonged spiritual crisis, seen from the inside and powerfully described."[7] In form it is interesting since she superimposes the predominating fantasy upon the superficial realism, depicting thereby the anarchy of a modern, disintegrated society, which produces the psychologically disoriented individual as the typical twentieth century protagonist.

The novel lends itself to several possible interpretations, as a metaphor for the South African racial situation; an allegorical rendering of the fight between good and evil in which the protagonist improves the lot of her group; the depiction of a woman's insanity, the fantasies of a sexually tormented woman intertwined with her religious growth.

The experience of a young woman, who has been demoralized by oppression in a seemingly hostile world, constituted the subject of the novel. She had been caught between the influence of two charismatic figures, one who wishes for the brotherhood of man and advocates non-violent resistance to evil and oppression and one who resists evil with violence and himself becomes an embodiment of evil power. The novel delineates how the protagonist, caught in a "hazy nightmare of eternal darkness," withstands the evil influence and develops a moral view of her own. The contribution this novel makes is one of insight and demonstration.

Elizabeth, the protagonist of *A Question of Power*, is a coloured South African exiled to Botswana where she goes as a teacher along with her young son. Elizabeth's mother fell in love with a black stable boy in the household of her English mother's family. Thus Elizabeth is the offspring of different racial and social classes. Moreover, she imbibes an urban syncretic culture which discards traditional ways. It is no wonder that she feels socially alienated in the largely tribal and traditional Botswana village of Motaberg. Elizabeth's social alienation and her habit of introspection lead her to a nervous breakdown during her first year in Botswana. However, she is restored to sanity by the generosity of white South African philanthropist Engine who gets her employed in a village co-operative project. Her work on the project and her responsibility towards her son partially help her to recover her sanity. It is largely due to an effort of will she recovers. Again, during her second mental breakdown, her rapport with the people working on the project and their innate goodness and her responsibility towards her son expedite her recovery. Finally, she assimilates herself into the new environment, assured of finding a philosophy for directing her life.

While depicting Elizabeth's story, Bessie Head draws analogies between the situation of the individual who has suffered from the force of prejudice and social oppression and that of a society which has been exploited by alien forces. The growing discontent in the society, which is in the process of adjusting to a new situation, is compared with the mental struggle taking place in the oppressed individual. Bessie Head extends the comparison between the individual who is groping for a guiding philosophy and the society which is trying to set its goals.

A Question of Power makes headway into the causes of cultural psychosis which is the result of colonization and also defines a cure for it. In a country like South Africa, where cultural colonization took place, the experiences of Elizabeth resonate the experiences of every colonized.

Before she starts a new life in Botswana, she wants to make a thorough search into her own self and eliminate the inveterate power-maniacs and culturally implanted demons within it to establish a free society. In Kierkegaardian terms, a society's only salvation lies in the reality of freedom in the lives of each of the individual members of that society.

In *Decolonising the Mind : The Politics of Language in African Literature,* Ngugi wa Thiong'o vividly describes the psychological struggle of the victims of cultural colonization such as Elizabeth. This cultural colonization, which induces a change in the psyche of the victim has the power

> to annihilate people's belief in their names, in their languages, in their environment, in their heritage of struggle, in their unity, in their capacities and ultimately in themselves.[8]

Just like economic neocolonialism, this cultural colonialism has in its wake the possibility of exploitation without the requirement of day-to-day responsibility. The dualities, represented in Elizabeth by Sello and Dan, exist as evidence of the power of cultural colonization. In the words of Paulo Friere:

> The oppressed suffer from the duality which has established itself in their innermost being. They discover that without freedom they cannot exist authentically. Yet, although they desire authentic existence, they fear it. They are at one and the same time themselves and the oppressor whose consciousness they have internalized. The conflict lies in the choice between being wholly themselves or being divided; between ejecting the oppressor within or not ejecting him; between human solidarity or alienation; between following prescriptions or having choices; between being spectators or actors; between acting or having the illusion of acting through the action of the oppressors; between speaking out or being silent, castrated in their power to create and recreate, in their power to transform the world. This is the tragic

dilemma of the oppressed which their education must take into account.[9]

Ngugi imparts a solution to this problem in his novel of, social satire *Devil on the Cross*. Bessie Head discusses the impact of cultural colonization in the form of a mental disease, a cultural schizophrenia. It is enacted through Elizabeth's internal struggle as an individual to liberate herself.

Unlike Ngugi who views the problem in its social dimensions and makes direct confrontation, Bessie Head's focus on Elizabeth's soul reveals the influence of contemporary French feminist thought. Bessie Head believes colonial situation is partially responsible for the oppression of African women.

Kate Millett in *Sexual Politics* identifies the oppressed women in the West with the victims of the cultural colonization. Just as writers like Bessie Head, Chinua Achebe and Wole Soyinka make writing instrumental to annihilate oppression, contemporary feminist theorists like Julia Kristeve and Helene Cixous deem writing as a means of escape from the oppression, of cultural colonization.[10] Cixous suggests that women have to allow their bodies to be heart, just as Elizabeth allows her body and soul to be heart in the novel, because a woman's personal history merges with the history of all women, of all the world. She argues that the liberation of the individual "will bring about a mutation in human relations, in thought, in all praxis."[11]

While interpreting Elizabeth's inner conflict, Bessie Head refers to symbolic paradigms in African, Eastern and Western mythologies. She draws motifs which advance the plot and metaphorical structures which relate the individual and social dilemmas explored in the novel. There is not, as Lewis Nkosi has suggested, any confusion in bringing the various sources together, for Bessie Head refers to key points which link the meanings of the myths from different traditions.[12] The myths introduced in the novel are related to mankind's quest for self-knowledge and self-mastery. Significantly, the novel reveals Bessie Head's endeavour to integrate themes of personal, social and universal significance.

The novel has two parts, and each part deals with an abnormal social reality for which Elizabeth suffers a mental breakdown. The oppression of the whites and her isolation in the Botswana society are the reasons behind the growing anger and resentment in her. There is an ingrained belief in the community that "if a man is alone with his thoughts, he may think of some mischief he can do."[13] Elizabeth's consciousness of her isolation also gives her a feeling of guilt. Her anger and resentment combined with her sense of guilt are like evil powers controlling her thoughts and thwarting her effort to live in harmony with the native community.

Bessie Head employs a series of dreams to reveal Elizabeth's inner mental conflict. As Elizabeth's mental state deteriorates, her dreams turn increasingly nightmarish. Obviously, in both African and Western traditions, the dream is regarded as an expression of inner conflict. In Africa, as Monica Wilson has observed:

> Long before Freud analysed the dreams of his Viennese patients, it was understood that dreams were an expression of inner conflict, before Erikson spoke of the loss of identity, African villagers talked of those with majestic authority, casting a shadow (*nesitunsi* in Xhosa) and those torn within casting no shadow.[14]

The novel renders a concrete image to the concept of Monica Wilson. Elizabeth is dominated by two figures who exist in her thoughts. She identifies them with black African men whom she has seen in the village. What she knows about these two people is scanty. One is Sello, a crop farmer and cattle breeder, who is admired by the villagers. He is well-known for keeping order in his family. Sello's role changes between a prophet and ordinary man in her dreams. As his appeal is spiritual, Elizabeth associates him with the power of the creative imagination. Dan is the other one who is an entrepreneur and politician. He is "greatly admired for being an African nationalist in a country where people were only concerned about tribal affairs" (104). He is one of the very few cattle millionaires of the country. "He ordered a fantastic array of suits from somewhere, and he was short, black and handsome" (104). He radiates force and energy and Elizabeth identifies him with power which is direct and intransigent.[15] Sello and Dan are the outward projections of Elizabeth's inner conflict and their assumed forms are a revelation of her social relation with the community. Being ostracized by the black and the white, Elizabeth is a contrast to the mental figures who "cast a shadow" over her, a powerless individual "torn within" and "casting no shadow."

Bessie Head employs most effectively the metaphor of dream to interpret and demonstrate her inner experience. Elizabeth's dreams are a sequel to her demented mind as a coloured woman in a hostile environment. The feeling that she does not resemble Africans is distressing to her. At this juncture her free mingling with the two black figures in her dreams can be viewed as a kind of wish-fulfilment which is denied to her in practice. Elizabeth's ruffled mental state emanates not only from a problem of identity but also from her conflicting reactions to cruel social pressures. Bessie Head transcends her personal experiences in her dreams. Elizabeth's involvement with figures who existed before her time and persons with whom she has never met personally indicates the large dimensions of the problem. Sello and Dan, in her dreams, are identified with those personalities whose names are linked with the use of non-violent or violent methods of social change. Thus her dreams have personal and social significance. These dreams are a manifestation of an individual's efforts to establish an identity of her own by coping with the personal and social problems.

The first section of the novel renders a vivid description of Elizabeth's encounters with Sello. Sello appears in Elizabeth's bedroom sitting on a chair three months after her arrival in Motabeng. Elizabeth herself does not recognize the dream from reality, "after that the dividing line between dream perceptions and waking reality was to become confused" (22). Sello's appearance and manner give the feeling that he had undergone spiritual and physical ordeals:

> He wore the soft, white, flowing robes of a monk, but in a peculiar fashion, with his shoulders slightly hunched forward,

> as though it were a prison garment. He stared straight at Elizabeth in a friendly way and said in a voice of quiet affection: "My friend" (22).

Elizabeth identifies the apparition with both Sello, an African living in Motabeng, and with a universal saviour figure:

> He looked like a man she had seen about the village of Motabeng who drove a green truck, but the name she associated in her mind with the monk-robed man was of an almost universally adored God (23).

To her amazement, Elizabeth finds Sello, an ordinary man in a brown suit who is the negative side of Sello, the monk. On the one hand, he is god-like and creative and, on the other, human and vulnerable. "Sello", in the words of Bessie Head, "is very similar to Maru but with greater projection of thought, torture and control."[16]

Sello represents a particular individual exerting moral or intellectual force in a society at a particular time and at the same time, he is an enduring spirit existing throughout human history. As a time-less spirit, he is identified not only with the heroes of religious myth but also with remarkable personalities who channelled their energy for racial equality or better social conditions in Africa. For instance, Sello's presence merges into that of an Asian who disseminates Gandhian ideas of tolerance and respect for the poor to Elizabeth. On one occasion, Sello "walks into" a figure who is referred to as "the Father" and who may be identified with the South African Philanthropist Patrick Van Rensburg, who organized various projects in Botswana.[17] In this connection, Bessie Head esteems historical figures like Gandhi and Patrick Van Rensburg and their unremitting motivation to the struggle for a humane and equitable society.

Just like her spiritual teacher Sello, Elizabeth has two dimensions to her character. Like Sello she is an ordinary individual within a particular time and place and the vesture of an enduring spirit. Our understanding of the novel is complicated by the fact that Elizabeth retains her personal identity and is at the same time transformed into a universal human type.[18] Images like Sello moving into Elizabeth's person or the mystic Madonna, Sello's spiritual country-part, entering Elizabeth's person testifies to this transformation. Thus Elizabeth turns to be Sello's companion on his spiritual journey. This spiritual journey is symbolic of the endeavours made by different individuals in various societies who aspire to achieve a balanced relationship with their society to create harmony in their personal lives.

Elizabeth's enlightening conversations with Sello extending for a period of approximately four years and later with Dan, constitute the major part of the novel. Dan's domination over Elizabeth is revealed through the second part of the novel. Elizabeth has the assurance that Sello can direct her thoughts and provide her with a philosophy to lead her. At first, Sello establishes himself as "the prophet of mankind" (44). He introduces a spectacular array of personalities and memories of the past which represent his work as "the prophet of mankind" (44). He directs her thoughts to those who have fought spiritual battles for the sake of mankind and attempts to teach her an ideal of fraternal love. Sello foresees a future in which mankind has got over a situation, in which the few entirely manipulated power to oppress the many to one in which ordinary people would begin to realize their own capabilities. Elizabeth hardly believes in Sello's beautiful future as she cannot obliterate the social reality from her mind.

Elizabeth turns desperate when Sello reveals his inner conflict. Since his way is the way of truth, Sello can conceal nothing from her. In his effort, to show the seamy side of his character, he had stripped himself of his veneer of goodness. He brings Elizabeth into contact with Medusa, a representation of the forces which undermine his spiritual powers. Mention of Medusa recalls the classical myth of the Gorgons which, as Erich Neumann has observed, are "images of the great pre-Hellenic Mother Goddess" in whom the opposed principles of life and death are combined.[19] Similarly, Medusa, in *A Question of Power* represents forces which have both creative and destructive potential but which may become totally destructive, if not brought under control. In this respect, obviously, she represents "the poor of Africa", especially the stubborn and reactionary elements in tribal society, which threaten to divide the new nation states in Africa. "Tradition, with its narrow outlook", Bessie Head has observed elsewhere, "does not combine happily with common sense, humanity and a broad outlook."[20] In relation to the society, Medusa is a representation of attitude and behaviour which stem from intolerance and irrationality.[21] With regard to an individual, she represents the intrinsic evil qualities which threaten to weaken his moral purpose. Elizabeth reflects that Medusa is "the direct and tangible form of the individual's own evils, his power lusts, his greeds, his self-importance" (40).

As for Sello, Medusa represents not only those irrepressible and unhealthy impulses within himself but also those external forces of irrationality and intolerance which try to weaken his purpose. Medusa dominates the Sello of the brow suit while Sello, the monk, looks on helplessly. With regard to Elizabeth, just as with Sello, Medusa represents Elizabeth's personal weaknesses as well as the external forces of parochial outlook. Naturally, Elizabeth's spiritual life and her social relationship with black Africans become the target of Medusa's attacks. Medusa instigates her to give up her spiritual journey and nurture hatred towards black Africans. Elizabeth views Medusa as an embodiment of sexual temptation and of negative social attitudes.

In the dreams of Elizabeth, Medusa contrasts her sexual powers with Elizabeth's. In the novel, as in the mythological sources on which Bessie Head draws, however, sexual excess is a metaphor for other types of excess and the emotions attached to sexual passion are opposed to the forces of reason and to the pursuit of spiritual perfection.[22] This is clearly an indication of life centred on the sensual rather than the spiritual. Reference to mythology further clarifies the significance of the contrast between Elizabeth's and Medusa's sexual powers; An Erich Neumann has observed the vagina is symbolic of the hell or the underworld that the mythic hero must survive:

> The opening of the vessel of doom is the womb, the gate, the gullet which actively swallows, devours, rends and kills. Its sucking power is mythologically symbolized as

> consciousness and the individual male can evade it only if he is a hero, and even then not always.[23]

Medusa's aim is to make Elizabeth feel ostracized from the black community. She scoffs at Elizabeth that she is not a genuine African and says again, "Africa is troubled waters. I'm a powerful swimmer in troubled waters, you'll only drown here. You're not linked up to the people. You don't know any African Language" (44). Suffering and poverty, as Bessie Head suggests, lead to a kind of arrogance, self-importance and exclusivity. By projecting the issue of Elizabeth's ethnic affiliation, Bessie Head is chiefly making a common cause with all those people who lost their identity in many post-independence societies.

Medusa's taunts precipitate Elizabeth's nervous breakdown. She loses her temper in a shop and abuses a Botswana clerk for which she is hospitalized. She engrosses herself in a co-operative farming scheme when she loses her job, after spending a brief period in the hospital. In order to survive the subversive power of Medusa, Elizabeth ensures the existence of goodness.

At the end of the first section of the novel Elizabeth comes to resent Sello's influence. She is incredulous of his ambiguous personality for he is both good and evil in one way. She could not rely on Sello as a guiding force as he himself is vulnerable to Medusa. Elizabeth discards those attitudes which made her vulnerable to Medusa. She infers that she has to find her own means to meet the exigencies of her particular situation.

The first section ends with her words of commitment to the "new day" heralded by the rising sun: 'O God,' she said softly. 'May I never contribute to creating dead worlds, only new worlds' (100).

In the second section of the novel, which records Elizabeth's encounter with Dan, Bessie Head examines a concept of power which is based on violence. Unlike Sello, Dan does not weaken his own purpose by an agonized soul-searching and is not prepared to compromise. Elizabeth at first identifies with his passionate commitment. Altogether Dan is Bessie Head's portrait of the popular nationalist leader, "a heroic father figure" and leader of the single party.[24] An example of how blatantly selfish and mean the nationalists can be is found in Bessie Head's first novel, *When Rain Clouds Gather*.

Dan, Elizabeth discovers later, is nothing more than a tyrannical lover. Dan's is "a sort of love so vehement and cruel that it is hardly fit for human society."[25] Her encounters with him seem to represent two different periods in the nationalist leader's career. The relationship which was established in the early period when the leader shared a common cause with the ordinary people rapidly develops into one in which he becomes more authoritarian, and invokes the mystique of the African personality.[26] As Elizabeth observes to the peace corps worker, Tom when the period of fascination with Dan is over, "Any heaven, like a black Power heaven, that existed for a few individuals alone was pointless and useless. It was an urge to throttle everyone else to death" (133). She observes further that the leader who tries to create a "heaven" for a select few will also turn his power against his own followers because his feeling of dominance makes him contemptuous of those without power. Elizabeth's observation comes true in her relationship with Dan. Like Medusa, he reminds her that she is not a 'genuine' African.

> A persistent theme was that she was not genuinely African. He too was a deep mystery she would never fathom. He could so subtly play on the earlier themes Sello had introduced to her mind about the poor, their central importance, and yet he twisted and prevented these themes with a merciless cruelty (159).

In giving Elizabeth, "the real African insight," Dan looks at the record of human behaviour mainly to uncover weakness; his is "the tough personality, facing the facts" in an essentially hostile world.[27] Dan is contemptuous of Sello's tentative efforts to create social harmony. Under the spell of Dan, Elizabeth views normal human relationship in a twisted way and can even believe that Sello is a pervert and child molester.

Dan's power is symbolized in the novel by his ability to dominate and use women. In her portrait of Dan, Bessie Head seems to be commenting on the kind of thinking which exalts sexual virility as a value in itself.[28] Dan's sexual excesses are a counterpart to Medusa's exhibitionism in the first section.[29] Dan also uses them to mock at her powerlessness. Dan's women may be seen as representations of political factions and interest groups with which the nationalist leader may be allied from time to time. In describing them, Bessie Head alludes to grass-roots groups such as peasants and agricultural workers, urban proletarian groups including displaced and unemployed workers and bourgeois nationalist groups. In some instances she seems to be referring to alliances with foreign agencies, liberal opinion in Europe and America, commercial interest and former colonial powers.

In the second section of the novel, the sexual act is clearly a metaphor for secret, underhand and corrupt political and business transactions. Unlike Sello, Dan had descended into the underworld to dominate the evil forces and had used them to increase his power. Evil though he is, Dan is himself a victim of his own power, spinning "away from himself in a dizzy kind of death-dance of will, distraction and dissipation."[30]

Being tormented by Dan, Elizabeth comes to resent even goodness in people. Her second mental breakdown is preceded by an incident in which she strikes a white woman who has been kind to her. During this mental breakdown, Elizabeth's anger at Dan is expressed in a hatred of everything African. A doctor, who feigns to share her feelings about Africans, helps her. After going home, she feels the presence of Sello again, who had withdrawn his presence for more than a year. Dan's attempts, to subject her to torture once again, are foiled by Elizabeth, who ultimately turns to Sello's teaching. Regarding Sello, Bessie Head writes in one of her letters, "It is argued that the man's perfection at the heights is based on what he did in his depths of degradation."[31] The kindness of the neighbours who look after her son during her illness, the constant concern of Tom, the Peace Corps volunteer and the generosity of the real Sello, who refuses to incriminate her are testimonials to the immanence of goodness in the people.

While discussing with Tom, she traces her illness to the loss of sense of goodness and her strong awareness of greed and arrogance around her. She compares Sello's teaching with a small light in a world of darkness, which had been obscured by an overwhelming evidence of evil, and he sees her personal conflicts as a reflection of an ongoing struggle between incompatible forces struggling for dominance in society.

Finally, Elizabeth is her proper self—the coloured woman from South Africa and an exile in Botswana who has undergone a traumatic social experience at a particular period in history. Bessie could visualize Martin Luther King's promised land "not for the black man alone but for all people alive on earth."[32] Elizabeth attains spiritual enlightenment and learns to control her rebellious instincts. Elizabeth's ability to control her inner conflict proves that the forces which promote social harmony will ultimately be stronger than the narrow loyalties which threaten to disintegrate the society. Violence, as Bessie Head tries to show, does not create harmony and violence in itself is not a proper basis for enduring social unity. Bessie Head thus declares herself a disciple of Gandhi and, at the same time, affirms the old Bantu ideal of "Commitment to the person."[33] The final sentence of the novel is fraught with symbolism "As she fell asleep, she placed one soft hand over her land. It was a gesture of belonging" (206).

NOTES

1. Cherry Wilhelm, "Bessie Head: The Face of Africa," *English in Africa* 10:1 (1983) 2.
2. Arthur Ravenscroft, "The Novels of Bessie Head," *Aspects of South African Literature,* ed. Christopher Heywood (London, Ibadan, Nairobi, Lusaka: Heinemann, 1976) 174.
3. Short biographical sketch preceding "Witchacraft," ms 4 Nov. (1975) 72.
4. Cecil A. Abrahams, "Introduction." *The Tragic Life of Bessie Head and Literature in South Africa.* (Tenton, New Jersey, Africa World Press, 1990) 4.
5. Besie Head, *A Question of Power,* African Writers Series 149 (London: Heinemann, 1977) 17. All further references are to this edition.
6. Ravenscroft 175.

7. Randolph Vigne, *A Gesture of Belonging: Letters from Bessie Head.* (London: Heinemann, 1999) 143.
8. Paul, H. Lorenz, "Colonization and the Feminine in Bessie Head's *A Question of Power." Modern Fiction Studies* 37, 3 (1991) 595.
9. Paulo, Freire, *Pedagogy of the Oppressed,* trans. Myre B. Ramos (New York: Continuum, 1990) 32-33.
10. Lorenz 597.
11. Lorenz 598.
12. Lewis Nkosi, *Tasks and Masks* (London: Longman, 1981) 101.
13. Bessie, Head, *Serowe-Village of the Rain Wind* (London: Heinemann Education, 1981) 10.
14. Monica Wilson, *Religion and Transformation of Society* (Cambridge: Cambridge UP, 1971) 40.
15. Heywood, Christopher, *Aspects of South African Literature* (London: Heinemann Educational, 1976) 184.
16. Vigne, Randolph, ed., *op. cit.*, 168.
17. Head, Bessie, *Serowe-Village of the Rain Wind* 135-38.
18. Hans Mayerhoff, *Time in Literature* (Berkeley: U of California P, 1974) 41.
19. Neumann, Erich, *The Great Mother,* trans. R. Manheim, 2nd ed. (Princeton: Princeton UP, 1963) 169.
20. *Serowe* xiii.
21. M.K. Gandhi, *Gandhi's India : Unity in Diversity* (New Delhi: National Book Trust, 1968) 28.
22. *Dreams,* trans R.F.C. Hull (Princeton : Princeton UP, 1974) 49.
23. Neumann, *The Great Mother* 171.
24. Claude Wautheir, *The Literature and Thought of Modern Africa,* 2nd ed. (Washington, D.C.: Three Continents Press, 1979) 276.
25. Randolph Vigne, *op. cit.*, 170.
26. V.S. Naipaul, *The Return of Eva Peron* (New York: Alfred A. Knopf, 1980) 175.
27. Joseph Campbell, ed., *Myths, Dreams and Religion* (New York: E.P. Dutton, 1970) 22.
28. Naipaul, *The Return of Eva Peron, op. cit.*, 175.
29. Neumann, *op. cit.*, 171.
30. Bessie Head, *The Collector of Treasures* (London: Heinemann Educational, 1977) 92-93.
31. Randolph Vigne, *A Gesture of Belonging, op. cit.*
32. Vigne 92.
33. Donald Burness, *Shaka King of the Zulus in African Literature* (Washington: Three Continents Press, 1976) 147.

16

AFFIRMATION OF SELF IN NGUGI'S *THE RIVER BETWEEN*

MOHAMED OSMAN GHELEWAY

Many established African writers in European languages have very often bitterly complained about the manner in which Western critics have judged and evaluated their work. Chinua Achebe, the well-known Nigerian writer, for example, states in his article 'Where Angels Fear to Tread': "We are not opposed to criticism but we are getting weary of all the special types of criticism which have been designed for us by people whose knowledge of us is very limited" (1973:5). Similarly, Wole Soyinka, the Nobel Prize winner in 1986, with reference to such critics goes to the extent of saying: "I sometimes think that the greatest professional hazard (to the African writer) is the critic" (1988:26).

The fact that the complaints made by such African writers as Soyinka and Achebe are justified and well-grounded can be seen, for example, from the remarks made by Albert Gerard, a Western critic, about creative writing in the sub-Saharan Africa. Gerard, arguing that the influence of tradition in the growth and development of modern sub-Saharan literature is "primarily negative," surprisingly maintains that critics are unanimous in "deploring the deficiencies in character delineation so conspicuous in most modern African novels," because according to him, "like most technologically underdeveloped cultures, African cultures are based on values that are fundamentally societal" (1970:35).

It is quite obvious for any scholar of African literature to see that such hasty generalizations, as the one made by Gerard, are biased and full of misconceptions to say the least. To counter the assertion of Western critics that modern African literature has mainly focused on society and not sufficiently on individual characters, and as a consequence of that "has lacked true aesthetic proportions" (Achebe), this article argues that modern African novels do not so much suffer from such 'deplorable' deficiencies or shortcomings with reference to Ngugi's novel, *The River Between.*

The Western critics' misinterpretation of African literary works written in European languages arise, in my opinion, due to the difference between the more or less communal nature of most African societies to which African writers belong and the individualistic nature of western societies to which the Western critics belong. It is perhaps the difference in perspective and worldview which has led to encouragement of "the misrepresentation of certain literary works, the underestimation of their human complexity and ambiguity, and the diminishing of their merit, when they are imposed on literature structured in different terms" (Kronenfield, 1975:203).

The unique personal experience of the individual character as an independent being in his own right and his continuous constructive efforts to affirm himself against all odds is one of the major themes in *The River Between.* This process of self-affirmation very often involves the courage to be oneself in spite of the threats of non-being to being, but since so man is an island, the courage to affirm oneself can take two main dimensions of being and becoming: Self-affirmation taken "individually" as well as taken in "participation" with others (Tillich 1980).

In Ngugi's *The River Between* this process of self-affirmation both individually and in participation with others (socially) can be observed in several characters but most noticeably in Muthoni, Joshua's eldest daughter. In spite of her father's conscious and unconscious efforts to obstruct her self-fulfillment as an independent human being in her own right, Muthoni courageously tries to be a self-affirmed person and lead a more worthwhile and meaningful life. To attain this state of personal freedom it becomes necessary for her to reject her father's confining brand of religion and way of life, and search for spiritual salvation elsewhere. In the process, Muthoni rigorously attempts to reconcile the numerous forces that strove to control and limit her life.

The main stumbling block in Muthoni's journey towards self-discovery was her father's rigid puritanical religion, which could not be reconciled with the rituals of the tribe, no matter what. So Muthoni had to rebel against this puritanical norms to lead a more meaningful and enriching life. This, of course, needed the full exertion of her will power to defy those forces, real or imagined, that hampered her progress. Defying her father through undergoing the act of circumcision, Muthoni, "cuts the psychological umbilical chord" which had prevented her development into a mature person in her own right. In contrast to Muthoni, Joshua, her father, lacks a proper sense of direction and orientation in his life, and he merely makes himself the white man's tool in being guided by the missionaries' do's and don'ts without using his own critical faculties as such. Unknowingly he has turned life in his own household into a sort of hell on earth. It is precisely under such brutal family circumstances that his daughters rebel against him. To his annoyance, Muthoni undergoes circumcision and Nyambura is in love with Wayiaki, who doesn't belong to the community of converts.

Muthoni's circumcision, an act of self-affirmation at the individual as well as the social level, contributes significantly to her maturity as a full-fledged person in her own right, particularly when she reconciles Christianity with the rituals of the tribe, as can be seen from her last words to Wayiaki: "'Wayiaki,' [...] tell Nyambura I see Jesus. And I am a woman, beautiful in the tribe [...]." Muthoni's circumcision provides the reader with a clear insight into her private experiences and emotions. Her great dilemma in the process of self-discovery, in fact, involves a subconscious conflict between the need to conform to her father's expectations, which prohibit participation in the tribal rituals and need to find her own true goals in life by overcoming these inhibiting forces. Such deep conflicts in her psyche are resolved only after she courageously rebels against her father's excessively demanding puritanical creed. It is precisely this healthy rebellion against the alienating forces represented by Joshua's brand of religion that brings about the birth of freedom of choice, integrity, and dignity in Muthoni.

Albert Gerard's remarks that the influence of tradition in the growth and development of modern sub-Saharan literature has been "primarily negative" and leads "deficiencies in character delineation" therefore do not apply to Ngugi's *The River Between* where tradition plays an important role at the individual and social levels. Thus, circumcision, an important ritual in the tribe, far from being detrimental to character delineation, makes characterization in the novel sound and effective. In fact, the spiritual and the social functions of circumcision in the novel are rather like the two sides of the same coin, with each side reinforcing the other. Binding the tribe, giving life to a person's life, circumcision is the core of the whole social structure among the Gikuyu people, as Ngugi's authorial voice puts it: "End the custom and the spiritual basis of the tribe's cohesion and integration would be no more" (79).

It is, therefore, the right merger of the social and individual aspects in the novel that gives characters such as Muthoni, Nyambura and Joshua, their own unique individuality. It is also through this blend of social and individual elements that the reader can get an insight into the motivations, emotions and private experiences of the characters in the novel. Hence, the influence of tradition in the African novel is not only primarily positive, but even can lead to more effective characterization and plot organization.

One can see a sharp contrast in character between the reflective and contemplative Muthoni and her father; Joshua is one who has failed to affirm either individually or in participation with others because he lacks the courage to do so. He is simply an imitator of the white man's way of life. Put in other words, he is 'a black white man' living in a no man's land after having uprooted himself from his origins in the tribe by completely rejecting all the values and rituals that held the tribe cohesively together as an organic whole. Concerning the uprooting of Joshua from his own culture Ngugi states in the novel: "He had clothed himself with a religion decorated and smeared with everything white. He renounced his past and cut himself away from those life-giving traditions of the tribe," and as a result, "he had nothing to rest upon, he had to cling to whatever the missionaries taught him promised future" (163). In this way, Ngugi using the omniscient point of view provides the reader with the emptiness in Joshua's inner self and its influence on his character.

Joshua represents, in psychological terms, a very harsh father figure in Muthoni's psyche, so much so that it became quite necessary for her to rebel against his confining creed to find her true self and live her own life as a free human being instead of remaining fixated in a state of permanent enslavement to his dictates. While undergoing this process of positive change in her life-style, Muthoni has been in a state of constant hesitation at first, but this wavering doesn't last long because she eventually overcomes the anxiety and guilt triggered by remembering her father's cruel words which she has unconsciously repressed since her childhood. The liberation from all these conscious and unconscious forces is eventually achieved when she independently decides to be initiated into womanhood through circumcision, which is an important ritual in the tribe. In this way, she disengages herself from the forces of alienation which previously prevented her from self-actualization. This, in turn, brings to her an inner equilibrium, which she had never experienced before in her life and had aspired to achieve for a long time. She achieves this only when she follows her own convictions about life, rather than following Joshua's dispiriting doctrines.

Circumcision, unimaginable to be put into actual practice in Joshua's superficially westernized household, brings Muthoni, as has been argued, into direct collision with her father's standards and expectations, and therefore deep in her soul she wants to reconcile Christianity with the rituals of the tribe. Although this attempt at reconciling two opposing value systems is a difficult process involving physical and mental suffering, Muthoni is determined to endure this agony because she has found meaning and salvation in it. As Wayiaki asserts, "Muthoni had found something, something that filled her soul and made her endure everything. Muthoni had tried to find salvation for herself, a surer ground on which to stand" (121). Circumcision, therefore, far from alienating her from Christianity enables her to get a new understanding of the religion itself. At the same time her sense of belonging and self-esteem are reinforced because as she says she has now become 'a true Christian in the tribe.' Thus when any religion is in harmony with the local customs and traditions of its believers it gets the right soil to flourish in and leads to a healthy growth of its followers.

While Muthoni's constructive efforts reinforce reconciliation between Christianity and the rituals of the tribe, Joshua consciously and unconsciously brings about the disintegration of the two opposing systems, *i.e.* the Western and African modes of life, by his divisive attitude. Joshua constantly suppresses and crushes the part in his own being that seeks fulfilment, understanding and growth as a person in his own right. To him faith has become a non-living process incapable of growth, and conversion to traditional roots in the tribe. In his philosophy of life, there is no room for dialogue and compromise. Commenting on Joshua's type of religion, Ngugi says: "A religion that took no account of people's way of life, was useless. It would not satisfy," adding "it would not be a living experience, a source of life and vitality. It would only maim a man's soul, making him fanatically cling to whatever promised security, otherwise he would be lost" (162-63).

Joshua's outright rejection of his African roots and cultural heritage, which has put his integrity and dignity into question, has also led to his alienation from himself and from the people of his country. As a victim of the colonial situation he has long ceased to be his true self, unwisely trying to live up to the standards and expectations of his colonial masters, the white missionaries. In this connection, Achebe, deploring the plight of those Africans who have lost their dignity as a result of the colonial impact, argues that the worst thing that can happen to a person is to lose his dignity as a human being and asserts that "it is this dignity that many African people all but lost during the colonial period and it is this dignity that they must regain" (1980:8). Hence, it is not surprising that Joshua has lost the respect of his two daughters who have rebelled against him by rejecting all that he stood for including his superficially Westernized religious views.

Most African literary works have themes in one way or another related to individual as well as social experiences depending upon literary sensibility, temperament, and single vision of the writer. It is indeed the right combination of these factors that leads to the creation of a good work of art which has a universal appeal to most readers. Any literary work as Hippolyte Taine argues "must be regarded as the expression of the psychology of the individual, which in its turn is the expression of the milieu and the period in which the individual lived, and of the race to which he belongs" (1992:9). In fact, too much unnecessary focus on individualism at the cost of the social dimensions, as is often demanded by western critics, far from being a measure of artistic craftsmanship is detrimental to it as Virgilio de Lemos put it "those who assert that the poet or any writer must speak with an individual voice to express his own experiences and interpretations are following the patterns of Western Culture" (1968:54). In *The River Between,* the individual and the social dimensions of reality are reflected in appropriate proportions, with each dimension mutually reinforcing the other, and this gives the novel good aesthetic proportions because the individual cannot be fully understood and appreciated unless he is put in the right social and cultural milieu. Moreover, besides expressing the uniqueness of the characters as human beings, the novel also mirrors the socio-political situation in Kenya during the early years of British colonization.

In preserving the outer symbols and signs of European way of life, unable to separate them from the Christian doctrine, Joshua has not only denied his African identity but he has also suppressed the emergence of his real self as a unique person. Stripped of all values, he has become, to use T.S. Eliot's expression, "a hollow man" and even worse, he has turned his household into an African "wasteland" as can be seen from Nyambura's agony: "Nyambura was not happy. Each day that she spent in her father's home seemed a greater weight added on to her. Her heart was restless and she knew that nothing at home would satisfy" (116). Pointing out how the Church of Scotland Mission, the religious sect Joshua belonged to, virtually mixed up Christian dogma with European customs and scale of values beyond recognition, Ngugi, for instance, comments: "[...] the measure of your Christian love and charity was in preserving the outer signs and symbols of European way of life, whether you are dressed as Europeans did, whether you had acquired European good manners, like European hymns and tunes, and of course whether you refused to have your daughter circumcised" (1972:31).

Muthoni's self-affirmation has two sides, which are clearly distinguishable but not so entirely separable. One is her affirmation of self, "of a separated, self-centred, individualized, incomparable, free self-determining self" (Tillich 1980:89). This is the self which Muthoni defends against non-being when she rebels against Joshua's alienating doctrine and way of life, and affirms courageously by "taking non-being upon herself." Muthoni's self-affirmation, however, would be incomplete without affirming herself in participation with others, which she achieves by going back to the rituals and values of the tribe, because "self is self only because it has a world, a structured universe, to which it belongs and from which it is separated at the same time" (Tillich 90). Since self and world are "correlated," individualization and participation are also correlated. Participation understood in this way means "being a part of something from which one is, at the same time, separated" (Tillich 91). This is precisely what gives meaning to Muthoni's life after she affirms herself at the two important levels because man's being, as opposed to non-being, includes his relation to meaning; in fact, man is human "only by understanding and shaping reality, both his world and himself, according to meanings and values" (Tillich 58). Hence Muthoni's struggle to find her own true goals in life boils down to her search for meaning in life.

The attempt to affirm one's own self courageously in *The River Between* can also be vividly seen in the person of Muthoni's younger sister, Nyambura, who, like Muthoni, rebels against the rigid norms of her father. Nyambura, however, affirms her unique individuality through love with Wayiaki, a love relationship which Joshua doesn't approve of simply because Wayiaki is not Christian. The authorial voice in the novel shedding light on the inner conflicts of Nyambura's life states: "Nyambura never rebelled before; not with deliberation. This was her first act of rebellion and she now knew that she was beyond the grasp of Joshua", and commenting on the nature of the urge she felt inside, the authorial voice continues, "the call of the inner voice that urged her on, the call of the land beyond Joshua's confining hand, was too strong" (157).

It is Wayiaki's love that sets Nyambura free from the shackles of Joshua, and enables her to come out of her narrow shell towards the path of light and meaningful life, leaving behind the darkness of the soul she went through. She could only be saved through Wayiaki who was then "her Savior, her black Messiah, the Promised one who would come and lead her into the light" (117).

WORKS CITED

Achebe, Chinua. "Where Angels Fear to Tread." *African Writers on African Writing*. Ed. G.D. Killam. Evaston: Northern UP, 1973.

——. "The Role of the Writer in a New Nation." *African Writers on African Writing*.

Gerard, Albert. "Preservation of Tradition in African Creative Writing." *Research in African Literatures* 1:1 (1970).

Kronenfield, J.Z. "The 'Communalistic' African and the 'Individualistic' Westerner: Some Comments on Misleading Generalizations in

Western Criticism of Soyinka and Achebe." *Research in African Literatures* 6:2 (1975).

Lemos, de Virgilio. *The Writer in Modern Africa.* Upsala: Scandinavian Institute of African Studies, 1968.

Ngugi wa Thiong'o. "Church, Culture and Politics." *Homecoming.* London: Heinemann, 1972.

——. *The River Between.* London: Heinemann, 1965.

Soyinka, Wole. "Ethics, Ideology and the Critic." *Criticism and Ideology.* Sweden: Nordiska Afrikainstitutet, 1988.

17

NATIONALISM IN MARGARET LAURENCE'S *THE DIVINERS*

P. MALLIKARJUNA RAO and M. PRABHAKAR

> [...] no man could own the land. The land was God's. Little did they know the concepts of the incoming European culture. They learned, however, in sorrow and pain.
>
> —Margaret Laurence

Canada has a three-part history of colonialism as a colony of French, British and the United States of America. A sense of complicity with the imperial power pervades colonial territory of Canada and it has influenced serious writers like Sarah Jeanette Duncan and Hugh Maclennan whose novels, *The Imperialist* (1904) and *Barometer Rising* (1941) respectively focused on anti-colonialism and anti-imperialism.

Margaret Laurence's sense of anti-imperialism and anti-authoritarianism is most powerfully expressed in her Manawaka novel, *The Diviners*, published in 1974. In her book, *Long Drums and Cannons*, Laurence expressed her credo which seemed to anticipate the theme of *The Diviners*:

> It (Literature) must be planted firmly in some soil. Even works of non-realism make use of spiritual landscapes which have been at least partially inherited by the writer. Despite some current fashions to the contrary, the main concern of the writer remains that of somehow creating the individual

> on the printed page [...] of settling down the conflicts of people who are as real to him as himself. If he does this well, and as truthful, as he can, his writing may sometimes reach out beyond any national boundary.[1]

Laurence is a 'Third World Writer' like Chinua Achebe. She proclaims:

> Canadian writers, like African writers, have had to find our, own voice and write of what is truly ours, in the face of an overwhelming cultural imperialism.[2]

In short, Laurence addresses herself to such issues as nationalism, regionalism, socio-political problems in her novels. The last of her five-volume Manawaka novels, *The Diviners*, remains an ample testimony to her concerns. The novel is "the so-called nation-building approach to the Canadian past."[3] Laurence, before beginning to write *The Diviners*, has obviously read Morton's book, *Manitoba: A History*, and has deeply been impressed by it. She cites it as the book about her land that has meant most to her. She says:

> When I first read (it), it was with a tremendous sense of excitement, combined with an angry sense of having been deprived, when young, of my own heritage. I have since done a great deal of reading priarie history, but it was Morton who first gave me the sense of my place's long and dramatic past.[4]

The Diviners is an anti-colonial piece of fiction. It has been described as a national allegory.[5] In the novel, personal relations are depicted as larger public concerns. It is a rejection of colonial ethos and literature and an assertion of native tradition based on orality. The novel, as a postcolonial text, strongly advocates the shedding of colonial burden. It could be interpreted as a re-writing of Shakespeare's *The Tempest*. Thus, Laurence writes against older traditions, "reworking epic quest and Shakespearean romance in a revision of a central myth, of our culture, that of the 'fortunate fall,' and proposing an alternative conception of 'paradise' and 'the artist.'[6]

Morag Gunn, the protagonist in *The Diviners* is herself a novelist. She is the mouthpiece of Laurence's nationalism. Morag uses her fiction to make her way in the world and make sense of the world. As Morag says: "If I hadn't been a writer I'd have been a first class mess."[7] In the novel, Laurence shows Morag as engaged in a quest for her ancestry and shows her maturing from an identification with 'Prospero's child' into the powers of Prospero himself. Laurence also portrays Morag, her artist, as a diviner, an alternative to Joyce's 'artificer.'

Morag Gunn invents national identity for herself using the cultural materials provided by "diviners" such as her foster father, Christie Logan. She rejects an identification with the imperialist image, but rather identifies with the indigenous, the dispossessed and the land of her birth. She embodies Laurence's view of Canadian national identity. Morag, the myth-maker-novelist writes a novel called *Prospero's Daughter* which is a postcolonial revision of Shakespeare's *The Tempest*. Morag who is the embodiment of Laurence's own myth has herself lived a revised version of Miranda's story.

Morag Gunn also advocates a myth of romance. According to Doris Sommer,[8] romance is the mode best suited to novels that would found a nation. Morag is an orphan fostered by Christie Logan. She is ashamed of her foster father, the town garbage collector, and feels constrained by Manawaka which she calls the 'small-town prison.' In university, she falls in love with her English Professor called Brooke Skelton. She is attracted by his Britishness. Brooke represents the culture and tradition of the imperial metropolis *i.e.*, London. He patronizes Morag, treats her condescendingly, and makes her feel like a child. The relationship itself proves to be barren as he refuses to entertain her desire for a child. It becomes clear that he wants it to be a dependency relationship of master and slave. Eventually Morag publishes her novel, *Spear of Innocence*, that gives her strength to leave Brooke. All along, she carried Manawaka with her in spite of her reluctance towards it, and now she finds solace in the company of Jules who belongs to the prairies. In the novel, she explains how 'paradise can be regained.' Thus, her writing becomes the process of regaining the lost paradise; it marks the break-up point with the cultural and literary traditions associated with Brooke.

The migration from the bigoted, class-ridden and provincial town of Manawaka to the glorious world of books of the ideal nation is strengthened by her matrimonial relationship with Brooke. But once she learns her bitter lesson that only alienation, falsehood, snobbishness, and dependence could be found in her association with the representative of colonial reality, she starts her journey back to the real nation of Manawaka. She forms a union with the representative of the indigenous population by means of her marriage with Jules. In her novel, *Prospero's Child,* Morag treats Brooke as Prospero, the coloniser, and develops her resistance to his powers. Through her involvement with Jules, Caliban, she gives expression to her creative powers in the form of songs and narratives and thus assumes the role of Miranda.

Brooke and Jules differ in many respects: In their social mores, and more significantly, in the demands they make on Morag. Jules gives her freedom to do what she likes about having a child, and drifts in and out of her life without exhibiting possessiveness. Brooke, on the other hand, orders every move of Morag like a parent instructing her on how to speak, what to wear and how to do her hair. In leaving him, Morag runs away from his efforts to control her life, to do the script for her.

Morag heard from Christie Logan tales of Piper Gunn who led Scottish highlanders to the Red River colony in 1814 and who fought against Louis Riel in 1870. Morag recognises these stories narrated by her foster father as myths in which history is the heroic cast. She patterns his heroic tales on literary models of oral narration. Thus, she has been given a Scottish identity through these stories. The national myth in *The Diviners* is manifested in Morag outgrowing her Scottish identity and recognising her true identity as a citizen of the Manawaka land. She returns to Ontario. "One is not born Canadian; one becomes Canadian"[9] is true in case of Morag's Canadian identity. Morag is inspired by Christie's oral tales although initially she feels ashamed of his Scottish identity and racial prejudice. She rejects race as a basis of identity in favour of nationality. Thus, she replaces in her writings, race by nation, since racial identities are human constructs. It does not, however mean that the novel replaces "the old imperialist divisions, of humanity by a new understanding of the world, now formally organised into homologous and theoretically equal nation states"[10] as argued by Kortenaar.

Laurence invests Morag Gunn with heroic qualities as Canada needs to invent national heroes according to her "Man of our People."[11] Morag has invented a national myth by her rejection of Brooke, the coloniser, and her acceptance of Jules, the metis. Morag's background as an orphan, her early awareness of the repression of Scottish and Metis culture create the desire to explore her ancestry. This genealogical quest comes to a climax when she decides to go to Britain and it continues to be important in the final sections of the text which describe her life after her return from Britain.

Morag goes to Britain, partly attracted to London as 'centre of writing,' and partly to visit Scotland from which her ancestors came, though she is unsure as to what she might 'learn' there. She thinks of this journey as a 'pilgrimage' (369). She leaves Scotland saying, 'It's a deep land here [...]. But it's not mine except a long, long way back' (390-91). She decides that her home is 'Christie's real country. Where I was born' (391) and when she hears that he is seriously ill, she decides she is going 'home.' 'Home,' then, signifies the place of one's Canadian origins, the small town of Manawaka, not the European place from which one's ancestors came.

Morag succeeds in asserting her national identity by giving her daughter a name that will define her completely. She names her daughter after Jules's sister, Piquette, who died in a tragic fire. She allows Pique to be free to write her own life history. Morag releases her daughter just as "the author lets her character go, free to develop her different voice [...] to enter into a loving and reciprocal relationship with the other, to let the daughter tell her own story."[12] Morag invents Canadian identity by inventing the past not for the sake of herself but for the next generation. That's why the novel has been regarded as a 'homecoming novel.'[13] The fusion of Scottish and metis heritages is seen in the way in which Pique attempts to embrace both sides of her ancestry. The union of Scottish and Metis strands holds out the possibility of a new multicultural identity for Canada in which English origins will no longer play a major role.

Pique and Morag become the centre of the re-telling mainly because as a family unit they provide a constant in a changing life, and also they are thrown into each other's company so much. The family focus points to all the 'old patterns' emerging from Morag and Jules into Pique. As a writer, Morag develops the skills of a diviner such as insight, intuition or "some other kind of sight" in order to fathom what goes on in outcasts, and poor people. She is in a position to understand Manawaka from a better perspective and make its people lead a better life. As a diviner, Morag, in her fiction, speaks for those who cannot speak for themselves—"fathoms the unfathomable, communicates the incommunicable, mentions the unmentionable."[14] In short, Morag uses her pen to divine the truths about the oppressed sections and the victimized people. In her writings, she raises her voice against colonialism and authoritarianism. In effect, she becomes a spokesperson of Laurence's postcolonial nationalism.

NOTES

1. Margaret Laurence, *Long Drums and Cannons* (London: Macmillan, 1968) 10.
2. Laurence, "Ivory Tower or Grassroots? the Novelist as Socio-Political Being." *A Political Art* (Vancouver: Univ. of British Columbia, 1978) 17.
3. Carl Berger, *The Writing of Canadian History* (Toronto: OUP, 1976) 256.
4. Margaret Laurence, "Books that Mattered to me." np.
5. Frederic Jameson, "Third-World Literature in the Era of Multi-national Capitalism." *Social Text* 15 (1986) 65-88.

6. Gayle Grene, "*The Diviners*: The Uses of the Past." *Critical Approaches to the Fiction of Margaret Laurence* ed. Colin Nicholson (Houndmills & London: Macmillan Press, 1990) 177.
7. Margaret Laurence, *The Diviners* (Toronto, New York, London: Bantam, 1974) 4. All subsequent references are to this edition.
8. Doris Sommer, *Foundational Fictions; The National Romance of Latin America* (Berkeley: Univ. of California, 1991).
9. Neil Ten Kortenaar, "The Trick of Divining a Postcolonial Canadian Identity: Margaret Laurence between Race and Nation." *Canadian Literature* 149 (Summer 1996) 16.
10. Kortenaar 21.
11. Margaret Laurence, "Man of Our people." *Heart of Stranger* (Toronto: Maclelland and Stewart, 1976) 204-12.
12. Barbara Godard, "*The Diviners* as Supplement: (m)othering the Text." *Open Letter* 7.7 (1990) 68.
13. Clara Thomas, *The Manawaka World of Margaret Laurence* (Toronto: Maclelland and Stewart, 1976) 172.
14. Greene 187.

18

The Context of Regionalism in Margaret Laurence's Manawaka Fiction

K. DAMODAR RAO and M. SURENDRA KUMAR

> The eastern point, the point of origin, was her feeling of being rooted in a particular place and time. She wrote of Canada, of her generation, and of the several generations preceding it. Because her voice and the contexts of many of her novels are so quintessentially Canadian [...].
>
> —John Thomas

Margaret Laurence's sense of being Canadian can be seen more obviously in her Manawaka fiction. Most of the novels of Laurence could be characterized as inner-space fiction. But the outer spaces of place and society play no less significant a part in her fiction. This paper is an attempt to look at her fiction from the standpoint of the outer space of Manawaka and its ethos. The fictional locale of Manawaka is modelled upon the Southwestern part of Manitoba, Neepawa, Laurence's home town. As Shirley Chew says, "Manawaka is a modest town of the mind."[1] The series of four novels published between 1964 and 1974 capture the cultural awakening of Canada during the sixties and early seventies. They hold a mirror to the lives of several generations settled in and around the town of Manitoba. As Clara Thomas puts it, "[...] in their dilemmas, her characters move us through four generations of the history of this country [...] through two world wars and the Depression, to the contemporary setting."[2] Laurence's fiction is an inter-connection of people and places. In fact, few novelists have captured the rhythms and mysteries of life in Canada as brilliantly as Laurence did. Manawaka is one of the interesting literary regions in which Laurence portrays her own place and her own people in a fascinating manner. Her fiction acquires a local and regional colouration and hence she is regarded as a regional writer and "a priarie writer."[3]

Laurence has many similarities with Chinua Achebe and Wole Soyinka of Nigeria and George Lamming of the West Indies in terms of her convictions about the writer's place in society and about handling the themes of her fiction. She also agrees with Achebe's avowed position that the writer should have strong sense of social mission in a changing, postcolonial world and that the writer cannot be excused from the task of re-education and regeneration. Laurence observes:

> For me fiction is primarily a matter of portraying individual, characters as faithfully as I am able to do. These characters, however, do not live in a vacuum. They live in specific places, and any writing about them must of necessity include social commentary.[4]

Laurence has created Hagar Shipley in *The Stone Angel* (1964), Rachel Cameron in *A Jest of God* (1966), Stacey MacAindra in *The Fire-Dwellers* (1969), Vanessa MacLeod in *A Bird in the House* (1970), and Morag Gunn in *The Diviners* (1974) who typify her Manawaka world from her own place and time through four generations of men and women in a Canadian western town. As her novels progressed from Hagar of *The Stone Angel* to Morag of *The Diviners,* Manawaka becomes more and more "a three-dimensional reality in our imaginations, with its interwoven families, its geographical landmarks and, above all, its climate of thought, as real to readers as their own backgrounds through time and across the country."[5] Her protagonists are caught within inherited codes and the social order of silence; they often express their deepest fears and desires and register contradictions between their outer and inner selves. Thus every narrator in her fiction reinvents and reconciles to Manawaka in her own idiom, her own way.

In *The Stone Angel*, Laurence begins the Manawaka cycle by setting the narrative within well-defined boundaries of geography and history. The ninty year old protagonist, Hagar Shipley represents the Manawaka ethos. She is proud, strong-willed and independent-spirited. She struggles hard to preserve her sanity and dignity in the face of severe limitations imposed by ageing limbs, sagging spirits and cracks in her personality that begin to expose contradictions within. Feeling desolate, she is, 'rampant with memory' (3). Yet, she refuses to acknowledge that she is fast becoming a victim of inundating memories. The split personality of Hagar, subtly portrayed, is in evidence right from the beginning of the narrative. She had married Bram Shipley despite the opposition from her father only to reject him later on. The rebellious and romantic spirit in her occasionally asserts only to be replaced by qualities of order, decorum, and respectability associated with Manawaka. Even after her marriage, she is unable to give up her class-conscious self-image and strongly disapproves of whatever Bram does. In fact, she likes to be remembered as the daughter of Jasson Currie rather than the wife of Bram Shipley. The basic contradiction in their marital life is articulated by Hagar herself:

> We'd each married for those qualities we later found we couldn't bear, he for my manners and speech, I for his flouting of them (79).

Laurence repeatedly indicates the fallibility of the narrator. Hagar thinks that she had inherited the cherished qualities and values of her father while her brothers, Dan and Matt, had taken after their mother who was meek, docile, and weak. Hagar has no sympathy for weakness. She detests her daughter-in-law, Doris, despite her generous attitude towards her in the old age. Similarly, she has no tender feelings left for her eldest son, Marvin. Instead, she pins high hopes on John to whom she presented the Currie family signet, a silver plaid-pin. It was much later that she learns that John had traded it for a knife. Ironically, it was John who drives home the point that she had all along pursued false values and misplaced priorities: 'You always bet on the wrong horses,' (237), he comments.

Hagar Shipley is the descendant of a family that could boast of rich class connections and self-made success in pioneering Canada. She thinks that she is strangely cast and has little or no concern for the larger issues of social order and justice. She relies heavily on the ethic of self-reliance and individualism and virtually has no sympathies for the dispossessed and the victims of power-structures. The novel subtly suggests that Hagar's indifference to the larger issues was to some extent typical of the self-made success stories of her generation. Hagar consciously avoids and steers herself clear of any contact or association with the farmers and the local metis who are favoured by her husband and son. She feels that her respectability is at stake and moves into her shell of self-imposed aloofness.

The novel effectively captures the energy, enterprise, success stories and the fast-paced development that was the hallmark of Manitoba, and Canada in general. At the fag end of her life, although Hagar is as defiant as ever, the realization dawns on her that she is alone. Pride, she bemoans the fact, was her wilderness, and the demon that led her there was fear. This realization brings her satisfaction but the fact remains that she is a symbol of death-in-life and life-in-death principle, the 'stone angel.' As Simone Vauthier rightly observes, Hagar is like a "verbal monument which representing life cannot but inscribe death, and inscribing death, ultimately asserts life."[6]

Since *The Stone Angel,* Laurence's fiction has illumined shades of her perceptions about Manitoba and its people. In her second novel, *A Jest of God,* she goes back to Manawaka projecting it through Rachel Cameron, daughter of Niall Cameron, an undertaker in Manawaka. Rachel is a spinster school teacher and she stands in stark contrast to Hagar. Laurence provides an account of Rachel thus:

The wind blows low, the wind blows high
The snow comes falling from the sky,
Rachel Cameron says she'll die
For the want of the golden city.
She is handsome, she is pretty,
She is the queen of the golden city.[7]

Thus, Laurence depicts Rachel as a young girl worrying in her servile existence with her widowed mother. Rachel could not finish her university education owing to financial constraints after her father's death. She does not want to undertake her father's occupation. She discontinues her education, settles as a school teacher in Manawaka. She is aware how she is put to loss by means of her servitude to her mother. When Nick, her former schoolmate meets and kisses her she realizes the urge for love relinquishing, in the process, all her false "crowing doubts and fears" imposed by her mother. As their love affair runs its course she voices her need for a child. She pleads with him: "Give me my children." But he replies: "I'm not God. I can't solve anything" (148). She mistakenly thinks that the tumour growing in her body as a symptom of pregnancy. Later she realizes:

> All that. And this at the end of it. I was always afraid that I might become a fool. Yet I could almost smile with some grotesque lightheadedness at that fool of a fear, that poor fear of fools, now that I really am one (181).

Rachel learns to accept that she has become a 'jest of God.' She realizes that her choices are humanly limited. She wants to be free of the geographical constraint, Manawaka, where she thinks, security rarely exists. But the fact is that she will carry with her, the strengths and constraints of Manawaka.

Of all the Manawaka novels, it is only in *The Fire-Dwellers* that Laurence portrays her protagonist as fulfilling the traditional wife-mother-housekeeper roles of a woman. Laurence creates a remarkable portrait of Stacey as a middle-aged mother of four children. She experiences the horrors of the Manawaka world and, attempts to free herself of the limitations. The town, in fact, batters her sensibilities so much that even the building appears for her as "charred, open to the impersonal winds, glass and steel broken like vulnerable live bones—"(11). At night, she has nightmares of fire engulfing her house in flames. She feels a sense of anguish and fear in bringing up her children all alone in a world, on fire. However she learns how to cope with the basic act of living in Manitoba. Thus, Stacey is always in life, not exactly apart from it. She thinks of herself as "common place and ordinary, but the great achievement of her anxious, rueful, urgent voice is to reveal her extraordinary qualities of love, fortitude, and especially, vitality."[8] The novel, thus, lays bare the dilemmas and problems of women in Manawaka through imprisoned consciousness of Stacey.

Laurence creates Vanessa MacLeod in *A Bird in the House*, and Morag Gunn in *The Diviner*s as imaginative writers. *A Bird in the House* is a fine piece of Manawaka fiction which is in the form of collection of stories. Laurence describes it as "the only semi-autobiographical fiction I have ever written."[9] Vanessa exposes the Manawaka codes of her grandparents' generation through her stories. She records her experiences in the family's Brick House. For her, the house never looks like a home. She says:

> That house in Manawaka is the one which, more than any other, I carry with me. Known to the rest of the town [...] and to the family as the Brick House [...]. Many other brick structures had existed in Manawaka for as much as half a century, but at the same time when my grandfather built his house, part dwelling place and part massive monument [...]. (3)

The house came to be associated with her grandfather's uprightness and his attitude towards others around him. As a writer, Vanessa is a sensitive observer of human relationships in Manawaka particularly of the earlier generation. The community history as narrated through Vanessa's stories is the record of the struggle during that period. Therefore, Laurence says that "there is a lot of history in my fiction."[10]

The Diviners is the last of the four-volume Manawaka series which has occupied a decade of Laurence's career as a regional writer concerned with Canadian history. The novel's beginning, the description of the river "that flows both ways" (3) is suggestive of the fact that the way forward is the way back through an understanding and recovery of the past. Morag realizes that though "You can't go home again [...]. You have to go home again, in some way or the other" (302). Once she realizes that her teacher-husband Brooke, was merely an epitome of colonial power, she does not hesitate to leave him and go back to her place where she marries Jules, a representative of the indigenous, dispossessed ones.

Morag uses her pen to expose the sorrow and misery of the oppressed ones in Manawaka. As Clara Thomas puts it, "*The Diviners* is a homecoming novel, containing within it an epic of this land and its people, culminating and closing the Manawaka works with a quiet assurance that is Morag Gunn's affirmation and Margaret Laurence's."[11] Through her novels, Morag speaks for the outcasts, the half-breeds and the metis. She opens up to an entirely new world with new ideas thereby breaking all the outdated Manawaka social structures.

A careful survey of Laurence's Manawaka fiction reveals that Manawaka world is every man's and every woman's but its particularities are emphatically Canadian as Laurence, like her protagonists, is firmly rooted in her soil. Even as they move out into the wider world, they still "carry Manawaka with them."[12]

NOTES

1. Shirley Chew, "Some Truer Image: A Reading of *The Stone Angel.*" *Critical Approaches to the Fiction of Margaret Laurence,* ed. Colin Nicholson (London: Macmillan, 1990) 35.
2. Clara Thomas, *The Manawaka World of Margaret Laurence* (Toronto: Maclelland and Stewart, 1976) 1.
3. Thomas 1.
4. Allan Twigg, *Strong Voices: Conversations with Fifty Canadian Authors* (British Columbia: Harbour Publications, 1988).
5. Clara Thomas, "Planted firmly in Some Soil: Margaret Laurence and the Canadian Tradition in Fiction." *Critical Approaches to the Fiction of Margaret Laurence* 3-4.
6. Simone Vauthier, "Images in Stones, Images in Words: Margaret Laurence's *The Stone Angel.*" *Critical Approaches to the Fiction of Margaret Laurence* (London: Macmillan, 1995) 69.
7. Margaret Laurence, *A Jest of God* (Toronto: Maclelland and Stewart 1966) 1.
8. Thomas 128.

9. George Woodcock, *A Place to Stand On: Essays by and about Margaret Laurence* (Edmonton: Newest P, 1983) 4.
10. Woodcock 208.
11. Thomas 172.
12. Thomas 177.

19

THE POLEMICS OF POSTCOLONIAL WRITING: MARLATT'S *ANA HISTORIC* AND NOURBESE'S 'DISCOURSE ON THE LOGIC OF LANGUAGE'

H. KALPANA

> I-na, I-no-longer, I can turn you into a story, there is this absence here, where the words stop (and then I remember-).
>
> *Ana Historic, 11*

> It was you who changed, you grew up, you learned the difference between story and history.
>
> *Ana Historic, 28*

Postcolonial has been used as an umbrella term to denote an imperialistic, hegemonic attitude and a colonized subordinate society. Yet the fact is that postcolonialism in spite of breaking down the standards and universality had not provided a suitable voice for women writers. It is true that women writers have found an intersection in terms of expressions of oppression, silence, marginalisation and they have also attempted to liberate themselves. Yet a major hindrance for the writers has been language and the concept of truth. Ashcroft *et al* in their seminal work, *The Empire Writes Back,* feel that the historical experience itself acts as a catalyst of postcolonial experiences, but for most women writers the question is whether history that they encounter is correct. The other problem, as already pointed out is to free oneself from the language, which is not only the language of the colonizers but also the language of the patriarchal fathers who in turn exhibit colonizers' mentality.

Postcolonial spirit has enabled the recovery and recognition of autonomous culture in society and yet, in the specific case of women's writing there has been the splitting of narrative to create a body of protest which in turn becomes a means of postmodern expression. Slemon adheres to this point when he states in his essay, "Modernism's Last Post":

> Whereas a post-modernist criticism would want to argue that literary practices such as these expose constructedness of all textuality—an interested postcolonial practice would want to allow for the positive production of oppositional truth claims in these texts—This referential assumption would appear to make what I am calling a postcolonial criticism radically fractured and contradictory for such a criticism would draw on post-structuralism's suspension of the referent in order to read the social "text" of colonialist power and at the same time would reinstate the referent in the services of colonized and postcolonial societies. (1997, 23)

The postcolonial polemic in Canada reveals to us that the women writers are displaying the use of innovative forms and techniques of applying language to creative work. It discloses the reality that women writers are creating a 'mosaic' of their own, a kaleidoscopic way of narration, breaking the existing boundaries.

Both Nourbese and Marlatt in their writings are concerned with the colonizing experience and the colonizer's attempt to thrust his language. They are also concerned about the problem of language. Nourbese herself addresses the Caribbean/African demotic and mentions, "I really can't say that language is less patriarchal. It is certainly less-white-Eurocentric, if you will—since so many of its tonal, linguistic, and rhythmic resources are African" (1989, 228).

The concern of this paper is to reflect on how these two writers attempt to transgress the patriarchal language, the experience of colonization and in this process for expression embrace a more feminine mode of writing. Nourbese and Marlatt deny any postmodern aspirations but the plurality that their writings depict and the purely feminine ethos that envelops the works create a new 'female' ethos.

Nourbese's poetry attempts not only to communicate the female experience but also convey the special place within the Black Diaspora. In attempting to understand the Black Diaspora in North America one need to at least explain the implications of the word, gender. Gender is associated with the cultural construct 'masculinity' and 'femininity' respectively. The fact is that not only, "socially constructed gender and reproductive roles restrict a woman's identity and behaviour" but socially constructed sexual roles make it difficult for a woman to identify and develop her own sexual desires and needs. This perception has percolated down to the North American society. What, however, is disconcerting is that even this gender construction when it comes to the races—namely the whites and the blacks—portrays a division. The white married woman in North American society had been able to realize the cultural ideal of caring for their homes and family while the Blacks were denied such luxury. The civil war changed this picture but this time their free husbands reconstituted the Black women's lives. Thus a "basic component of the black ideal of family life, significantly was female domesticity" (1984, 225). Therefore, for the Black women a new sense of women's space emerged. Moreover, a cause for stronger women's consciousness was a strong matriarchal base among the Blacks. One, thus, notices at this point the development of the Afro-American women who are endowed with not only a feminist consciousness but also with an understanding of racist tendencies.

Another important feature of imperial rule is the control they have inscribed on the colonizers through language. As Ashcroft *et al* state, "language becomes the medium through which a hierarchical structure of power is perpetuated and the medium through which conceptions of truth, order and reality become established" (1979, 7). In this imperialistic enforcement the natives not only lost their language but they were also ashamed of their own language and ideas. As such images of the imperial language is used by the writers even when they write about their own culture. Norbese substantiates this when she says:

> I-mages that comprised the African aesthetic had previously thought to be primitive, naive and ugly, and consequently had been dismissed not only by white westerners but by the Africans themselves living outside Africa—so far were Africans themselves removed from the poem to create I-mages. (1989, 13)

The new world developed a consciousness among the people and created an urge to subvert the language. This language was, in other words, a deconstruction of the formal imposed language. The result was the use of indigenous words, phrases and structures. Thus, the writers, such as Marlatt and Nourbese played around and created their own language.

In this process the women writers had a greater responsibility for their language was not their own. It was the search for a new language, a language that was not created by men. Therefore, they tried to find a true 'mother tongue.' Both Marlatt and Nourbese achieve their purpose by crossing boundaries, while one treads past the white imposed image and structure the other crosses the structure of a genre itself by breaking language codes. In reality Nourbese's poetry reinstates her existence in the white Canadian province. The back cover of her book carries a statement by Rozena Maart:

> —is a political statement of the tenacity of black female livelihood, of our rebellion against our colonizers, of our defiance through speech—and the continuity of our history through the verbal tradition—of the uncut umbilical cord with the continent from which we were forcibly removed, of the knot tied tightly and still bursting with speech. (1989)

It is significant that works of writers such as Nourbese Philip, Gail Scott, Daphne Marlatt and others are categorised as post-modernist. Post-modernist feminist theory attempts to distract the phallogocentric thought that has been created around feminist theories. They provide a ground for creating a pluralistic, multiplistic and difference muted theory. Whether this can be termed post-modern is questionable but it is definitely a different and newer form of writing. The women writers are producing writing that question and provoke rethinking of cultural values and ideology in their writing. Three feminists who have initiated post-modernism in feminist circles are Helene Cixous, Luce Irigaray and Julia Kristeva. These French critics provide a freedom in writing circles and celebrate the 'other.'

Helene Cixous challenged women to write themselves -I'ecriture. She investigated a woman's own type of writing, namely, marking, scratching, scribbling and jotting down. She feels that feminist writing is open and multiple, varied and rhythmic:

> Her writing can keep going, without inscribing or discerning contours—She lets the other language speak in the language of 1000 tongues which knows neither enclosure nor death—Her language does not contain, it carries, it does not hold back, it makes possible (1981, 259-60).

This can be illustrated by viewing small extracts from the works of Nourbese and Marlatt:

> English
> is my mother tongue
> A mother tongue is not
> not a foreign lan lan ang
> Language
> I/anguish
> anguish
> —a foreign anguish (58).

> We give place, giving words, giving birth, to
> each other—she and me. You. hot skin writing
> skin, fluid edge, wick, wick.
> she draws me out. You she breathes, is where we meet.
> breeze from the window reaching you know, trees
> out there, streets you might walk down, will
> soon, it isn't dark but the luxury of being
> has woken you, the reach of you desire, reading
> us into the page ahead (153).

One notices in these lines rhythm, as well as a sense of continuity and cyclicality.

Luce Irigaray, on the other hand, attempts to free the feminine from the male philosophical thoughts. She suggested three things which women have to pay attention to. The nature of the language was to be thought about by women. Women need to talk in the active voice, avoid passive and to take responsibility for one's words. Secondly, women have to know their body, know what is feminine. Finally, women have to magnify the images imposed on them by men and portray them back to the men. By such gestures, women can undo the power of patriarchy. Once again one observes that Nourbese and Marlatt attempt all the three strategies in their works. They use oral form of narrative that is in the active, the body and sexual activity are foregrounded as noticed by the words:

WHEN IT WAS BORN, THE MOTHER—. THE CREAMY WHITE SUBSTANCE COVERING ITS BODY (58).

> history. the excision of women (who do not act but are acted upon), hysterectomy, the excision of wombs and ovaries by repression, by mechanical compression, by ice, by the knife, because we were 'wrong' from the start, our physiology faulty, preoccupied as we are with the things of the flesh. (88)

Kristeva goes a bit further than Cixious and Irigaray. She felt that woman is always in the act of becoming and does not exist *per se*. She states:

> The belief that "one is a woman" is almost as absurd and obscurantist as the belief that "one is a man." I say "almost" because there are still many goals which women can achieve: freedom of abortion and contraception, day-care centres for children, equality on the job, etc. Therefore, we must use "we are women" as an advertisement or slogan for our demands. On a deeper level, however, a woman cannot "be"; it is something which does not even belong in the order of being. (1974, 157)

It is this aspect that Nourbese probes when she uses a semi-scientific passage and two edicts next to the poem along with a multiple choice questionnaire at the other part of the poem:

Edict 1
Every owner of slaves
shall, wherever possible,
ensure that his slaves
belong to as many
ethno-linguistic groups as
possible. If they cannot
speak to each other,
they cannot then foment
rebellion and revolution.

Marlatt teases this aspect by adopting a repetition of scientific or other facts which can be identified by the writing in italics:

> *Mechanical devices were invented for compressing ovaries or for packing them in ice. In Germany, Hegar (1830-1914) and Friedrich (1825-82) were using even more radical methods, including ovarectomy and cauterization of the clitoris. The source of hysteria was still, as in Plato's time, sought in the matrix of the female body, upon which surgical attacks were unleashed.*

They thus attempt through their narratives a rupture of the linguistic structure. Moreover their writing helps to subvert the patriarchal existing structure/form. They employ the feminist concept of perception a sense of words and taste by using sensually rich words. The female voice is emphasized by repeatedly using the word 'mother tongue' or images pertaining to the mother. The reading of these works enhances the silence and noise creeping through them when one's senses are percolated by the semantics of the narratives.

One has noticed that though Cixous, Kristeva and Irigaray share different ideas about women and their writing, yet these critics have also paved the way for a non-linear, irrational writing that has colour, sound, rhythms and breaks up syntax and grammar and is unrepressed; it has room for what disgusts us.

It also exhibits the fact that such types of gyno-centric writing are needed to foreground the feminine. Moreover, at another level, such writing enables one to overcome differences and to understand the 'other'—the 'other', who is repressed, marginalised and decentred. The statement made by Rosemarie Tong also emphasizes this:

> Whether women can by breaking silence, by speaking and writing help overcome binary opposition, phallocentrism and logocentrism, I do not know. All that I do know is that we humans could do with a new conceptual start. In our desire to achieve unity, we have excluded, ostracized and alienated so-called abnormal, deviant and marginal people. As a result of this policy of exclusion, we have impoverished the human continuity. We have, it seems, very little to lose and much to gain by joining a variety of post-modern feminists in their celebration of multiplicity. For even if we cannot all be One, we can all be Many (1989, 233).

WORKS CITED

Ashcroft et al. *The Empire Writes Back: Theory and Practice in Post-colonial Literatures.* London and New York: Routledge, 1989.

Cixous, Helene. "The Laugh of the Medusa." *New French Feminisms* ed. Elaine Marks and Isabella de Courrivron (New York: Shocken Books, 1981) 245-64.

Irigaray, Luce. *This Sex which is not One.* Tran. Catherine Porter. Ithaca: NY Cornell UP, 1985.

Kristeva, Julia. "Interview with Tel Quel." *New French Feminisms.*

Nourbese, Philip Marlene. *She Tries Her Tongue: her silence softly breaks.* Canada: Ragweed Press, 1989.

Marlatt, Daphne. *Ana Historic.* Toronto: Coach House Press, 1988.

Tong, Rosemarie. *Feminist Thought: A Comprehensive Introduction* Colorado: Westview Press, 1989.

Woloch, Nancy. *Women and the American Experience.* New York: Alfred A. Knopf.

Williamson, Janice. *Sounding Differences: Conversations with Seventeen Canadian Women Writers* (Toronto: U of Toronto P, 1993) 226-46.